SWIFT

THE MAN, HIS WORKS, AND THE AGE

VOLUME ONE

Mr Swift and his Contemporaries

by Irvin Ehrenpreis

HARVARD UNIVERSITY PRESS
CAMBRIDGE · MASSACHUSETTS

First published in 1962
Printed in Great Britain

An index to the complete work
will appear at the end of the
last volume

SWIFT

The Man, his Works, and the Age

VOLUME I

by the same author

THE PERSONALITY OF JONATHAN SWIFT

CONTENTS

Appendices

PREFACE

Compared with the ideal of a definitive biography, the present volume has more faults than its author has blushes; compared with available biographies, it aims at a new standard of thoroughness and accuracy. The two remaining volumes are already complete in a preliminary draft, and will appear in reasonably quick succession to the first.

Biographers find Swift's character so fascinating that often they treat him in comparative isolation, telling the single story of his inner development and employing other people, as well as public events, only as these bear unavoidably upon the man or his works. Presented with so stark an image, the reader must come with unusual resources if he hopes to judge both the degree to which Swift was representative of his generation and the degree to which he was either independent or eccentric. Since I think this judgment is important, I have drawn many parallels between Swift and his contemporaries. I have tried, by revealing unexpected connections and relationships, to suggest the narrow, close-knit nature of the social fabric to which he belonged. I have further tried to indicate how far intellectual traditions and public events could, as it were, endow Swift with principles which might seem arbitrary to us.

I have been less concerned to add than to eliminate fables; and those readers who look for my views on a long train of legendary Swiftiana will search in vain. Here, neither Swift nor Stella is made a bastard; Swift does not say, 'My uncle gave me the education of a dog'; Dryden does not say, 'Cousin Swift, you will never be a poet'; and Temple does not seat Swift and Stella at the servants' table. But I have looked minutely into Swift's intentions and principles. Since his early works contain bold expressions of his ideals and intricate examples of his satirical methods, I have given them a detailed examination. Because *A Tale of a Tub*, his hardest and most brilliant work, has been misunderstood by many critics, I have gone over it with unusual care.

For early encouragement, steady guidance, and innumerable kindnesses, I am indebted to my teachers, George Sherburn, Louis Landa, and Sir Harold Williams.

For generous support of the work, I am indebted to Indiana University, the U.S. Educational ('Fulbright') Commission, the John Simon Guggenheim Memorial Foundation, the American Council of Learned Societies, and the American Philosophical Society.

For their incredible patience and hospitality, I am indebted to Dr William O'Sullivan, Dr Richard Hayes, Mr L. W. Hanson, and the other librarians of those sanctuaries where my work was mainly done: Indiana University, the British Museum, Trinity College (Dublin), the National Library of Ireland, and—condition to which all others naturally aspire—the Bodleian Library, Oxford.

For generously permitting me to use manuscript materials, I thank the Board of Trinity College, Dublin, the Trustees of the British Museum, the officers of the Leicester City Museum, Bodley's Librarian, and Mr James Osborn. I thank the Syndics of the Cambridge University Press for allowing me to quote from R. L. Colie, *Light and Enlightenment*, and A. R. Hall, *Ballistics in the Seventeenth Century*; the Delegates of the Clarendon Press for L. A. Landa, *Swift and the Church of Ireland*; and the officers of the University Press, Dublin, for C. E. Maxwell, *A History of Trinity College, Dublin*.

For many kinds of assistance over many years of work, I am indebted to Mr Giles Barber, Professor Frederick L. Beaty, Mr James T. Boulton, Mr John Russell Brown, Mr G. A. Chinnery, Professor James L. Clifford, Professor Rosalie L. Colie, Professor Ronald S. Crane, Professor Philip B. Daghlian, Professor Herbert Davis, Professor Oliver W. Ferguson, Mr Alastair D. S. Fowler, the Rev. J. G. Frostick, Professor Rudolf B. Gottfried, Professor Donald J. Gray, Professor John C. Hodges, Professor A. Rupert Hall, Professor Colin J. Horne, Mr Emrys Jones, Professor Alexander C. Judson, Mr Hugh F. Kearney, Professor

Part I

Chapter One

ERICKS, DRYDENS, AND SWIFTS

For a man who claimed that his family were 'of all mortals what I despise and hate',[1] Swift surely had much to do with them. His early years were sheltered by an uncle's hospitality; the last years were eased by a cousin's devotion. He paid a lifetime allowance to a needy sister; he supported and regularly visited a widowed and distant mother. In his era of intimacy with peers and statesmen, he saw and gave help to humble relations. When, ageing and ill, he lived withdrawn from the world, he lent a fortune to a young cousin; another cousin's husband was for a while his curate. Probably, Swift's ironical, ostentatious contempt for 'what the world calls natural affection'[2] betokens an instinct grown too powerful for him to handle directly.

Contrary both to received opinion and to the hints dropped by Swift himself, his relatives influenced in fundamental ways his literary ambitions, his political sympathies, and his religious convictions. He was born into a family allied with two of the great names of seventeenth-century literature, Dryden and Davenant: his cousinship with Dryden he repeatedly mentioned; Davenant's grandson played the part of a brother to Swift during his childhood and youth. The high church, anti-Whig political alignment of Swift as an adult follows the course of his father's generation and of the father's father. In his vocation of priest and dean Swift, with belligerent persistence, supported policies which not only tie him to one grandfather but oppose him to the other; for though both were parsons, one had been persecuted by Puritans and the other by Laudians.

But Swift has not only misled us as to the effect of his forebears

[1] Ball VI. 113. [2] *Ibid.*, p. 126.

upon him; he has even misled us as to plain facts of his ancestry; and several early biographers have deepened the darkness by assertions and conjectures which can now be dismissed. Swift's exact relationship to Dryden, the identity of his mother's father, the large number of clergymen in his background, the early division, in associations, between his sister and himself—these are some of the points established by a survey of his descent. We shall discover how, in a literal sense, 'natural' it was for Swift to grow up into a high church Anglican priest, bitterly opposed to nonconformity, separated from his sister, and preoccupied with literary ambitions.

One ancestor he venerated above all, his parson grandfather Thomas Swift. Writing toward the end of his life, when he was almost seventy-two, Swift still flamed at the idea of that royalist vicar's sufferings from the Puritans—'persecuted and plundered two and fifty times by the barbarity of Cromwell's hellish crew'.[1] Yet Swift knew little about his own extraction, and that little was often wrong. In a fragment of autobiography, he traced his paternal line to a Yorkshire family which had really a negligible tie or none with the Reverend Thomas Swift (1595–1658), vicar of Goodrich and rector of Bridstow, Herefordshire.

His own maternal grandparents Swift skips over in this account, blandly tying his mother, Abigail Erick, to 'the most antient family of the Ericks, who derive their lineage from Erick the Forester'. Genealogists believe it more likely that she belonged to a modest branch of the Erick or Herrick family of Leicestershire, 'very private gentlemen' in her son's odd phrase[2]; her father was no doubt the Reverend James Ericke (B.A., Cambridge, 1624), vicar of Thornton, Leicestershire, from 1627 to 1634.[3] (Although she is supposed to have been related to Dorothy Osborne, the connection has not been traced.)[4]

Swift owed his Christian name, in the last instance, to neither the Ericks nor the Swifts, but to the family of his father's mother.

[1] Ball VI. 127. [2] *Autob.*, f. 6^{v}. [3] See Appendix B.

[4] When Sir William Temple died, Swift's mother was one of those who received an allowance for mourning.

From these more remote ancestors were descended cousins with whom he was to spend much time when he lived in England; and from the same ancestors, as Swift readily pointed out, John Dryden was also derived. Both writers—Dryden in the male line, Swift in the female—are traced to a Northamptonshire gentleman, John Dryden of Canons Ashby; for one of his sons was Dryden's grandfather, and another, Nicholas, was Swift's great grandfather. This—second cousinship once removed—is what Swift termed a 'near relation'.[1]

The name 'Jonathan' appears only after Nicholas Dryden's marriage; and with it we meet other names belonging to the generation of Swift's father. Nicholas Dryden married a Mary Emyley, both whose grandfather, Thomas Godwin, and uncle, Francis Godwin, were bishops. Nicholas and Mary Dryden called their eldest son Jonathan and their eldest daughter Elizabeth. A son who died in infancy was called Godwin, after (one assumes) either or both of his episcopal forebears.

Here begins the tale which Swift knew: for it was Jonathan Dryden's sister Elizabeth who married the Reverend Thomas Swift of Goodrich; and their fifth son, Swift's father, was named Jonathan, probably after his Dryden uncle. The eldest and by far the most important uncle of Swift himself was named Godwin; another uncle, Dryden. Such names and such connections show that Swift's links with literature and the church go back in one direction as far as the female side of this favourite grandfather's family.

On the other side, Thomas Swift came not of Northamptonshire gentry but of Kentish clerics. Both his father, William Swift (1566–1624), and his grandfather, Thomas Swyfte (1535–92), had been rectors of St Andrew's, Canterbury; and his great grandfather, William Swyfte, had also lived in Canterbury.[2] In

[1] Ball v. 162, 452–3; P. D. Mundy, *N. & Q.*, 4 Oct. 1924, pp. 243–4; 18 Oct. 1924, pp. 279–80, 334; 30 Oct. 1948, pp. 470–4; J. M. Osborn, *John Dryden: Some Biographical Facts and Problems* (New York 1940), p. 237. Swift was not—as has been said—also related to Dryden through descent from Bishop Thomas Godwin: see Mundy, *N. & Q.*, 1 Sept. 1951, pp. 383–4.

[2] Mundy, *N. & Q.*, 1 Sept. 1951, pp. 381–7.

naming his many sons, however, Thomas Swift seems to have drawn more on his wife's family than his own. Godwin, the eldest son (1628–95), must go back ultimately to one of the bishops—probably Francis (1562–1633, Bishop of Hereford), who had collated Thomas Swift (his cousin) to the Goodrich living and, being alive, might still do some duty.[1] Dryden, the second son (born 1629), obviously perpetuates Elizabeth Swift's maiden surname. Thomas, the third (born 1633), continued one Swift tradition; and William, the fourth (1637–*c.* 1705), continued another. Jonathan, the fifth (baptized 24 May 1640, died March or April 1667), has already been linked to Mrs Swift's brother.

Swift's fragment of autobiography reflects more concern with the parson Thomas than the parson's children; for Uncle Godwin is dismissed in five sentences, Thomas in three, and Dryden, William, and Adam,[2] all together, in one. Of the three last, Swift remarks that 'none of them left male issue', but that Jonathan, 'besides a daughter left one son'.[3] This daughter's name may yet again have significance: it was Jane, and it must belong to Abigail Swift's family; we know that Mrs Swift had a niece, Jane, daughter of a brother, the Reverend Thomas Errick, whose wife was named Jane as well. On his father's side, Swift had many female cousins, and they had many female offspring; but none of them seem, like his sister, to be called Jane. By every token, Swift counted himself as belonging to his paternal grandfather's family, not to his mother's. By sex and by name, by earlier birth, and—as we shall find—by constant association, Jane would belong to his mother's side.

It is not certain that Swift's mother knew much of her father, since he may have died when she was a child; it is far less certain that her son did. Yet Swift made many visits to Leicester; so he must have been familiar with the city's Puritan tradition and its anti-royalist role in the Civil War. Thomas Errick, Swift's mother's brother, only died in 1681, but there were other ways as well to pick up hints of James Ericke's sympathies; and no admirer of the Laudian tradition would have welcomed these

[1] Mundy, *N. & Q.*, 1 Sept. 1951, p. 384. [2] See Appendix A. [3] *Autob.*, f. 6.

hints. For after seven years as vicar of Thornton, James Ericke had confessed to holding an unlawful conventicle in his brother-in-law's house. He had been brought before the Court of High Commission; and though that court had first 'resolued to make tryall of him for a tyme to see how and in what manner he did demeane and carry him selfe in the execution of his ministry',[1] he was probably, in the end, deprived of his living.[2] If Swift was at all aware of the Puritan strain in his mother's background, his remarkably intense devotion to the royalist Anglican of Goodrich would seem to imply a corresponding repudiation of the vicar of Thornton's family.[3] I am confident that he was indeed aware of the strain and that while Swift's lifelong polemic against nonconformity could not be simply due to this element in his background, it does reflect the degree to which he considered himself a 'Swift' rather than an 'Erick'.

[1] P.R.O. MS. SP 16/ 261, 8 May 1634.

[2] On the Induction Mandate for his successor, John Summerfield, the parish is stated to be vacant 'per cessionem derelictionem sive deprivationem Jacobi Ericke', which suggests but does not confirm deprivation (Leicester City Archives MS. 1D41/ 28/ 442).

[3] See Appendix C.

Chapter Two

IRELAND

The meaning of Swift's work will escape anybody who forgets that his English career, long and important as it was, only interrupted an Irish life. Although a residence in Whitehaven during infancy was to remain a cherished fact for Swift (and though he may perhaps have briefly visited England during his adolescence), he had no real experience of Leicester, London, or Surrey till he left the university of his native city as a young adult. The traditions of his Herefordshire and Kentish ancestors had to receive a strange Irish setting before he was introduced to them; and around the immediate frame of a Protestant English family living in Ireland extended the larger frame of the so-called 'English interest' there. Let us understand the evolution of the unstable social order to which Swift belonged—with its splits between the native Irish and their conquerors, nonconformity and the Established Church, landlord and priest, old settlers and new administrators—and we shall see many of his distinguishing features emerge not as eccentricities but as intelligible reflections of the backgrounds of his career: for example, his conservative morality, or his uneasiness about property and wealth, or his unwillingness to call himself a Tory; his attacks upon Presbyterianism, his sympathy with the sufferings of the native Irish, coupled with his contempt for Roman Catholicism; his aggressive identification of himself with England, matched by his violent criticism of English policies in Ireland; his love of the church and his loathing of bishops.

In the development of that uneasy social order, however, certain forces did touch the dependent and half-orphaned boy more than most of his contemporaries: one was the shaky condition both of property titles and of money; another, the mutual distrust of northern, Scottish Presbyterians and the Anglican population of Ireland. Under such influences, Swift struggled to accumulate an estate for himself; he battled all his life for the strengthening of the Church of Ireland; and in his greatest political essays, *The Drapier's Letters*, he evoked the principles of human freedom out of a controversy over the coinage of money. Yet it is in the more general pattern of Irish history that we can observe not only what brought the Swifts to Dublin originally but also how they became involved with two great families, the Temples and the Ormondes; for the Temples directly and the Ormondes by way of the institutions they controlled were to guide young Jonathan Swift through the first stages of his career. At the same time, moreover, these families embodied the polar traditions of the English in Ireland: the Ormondes or Butlers, anciently established there, accepting responsibility for the whole population's welfare; the Temples, come over as administrators, regarding the kingdom only as a province that should be of some use to the rulers and their dependents, with no care for the condition of the vast, stubborn majority. We shall see that Swift, assigned by birth to the social philosophy of the Temples, educated himself to transcend it and to support that of the Ormondes. In remarking this movement, however, as in studying any aspect of Restoration Ireland, we shall acknowledge that it derives in turn from the ultimate principle of the history of the kingdom, the difference in number and religion between the rulers and the ruled.

Swift, then, grew up in a middle-class, Anglican community within a much greater population of rural Irish Roman Catholics. The Ireland he knew was the result of several violent but inconclusive military and colonizing projects of the English. The earliest effort, accompanying the invasion of Strongbow and the Normans in the twelfth century, planted among the Irish a number of great ruling families whose interests merged only very gradually with those of the natives. Into the seventeenth century the descendants of these invaders continued to wield something of their traditional power. From one of them, the Butlers, came the first Duke of Ormonde, who dominated the institutions which shaped Swift's career; and the second Duke, his grandson, whom Swift well knew and too much admired. By the end of the thirteenth century such families possessed (at least, nominally) most of arable Ireland.

During the next three hundred years the English settler did not exterminate the Irish; he did not admit the Irish to civil or political rights; and he did not multiply so as to outnumber the Irish. Instead, he continued to live in the conquered land as overlord, holding high offices under the crown, and despising the natives until their resentment boiled over into armed rebellion. A ferocious suppression would regularly end each uprising, with confiscation of the land of the leaders. Undisputed English supremacy, however, hovered around the dimensions of the Pale. This enclave, where English law was regularly enforced, had been established by Henry II; it centred on Dublin, but varied in extent, generally including most of what is now the county of Dublin and much of Louth, Meath, and Kildare. Sir John Temple, writing about 1646, described it as 'a large circuit of land possessed at the time of the first conquest of Ireland by the English, and ever since inhabited by them; it contains several counties, viz., the counties of Dublin, Meath, Lowth, Kildare, &c.'[1]

The feckless but mercenary administration, by the king's officers, of the English colony itself, fed a spirit of separatism. During the fifteenth century this grew into a resentful hostility toward England and English interests; what mainly irritated the settlers was the steady neglect of the authorities to assist in their defence. By Elizabeth's time three of the most pervasive elements in Irish history were established: the political alienation of the natives, who remained by far in the majority; the distrust of the so-called Anglo-Irish and the natives for each other—a hatred nourished by the long history of mutual terrorism; and the clash of interests between the descendants of the English born in Ire-

[1] *The Irish Rebellion*, 1679, p. 63.

land, and those Englishmen either directing Irish affairs from England or recently arrived in Ireland on administrative or plundering missions.

It is always to the interest of a mother country to prevent individual colonists from winning entrenched power for their families through the cumulative effect of intermarriage, legacies, hereditary perquisites, and traditional apportionments of privilege. At least, it is to the interest of ambitious statesmen, who must control every source of preferment. For this end, and to keep the colonists' regime generally subservient, it is common for the home government to bring in, as administrators, new men who will not direct their superiors but obey them. Thus the Domviles, Boltons, Percivals, Doppings, and Temples, whom Swift was to consider proper (if imperfect) leaders of Irish society, would only have risen to high office in the latter half of the sixteenth century.[1] In Ireland, moreover, just as 'old' English Catholic landowners saw themselves ousted, under Elizabeth and James, by new Anglican families associated with the army or the plantations, so the heirs of those recently established families were to find themselves displaced, under the later Stuarts and George I, by fresh carpet-baggers sent over from England.

A further complication was introduced with the plantation of Ulster, early in the seventeenth century. In that northern province a tremendous conspiracy had been smashed, and the usual confiscations had taken place. These in due course opened the way to a new settlement of loyal Britishers; and because careful limits were put on the type of participation allowed, the project did achieve permanent success. Of all the undertakers, the Scots were the most energetic. Since, in addition, the counties of Antrim and Down, bordering on the escheated lands, were already well colonized by Scots, the enduring character of the new settlement was Scottish. When the Presbyterian ministers, persecuted by James's episcopacy, came after their people, they established a religious bent which has remained a distinguishing mark of northern Ireland.

[1] H. F. Kearney, *Strafford in Ireland* (Manchester 1959), p. 18.

The strongest block to Anglo-Irish amity may also be blamed on the Tudors. This was the failure of the Reformation in Ireland. Although a parliament sat in Dublin 1536–7 for the purpose of establishing the new church, such legislation had negligible effect outside the Pale. The Roman Catholic Church had always commiserated the sufferings of the Irish, and there was in the country no sentiment favouring a break. The suppression of the regular clergy and the reversion of ecclesiastical property to the crown gave the whole movement a venal, lawless stamp which was attended by neither the piety nor even the proselytizing which might have relieved it. Recognizing their advantage, the Roman Catholic clergy laid down a policy of complete loyalty to Ireland and relentless opposition to English Protestant ascendancy. This strategy was so successful that, by Swift's time, to be Irish was to be Roman Catholic, although to be English was not always to be Anglican.

The forces behind all these developments came into play during the vast rebellion which started in 1641 in Ulster, spread over the whole of Ireland, and was not finally suppressed until 1652. The results of it gave Irish history its direction at least up to Swift's death. At the centre of the conspiracy was a group of prominent Irish Catholic clan leaders and landowners. Worried by the progress of the Puritans but encouraged by the vacillations of Charles I, they acted as though they thought the last opportunity had come for them at one stroke to preserve their church from extinction, to frustrate a final seizure of their estates, and to rectify the abuses of centuries. As the Civil War went on in England, a split developed within both this group and the British power which opposed them, so that the Irish divided between those who remained loyal to the king himself and those who demanded complete independence, while the British in Ireland divided between Parliamentarians (including, naturally, the Scottish Presbyterians) and loyalists (including the Anglicans). In August 1649—six and a half months after the execution of the king—the Irish Rebellion reached the point where Cromwell himself marched in. But though he spread a ferocious, if uniform, terror for nine months, active resistance endured into the spring of 1652. Then at last, under the Articles of Kilkenny, the utter conquest of a nation was done.

By this date, unfortunately, the cost to Parliament of putting down the Rebellion had swollen so high that out of the twelve million acres of arable land in Ireland, five would be wanted to pay the accumulated debt. In the summer of 1652, therefore, an Act of Settlement was passed—as arrogant and arbitrary as it was inevitable—by which the whole territory of Ireland was treated as confiscated property. The basis of this expropriation (and later ones) was no longer racial but religious. Every Irishman, whether English, Scots, or Gaelic, who could not demonstrate his innocence in the Rebellion and his constant good affection to the Commonwealth of England, was to suffer punishment by loss either of life or of property or of both, 'wholly or partial according to the degree of their guilt'.[1] Such was the so-called 'Cromwellian Settlement'. But if the Rebellion was thus extinguished, its primitive causes remained untouched and continued to flourish: land titles were still not secure; the English renewed their mistreatment of the Irish and their neglect of 'Anglo-Irish' families; and the Roman Catholic Church still underwent a harsh, though unsystematic, suppression.

While the main victim of Cromwell's army was the native Irish Catholic population, the Parliamentary troops were not, of course, careful of Anglican property. When Swift went to school at Kilkenny, he was to see a monument to their energy in the cathedral of St Canice: 'They left it roofless,' writes the first Restoration bishop, 'took away five great and goodly bells, broke down all the windows and carried away the glass, also broke down the doors, the font, and many goodly marble monuments.'[2] Cromwell's administration of Ireland, intended, in Macaulay's words, 'to make Ireland thoroughly English, to make it another Yorkshire or Norfolk', went far toward its goal. There was a 'con-

[1] Dunlop, p. 116.

[2] George Seaver, *The Cathedral Church of St Canice, Kilkenny* (Kilkenny 1953), p. 19, quoting Griffith Williams.

stant and large emigration from England to Ireland', and 'the native race was driven back before the advancing van of the Anglo-Saxon population.'[1] In general, hideous agonies were inflicted upon the Irish Catholics; for although some managed to find either farms they could rent or else other employment, many were transported to the West Indies and many became simply vagabonds.

At the Restoration, the trend naturally reversed itself, in a movement which did not cease until 1691. The Act of Settlement (1662) and the Bill for the Explanation of the Act of Settlement (1665) re-established many of the old proprietors. Numbers of them had indeed returned to their homes when Charles II became king, since they had no reason to think he would deal kindly with the Cromwellians. Very roughly, the outcome was that a third of the pasture and plough land went to native Roman Catholic landlords, a third to the older Protestant colonial families, and a third to the more recent 'adventurers' and soldiers. All serious attempts to modify this Act failed until the death of Charles.

With the accession of James II, the native Irish, led by Richard Talbot, now Earl of Tyrconnel, found their opportunity. A younger brother of the Roman Catholic Archbishop of Dublin, and a crony of James II when Duke of York, Tyrconnel had long been the most influential spokesman for the Irish Catholics at the court of Charles II. Not until the Revolution, however, did he have his way. Then, during the War of Williamites and Jacobites in Ireland, an irregular Irish Parliament—packed with Catholics—repealed the 1662 Act of Settlement. Yet even this change had no real effect, since in October 1691 the war ended.

On this occasion the famous Treaty of Limerick was signed, among the civil provisions of which appeared the last grand attempt to regulate the tenure of land in Swift's lifetime. This was the agreement that all submissive Roman Catholics should 'be secured in the free and undisputed possession of their estates as

[1] Macaulay, *Constitutional Essays*, World's Classics ed., p. 332.

they possessed them under the Act of Settlement'.[1] However, the civil Treaty (unlike the military) was never ratified by the Irish—i.e., 'Anglo-Irish'—Parliament, which on the contrary rejected it at last in 1697; and so it remained invalid.

Under William and Mary, the confiscations, grants, and resumptions made by crown and parliament had effects too elaborate to be detailed; but they can be roughly summarized. In 1688, between a quarter and a fifth of the profitable land of Ireland had belonged to Roman Catholics, whether of Gaelic Irish or of 'old English' extraction. By 1703, this fraction had declined to something like a seventh. Yet the area forfeited over these fifteen years was much less than what such proprietors had lost through the combined effects of the Cromwellian and the Restoration settlements. 'After 1703 there were no more confiscations on the wholesale scale of the sixteenth and seventeenth centuries. Stability had at last been reached.'[2]

Through the evolution of this land problem, the fundamental instability of Irish society during Swift's early years becomes unpleasantly clear. The basic form of wealth was real estate. From the outbreak of the Rebellion, however, the titles to thousands of acres changed hands with crumbling rapidity. Not regard for justice, but political and ecclesiastical expediency, guided these shifts. And if even property in land seemed shaky, money was more so. From the year of the Restoration until well into the reign of William and Mary, Irish coinage passed through alchemical transformations. Under Charles II a series of private persons obtained licences to supply the kingdom with copper and brass small change; but as each licencee failed to honour his pledge to redeem these pieces with gold and silver, the public always suffered from the consequent depreciation. James II, during his Irish campaigns, made a chaos of the coinage. He raised the price of gold and silver, struck brass sixpences, issued coins from two mints as fast as materials could be collected: church bells, cooking utensils, old cannon; he even recalled his

[1] Dunlop, p. 128.
[2] J. G. Simms, *The Williamite Confiscation*, 1956, pp. 17, 160–2.

own large half-crowns and restamped them as crowns. Then in 1691 all these coins ceased to be current. But still under William III one patentee flooded the kingdom with halfpence until it became common—a historian writes—for creditors to compound for 'one fourth copper'.[1] And all the time, of course, by inexorable, universal process, the value of gold and silver fell gradually in both England and Ireland; for Swift well knew that it took thirty pounds under Queen Anne to buy the equivalent of five pounds under Henry VI.[2]

To Swift's private reasons for worrying about his material fortunes, such a history would have given a special sharpness. The English for centuries have found prestige in the ownership of land, and put a price upon estates beyond the economic value. In Swift's day it was a truism that 'power follows property' (i.e., ownership of land); and although the maxim was often realized in reverse—through the alleged effect's giving rise to the supposed cause (power likes to be respectable)—Swift's obsession with 'real' property, as superior both morally and substantially to moneyed wealth, would have had all the weight of tradition behind it. If to this common tradition and to Swift's early poverty and dependence we join the peculiar course of Irish history, we shall not feel puzzled by his fear of inflationary trends ('the perpetual decrease of the value of gold and silver')[3] and his consequent insistence that land is the only sound bottom of a man's prosperity. As he struggled to build 'some little oeconomy of [his] own',[4] Swift was to reflect that within his memory even the most stable form of capital had several times been shaken.

Over this same period, of course, the 'settlement' acts and penal laws (against the Papists' acquiring large estates) operated so severely that there were few Roman Catholic freeholdings of any size, and those were constantly dwindling.[5] Yet for ordinary natives, in this period, emigration was hardly a practicable

[1] Davis, *Drapier*, p. 233.

[2] William Fleetwood, *Chronicon Preciosum*, 1707, p. 167. Swift owned and apparently used a copy of this book.

[3] Davis IX. 48. [4] Sherburn III. 96.

[5] For a detailed analysis of Protestant and Catholic landowners, see Simms.

possibility; they generally lived so near starvation that a failure of crops meant immediate famine. With conditions of existence that could not be much depressed by war, and with normal ways of improvement closed to them, the Irish were indifferent to prospects and obstacles alike which would have moved a happier nation.

To Englishmen who were seeking financial opportunities, the case was alluring. 'In those days,' a cousinly biographer of Swift says, with exquisite though unintentional irony, 'Ireland was very moderately supplied with lawyers.'[1] Particularly at the Restoration, men whom the Irish must have considered carpet-baggers found their chance to swarm into the gaps which a succession of upheavals had opened in officialdom and the professions. For Swift's father's family these attractions were probably improved both by the confidence they felt in their record of loyalty, and by some direct ties with a few high personages, especially the great Duke of Ormonde and Sir John Temple.

At the head of the Anglican, royalist interest, almost throughout the Rebellion, had stood James Butler, Marquess, and in 1661 Duke, of Ormonde (whose grandson was to be one of Jonathan Swift's heroes). The great duke's lineage, his vast fortune, handsome appearance, intelligence, charm, honesty, and energy made him the first man of his age in Ireland. For the opening five years of the Rebellion he led the campaign on behalf of the king, first against the Irish Catholic rebels, later against both them and the Parliamentarians. When in 1647 he had to choose between the two, he handed Dublin over to the Parliamentary troops, aligning himself with the England of Puritan republicans rather than the Ireland of the Popish separatists. Afterward, 'in foreign fields he won renown', through military and diplomatic errands which took him to England, France, and Germany. Upon the Restoration, which he helped to plan, the king heaped him with honours and estates; Dryden celebrated him as Barzillai—'Large was his wealth, but larger was his heart.' Nevertheless, his integrity became a fault, and the devious politics of Charles and

[1] D. Swift, p. 15.

James finally forced him out of public affairs. Ormonde was, we are told, connected with the Swifts through his wife (one of her relatives married Swift's eldest uncle, Godwin); and he gave essential aid in establishing the family in Ireland.

The other great support for Godwin and his brothers was allegedly Sir John Temple, Master of the Rolls in Ireland, whose son, Sir William, was to become Swift's patron. The older Temple, according to Swift, was 'a great friend' to the whole Swift family.[1] Sir William Temple, describing Swift, said that 'his whole family' had been 'long known to me'.[2] Even stronger expressions were used by Deane Swift; for he averred that Godwin (his own grandfather) had been on terms of the warmest friendship with Sir John, that the two men passed a great deal of time together, and that they worked in each other's interest. This account might seem more convincing if it were less minute.[3]

At the outbreak of the Rebellion, Sir John Temple happened to be in Ireland as a member of the Privy Council. His father, Sir Philip Sidney's friend, had brought the Temple family to this country upon his own appointment as provost of the young Trinity College, Dublin. Sir John, born in Ireland, was educated at Trinity College, but eventually made his home in London, and visited his native land only on business.[4] His notable achievement in the 1641 crisis was to supply Dublin Castle with food. Since the merchants were deeply anxious for their property, he not only invited some of the foremost provisioners to use the castle as a warehouse, but also made himself responsible for the safety of their stores. As they accepted the offer and moved in large supplies of beef, herring, and wheat, Temple (then Master of the Rolls) was able to victual the Castle and feed the army.[5]

In spite of his ingenuity, Sir John took the most bigoted view of the uprisings and freely exaggerated both the atrocities committed by the rebels and the stubbornness of their leaders. The language of the preface to a reprint (1679) of his book will convey his

[1] *Autob.*, f. 8. [2] Ball I. 2. [3] D. Swift, pp. 33–4.
[4] Woodbridge, pp. 2–4.
[5] Sir John Temple, *The Irish Rebellion . . . Now Reprinted*, 1679, p. 31.

attitude; here spotless virtue shrieks with that indignation which wolves always mouth against sheep who bite: he places entire blame upon the natives for

> a rebellion so execrable in itself, so odious to God and the whole world, as no age, no kingdom, no people can parallel the horrid cruelties, the abominable murders, that have been without number, as well as without mercy committed upon the British inhabitants throughout the land, of what sex or age, of what quality or condition soever they were.[1]

In an age when at the most a few hundred men directed all the affairs of Ireland, and the same figures appeared now as lords justices, now as bishops, and now as college provosts, nobody in Sir John's station could fail to have dealings with Ormonde. Even outside the continual shoulder-rubbing of a small viceregal society, Temple as a privy councillor would regularly meet the lord lieutenant, argue with him, and help draft official messages from the council to the king's own deputy.[2] But while Ormonde felt sympathetic with the people among whom his ancestors had lived and died, Temple had two feet in England. Carte, the biographer of Ormonde, indicates that the councillors did all they could to aggravate the differences between the Irish and the king. Evidently they expected that with the end of the war great territories in Ireland would, as they wrote to the lord lieutenant, 'lie the more open to his majesty's free disposal, and to a general settlement of peace and religion by introducing of English'.[3]

> By their own hopes of greater gains from forfeited estates by the spreading of the Rebellion, they did not care to have it crushed in the bud.[4]

The venal calculations were not wholly belied by the event. Only three years after the Cromwellian (1652) Settlement, Gen-

[1] J. Temple, *The Irish Rebellion*, p. 31.

[2] Among the Carte MSS. in the Bodleian Library are many messages from the Irish Privy Councillors, including Sir John Temple, to Ormonde; there are also letters from Sir William Temple, much later, to Ormonde.

[3] Carte II. 140. [4] *Ibid.*, p. 6.

eral Fleetwood was writing that the country was quiet: English people might come over and buy land confidently, for they would find Ireland little different from home; considering what the devastation had been, the 'plenty' that had sprung up—for the 'Anglo-Irish'—was 'wonderful'.[1] Among those who took advantage of this situation were, of course, the Swifts.

[1] Froude I. 138–9.

Chapter Three

DUBLIN

About the immediate setting, material and human, of Swift's childhood, we do know a little. It was either at the Restoration or shortly before—when the royalist reaction was obviously setting in and Ireland was calm—that Swift's father and uncles crossed St George's Channel. Deane Swift, grandson of Godwin, says they left England shortly after their father's death in 1658,[1] but allusions to them in Ireland seem to commence only about 1660. Godwin, the eldest (and executor of his father's will), was called to the English bar July 1660, and to the Irish bar not until May 1663.[2] But William, the fourth son, was admitted a solicitor in Dublin in November 1661; and Jonathan had begun to work at the King's Inns, Dublin (hall of the lawyers' corporation of Ireland), about 1660.[3] Adam, the youngest, seems to have come over last; and Dryden, the second son, does not seem to have reached Ireland at all. Thomas stayed in England and followed his father's profession. Although Jonathan, like Dryden, died young, the remaining three immigrants managed to set themselves up in prosperous comfort.

When Godwin and his brothers arrived in Ireland, they settled in Dublin, the seat of government and centre of wealth. Even Adam, who eventually got himself an estate in the north (where he became a Member of Parliament), kept a place in the capital.[4] To an unpleasant degree, Dublin was an island of Anglican civili-

[1] D. Swift, p. 15. [2] Ball I. 371–2, n.; Fletcher, *Gray's Inn* I. 4–31.

[3] D. Swift, p. 15; Ball I. 8–9, n. 4; *N. & Q.*, 15 Nov. 1947, p. 497; see Appendix A.

[4] *N. & Q.*, 15 Aug. 1857, pp. 124–5; 10 Jul. 1858, p. 24. In his will, 27 May 1704, Adam Swift describes himself as of Greencastle, county Down, but he probably lived much of the year in Dublin (Ball I. 24, n. 2).

zation. Yet during the decade following the Restoration it held upwards of thirty or forty thousand inhabitants—possibly as many as seventy thousand—and was considered one of the first five or six cities of western Europe.[1] In the British Isles it was larger than any city outside the capital—supposedly more populous even than Bristol, then the second city of England. On the Continent only Paris, Rome, Amsterdam, and Venice seem to have been larger.

The city had long since burst through its medieval walls but was not yet distinguished by the great neo-classical or Palladian edifices which in the eighteenth century came to dominate its architecture. The landmarks were still the two cathedrals, the castle, and the single-colleged university. Nevertheless, a Parisian touring Ireland about the time of Swift's birth called Dublin 'one of the greatest and best-populated towns in Europe'.[2]

The river Liffey crossed the city from west to east, going on to empty into the Bay of Dublin. South of the river lay the oldest quarter, including what remained of the medieval walls, with their seventeen towers and gate-towers generally in poor repair. Within these walls and nearly at the centre of the ancient town stood Christ Church Cathedral. South-east of it, forming a corner of the fortifications, Dublin Castle rose, 'with the miserable trickle of the Poddle river serving as a ditch round two of its sides'.[3] St Patrick's Cathedral (not yet steepled) was outside this district, about half a mile south of Christ Church; and due east of the castle, on rising ground near the widening Liffey and—in Swift's youth—on the border of the expanding city, lay the buildings of Trinity College.

Close to the west edge of the castle, and containing its parish church, was the parish of St Werburgh's, one of the oldest sections of Dublin. Here, adjoining St Werburgh's Street, and just under the old south-east wall (then still standing), was the group

[1] Jouvin, p. 414; Petty II. 498, 538–9; Maxwell, p. 102, n. Petty, *c.* 1686, estimated the Dublin population at 69,000; Connell, p. 25 and *passim*, shows that Petty tended grossly to underestimate population figures. Edmund Lloyd, in his *Description of Dublin*, 1732, reckoned the city's population to be 150,000 (p. 4).

[2] Jouvin, p. 414. [3] Maurice James Craig, *Dublin 1660–1860*, 1952, p. 5.

of buildings called Hoey's Court, where Swift's mother was living when he was born. Describing the location, Sir Henry Craik remarks that it

> was then one of the best [neighbourhoods] in Dublin, and the houses, though conveniently close to the principal street, were approached only by sedan chairs, and thus relieved from the noise of the thoroughfare. The street close by (St. Werburg Street), was the busy street of Dublin.[1]

During Swift's early years Hoey's Court (erected in the seventeenth century) and St Werburgh's Street were where prominent lawyers lived. At the fashionable parish church the services were thronged, and there was a state seat for the lord lieutenant. In Fishamble Street, the northerly continuation of St Werburgh's, lived some of the Grattans, whose illustrious men were to be cherished and admired by Swift.[2] In the southerly continuation, Bride Street, lived William Swift, close by his brothers Godwin and Adam in Bull Alley (which belonged to the same street). Their parish church was St Bride's, where Godwin and Adam were vestrymen. Richard Steele's father, an attorney, established his family in this parish; and Steele was baptized in St Bride's.[3]

When Abigail Erick came to Dublin, and how she met her husband, we are not sure. Since her parents apparently emigrated to Ireland in 1634, however, she was probably born there.[4] In her marriage licence she was described as 'of the city of Dublin spinster'.[5] With a persecuted Nonconformist minister for a father, she must have had a sober, devout upbringing. Of her character and opinions when she was betrothed to Swift's father, nothing more definite can be said.

But several hints are preserved concerning the affiliations of the Swifts as her son was to see them. Those of his uncles who moved to Dublin carried with them an admiration for their father who had just died. For this, the main reasons were his own

[1] Craik I. 11. [2] Gilbert I. 6, 13, 14, 30, 36, 44, 57.

[3] G. A. Aitken, *The Life of Richard Steele*, 1889, I. 13, 14, n. 1; also C. Winton in *JEGP.*, LVIII (1959), 264–9.

[4] See Appendix C. [5] Ball IV. 475.

devotion to the cause of Charles I, and the drastic punishments which that loyalty had brought down upon him. He was certainly ejected from his two livings in 1646, and imprisoned for a time in Raglan Castle; and some of his belongings were certainly seized; he was accused of being 'active', 'incendious', and in arms against Parliament.[1] The Cromwellians are less reliably reported to have looted his home several times, attacked his large family, and ruined his property. The harassment may not have been quite so devilish as portrayed in the accounts of royalist sympathizers. That his wife and children did undergo painful hardships, however, is clear. Rooted in the family and household where Swift was to grow up, there lived a deep pride in this record of truth to the crown. The Goodrich vicar's son, the elder Jonathan Swift, showed not only a respect for the legend but an appreciation of its political utility, in a petition for the stewardship of the King's Inns: 'Your petitioner, his father and theire whole family have been always very loyall and faithfull to his sacred majestie and his royall father and have beene very greate sufferers upon that account.'[2] Swift himself, writing his fragment of an autobiography, went into much more detail about this ancestor and his trials than about anyone else except Swift. In 1726 he presented to the Goodrich church a chalice which his grandfather had used, with a Latin inscription running in part, 'notus in historiis ob ea quae fecit et passus est pro Carolo primo'.[3] Thirteen years later, writing to Pope, he recalled the 'poor old gentleman's' sufferings.[4] Even Deane Swift, a great-grandson, kept up the proud tone, and called his forebear 'one of the greatest examples of patience, constancy, and spirit' to have appeared in England.[5]

In addition to these social and political traditions, the family had two literary ties which Swift would not consider negligible. The obvious one was the Dryden connection. But besides that, Sir William Davenant was allied to them through his daughter Mary, who married Swift's non-migrating uncle Thomas, the

[1] A. G. Matthews, *Walker Revised* (Oxford 1948), p. 196, where there are further references.

[2] King's Inns, Dublin, MS. *The Black Book*, f. 203.

[3] D. Swift, Appendix, p. 22. [4] Sherburn IV. 174. [5] D. Swift, p. 14.

clergyman. This uncle took his B.A. degree at Balliol, establishing a pattern which his son was eventually to imitate for the M.A. degree and which through him in turn influenced Jonathan Swift to follow a similar course at Hart Hall, Oxford. Uncle Thomas, after some service as a country parson, managed to obtain a church in London; but like Swift's father he died both unexpectedly and without accumulating much wealth. At the time he was only thirty-six,[1] and left an infant son, also named Thomas, who had probably been born in the Davenant family's Oxford home. Since this boy, a year or two older than Swift, was to share most of his early experiences, the Davenant connection could not have seemed remote. In a dry comment upon the aftermath of the death, Swift suggests that he appreciated the degree of analogy between the bereaved family and his own: 'His widow lived long, was extremely poor, and in part supported by the famous Dr South, who had been her husband's intimate friend.'[2] The child of such a marriage would have seemed to live in a situation close enough to Swift's to allow each boy easily to identify himself with the other.

For a happier story, Swift could have looked to the career of his uncle Godwin (1628–95). Yet Godwin's hopeful beginnings reveal just the possibilities which failed to excite his nephew. This uncle had received a legal education, entering Gray's Inn as a student in 1650.[3] His success as a lawyer was enhanced by his marriage to Elizabeth Wheeler, first of his four wives; for she had a distant connection with the Duchess of Ormonde.[4] There is no doubt that the great Duke—'who well the noblest objects knew to choose'—used his influence on Godwin's behalf. In Ireland, Godwin flourished. His application for the office of filacer in the Court of Common Pleas was granted in 1660.[5] This post, originally charged with the filing of writs, the issuing of processes, etc.,

[1] See Foster; Henry Isham Longden, *Northamptonshire and Rutland Clergy* (Northampton 1938–52), XIII, 131; George Hennessy, *Novum Repertorium Ecclesiasticum Parochiale Londinense*, 1898, p. 143; Arthur H. Nethercot, *Sir William Davenant* (Chicago 1938), pp. 345, 406; Ball VI. 215.

[2] *Autob.*, f. 5v. [3] Ball I. 371–2, n. 3; VI. 212.

[4] Mason, p. 227; Ball I. 11, n. 1. [5] *SPI.*, *1660–2*, p. 83; *1663–5*, p. 469.

had become a sinecure; and it was later held by Godwin's younger brother, William.[1] Furthermore, among the estates which Ormonde regained was the county palatine of Tipperary, to which an attorney-generalship belonged. This office too he bestowed upon Godwin Swift, though only until 1668.[2] Neither appointment should imply that Godwin actually appeared much in courts of law, whether in his public duties or his private career: Swift says he was 'an ill pleader, but perhaps a little too dextrous in the subtil parts of the law'.[3] His business was that of attorney or solicitor, and people often employed him—as Deane Swift, his grandson, writes—to draw up 'great settlements'.[4] When in 1664 he was slandered as having cheated when drafting a will, he petitioned Ormonde for freedom to take action against his accusers.[5]

[1] Ball I. 8–9, n. 4.

[2] *Ibid.* VI. 212. A letter of 13 June 1668 from Ormonde to Godwin Swift, removing him, is among the unpublished Ormonde MSS. in the National Library, Dublin.

[3] *Autob.*, ff. 9–9ᵛ. [4] D. Swift, Appendix, p. 32.

[5] *HMC.*, IX, pt. II, pp. 127a, 145a.

Chapter Four

INFANCY

When her son was born, 30 November 1667, Abigail Swift was a widow. Her husband had died in March or April; but, as Swift is reported to have said, the new child 'came time enough to save his mother's credit'.[1] The elder Jonathan Swift had settled in Ireland about 1660 and perhaps through his brother Godwin's influence obtained a post at the King's Inns. This was the legal society of Ireland, corresponding to such English bodies as Lincoln's or Gray's Inns; Sir John Temple was on the governing board. Here the young newcomer began as assistant to Thomas Wale, the steward of the society. In the summer of 1664 he married Abigail Erick: both bride and groom were twenty-four years old. When, more than a year later, Thomas Wale died, Jonathan Swift petitioned for his place. By an order dated 25 January 1665/6 and signed, among others, by Sir John Temple, he was 'admitted steward of this house'; and the following day he was made a member of the society. A few months later the first child of Jonathan and Abigail Swift was born, a daughter named Jane, baptized 1 May 1666.[2]

Swift wrote of his father as a person only that 'he had some employments, and agencyes; his death was much lamented on account of his reputation for integrity with a tolerable good understanding'.[3] On the improvidence of the marriage, however, he was almost eloquent; and the personal note in his comment should temper any surprise one might be inclined to feel over Swift's later attitude toward wedlock:

[1] Pilkington, p. 57.
[2] For the facts in this paragraph, see *N. & Q.*, 15 Nov. 1947, pp. 496–8.
[3] *Autob.*, f. 6.

> This marriage was on both sides very indiscreet, for his wife brought her husband little or no fortune, and his death happening so suddenly before he could make a sufficient establishment for his family: and his son (not then born) hath often been heard to say that he felt the consequences of that marriage not onely through the whole course of his education, but during the greatest part of his life.[1]

The death of her husband left Mrs Swift dependent upon the generosity of her brothers-in-law. Yet even with the assistance of William Swift and the encouragement of the officers of the society, she recovered 'but a very inconsiderable sum'[2] out of the fees—totalling something like a hundred pounds—due her late spouse. If (as her husband's great-nephew unreliably reports) the income she was left with came to only twenty pounds a year, it could not have supported her family of three.[3]

The relations between Swift and his mother make one of the puzzles in his life. His words about her are all in praise, and by every account she was an unusual woman. However, only one direct indication remains of his attitude towards her, the private comment which he wrote in his memoranda when he was notified of her death:

> On Wednesday, between seven and eight, in the evening, May 10, 1710, I received a letter in my chamber at Laracor, (Mr. Percivall and [Jo] Beaumont being by) from Mrs. Fenton [i.e., his sister Jane], dated May 9th, with one enclosed, sent from Mrs. Worrall at Leicester to Mrs. Fenton, giving an account, that my dear mother Mrs. Abigail Swift died that morning, Monday, April 24, 1710, about ten o'clock, after a long sickness, being ill all winter, and lame, and extremely ill a month or six weeks before her death. I have now lost my barrier between me and death; God grant I may live to be as well prepared for it, as I confidently believe her to have been! If the way to Heaven be through piety, truth, justice, and charity, she is there.[4]

One does not doubt the sincerity of this tribute. There is no

[1] *Autob.*, f. 6. [2] *Black Book*, f. 250v. [3] D. Swift, p. 23.

[4] Nichols x. 104–5, from a page now lacking in Swift's account book for 1709–10.

equivocation, and Swift expected no one besides himself to read the words. His affection and respect for Abigail Swift are delivered with intense feeling. To the 'piety, truth, justice, and charity' which he lists as characteristic of her, he added, in a letter almost two decades later, the trait of prudence.[1] People who knew the family have told some anecdotes which give her also a liveliness unmentioned in her son's allusions. The most entertaining is John Lyon's story of her visit to Dublin, after Swift received a benefice not far from the capital. She stayed with Mrs Brent, a printer's wife, who was later to be Swift's housekeeper. Upon her arrival, Mrs Swift disclosed to her landlady that she had an admirer in Dublin who had been corresponding with her, and that he would soon come to pay his addresses. Of course, the gentleman who presently appeared was Swift. His mother spoke with him alone for a while, then called Mrs Brent in. The son was presented as the lover, supposedly the only one, of Mrs Swift. 'The doctor smiled at his mother's humour', writes Lyon, and he 'afterwards paid his duty to her every day as expected by Mrs. Brent'.[2]

It is easy to accept the portrait of Mrs Swift as a good Christian, honest and prudent, but cheerful and willing to make up an innocent practical joke. Swift's personality reflects such influences. The difficulty is in her treatment of him during his childhood. Or perhaps it is in her lack of treatment. Among good English families it was customary for infants to be boarded out with wet nurses who were usually country women. How common the practice was, may be judged from Jeremy Taylor's protest against the physical and moral corruptions to which the vulgarity, ignorance, and carelessness of most nurses exposed their victims.[3] Although his attack has antecedents going back to Plutarch and beyond, the custom persisted long after the reign of Queen Anne. The *Spectator's* complaint is well known.[4] Swift's nurse was not, however, the monster whom Taylor and Steele feared. His mother, moreover, was evidently wise enough to have him breast-fed rather than submitted to the usual alternative, rearing by

[1] Ball IV. 55. [2] Lyon, f. 9 of preliminaries.
[3] *Works*, 3rd ed., 1839, II, 38. [4] 12 Dec. 1711, by Steele.

hand—on bread-and-water pap, or a flour-and-sugar posset, or syrup of violets.[1]

In Swift's case the difficulty was too much, not too little, attention from the foster-parent. 'Irish nurses', an English visitor wrote in 1681, 'are very tender and good to the children of others of higher degree, and most commonly their love is more to them than to their own.'[2] Although Swift said his nurse was English by birth, her attitude fits the native pattern. In fact, she fell in love with him. To quote the victim's own words,

> his nurse who was a woman of Whitehaven, being under an absolute necessity of seeing one of her relations, who was then extremely sick, and from whom she expected a legacy; and being at the same time extremely fond of the infant, she stole him on ship board unknown to his mother and uncles, and carried him with her to Whitehaven, where he continued for almost three years. For, when the matter was discovered, his mother sent orders by all means not to hazard a second voyage, till he could be better able to bear it.[3]

He adds that the nurse taught him to spell and that when he was three years old, he could read 'any chapter in the Bible' (meaning, perhaps, the New Testament only). While the authority for the kidnapping is unimpeachable, the comment of Emile Pons, that it sounds like '*un conte de fées*', seems pertinent.[4] Swift wrote out the received version when he was over seventy and notoriously forgetful; his fragment of an autobiography has as many errors as facts.[5] The details must be handled with caution. In 1734 he wrote, 'I happened indeed by a perfect accident, to be born here [i.e., in Ireland], my mother being left here from returning to her

[1] Rosamond Bayne-Powell, *The English Child in the Eighteenth Century*, 1939, p. 163.

[2] Thomas Dineley, from extracts in *Journal of the Kilkenny . . . Archaeological Society*, new ser., I (1856–7), 185.

[3] *Autob.*, ff. 7–7^{v}. The 's' in 'uncles' is not certain.

[4] Pons, p. 117.

[5] D. Swift, *c.* 1754, says the fragment was composed 'about six or eight and twenty years ago'; but in the fragment itself Swift says his grandfather's house, dated 1636, 'is above a hundred years old' (f. 2^{v}); and in a letter of April 1739 he echoes the language of the fragment in a way that suggests he was writing both near the same time (Sherburn IV. 174). Monck Mason also mentions an extract from the *Mercurius Rusticus* account of the vicar of Goodrich, endorsed by Swift, 'Memoirs of my grand-father, Thomas Swift, by Mr. Lyon; April 1738' (p. 228, n. c).

house at Leicester, and I was a year old before I was sent to England.'[1]

That Swift accepted the kidnapping as truth cannot be denied. He tells it in a straightforward passage of a factual account. An acquaintance close to him in his last years says that Swift loved Whitehaven as though he had been born there. Even toward the end of his life, in 1740, he was happy to hear that a merchant from the town was in Dublin with his son and daughters. Swift 'invited them to dine with him and paid them many civilities while they stayed'.[2] Deane Swift, who speaks here with authority, says,

> His return to Ireland about three years after [the kidnapping], gave occasion to many ludicrous whims and extravagancies in the gaiety of his conversation. Sometimes he would declare, that he was not born in Ireland at all; and seem to lament his condition, that he should be looked upon as a native of that country; and would insist, that he was stolen from England when a child, and brought over to Ireland in a band-box.[3]

Whenever the child was returned to his mother, he did not remain long with her. At the age of six—around 1673[4]—he was sent to the excellent grammar school in Kilkenny (a little over

[1] Ball v. 64. [2] Lyon, p. 10.

[3] P. 26. Letitia Pilkington gives what reads like a garbled recollection of Swift's stories about his infancy: 'The account I have frequently heard the Dean give of himself was that he was born in Hoy's Alley, in Warburgh's parish, Dublin; his father was a lawyer, and, returning from the circuit, he unfortunately brought home the itch with him, which he had got by lying in some foul bed on the road. Somebody advised him to use mercury to cure it, which prescription cost him his life in a very few days after his return. The Dean was a posthumous son to this gentleman, but, as he said, came time enough to save his mother's credit. He was given to an Irish woman to nurse, whose husband being in England and writing to her to come to him; as she could not bear the thoughts of parting with the child, she very fairly took him with her, unknown to his mother or any of his relations, who could learn no tidings either of him or her for three years; at the end of which time she returned to Ireland, and restored the child to his mother, from whom she easily obtained a pardon, both on account of the joy she conceived at seeing her only son again, when she had in a manner lost all hope of it, as also that it was plain the nurse had no other motive for stealing him but pure affection, which the women of Ireland generally have in as eminent degree for the children they nurse as for their own offspring' (pp. 57–8).

[4] So Swift says. He may be wrong, since boys admitted to Kilkenny College 1684–6 ranged in age from nine to fifteen; see Hodges, p. 14, n.

seventy miles south-west of Dublin), which had been established by the Ormonde family. While her son was at school, Mrs Swift did not remain in Ireland but moved with his sister to Leicester.[1] She may have visited Dublin and seen him there from time to time; however, there is no proof that they met again until he left the university. It is certain that if Swift went to England during the interval, he did so only once.[2]

One is left with the impression that Mrs Swift had access to her son for the first year of his life, for a year or two before he entered school, and for short periods during infrequent visits afterwards. The behaviour did not appear odd, as no early biographer of Swift picked it out for special comment. He himself implies that his mother's conduct seemed normal to him.[3] During the late seventeenth century, of course, the rate of infant mortality, the teachings of religion, and the demands of a harsh environment were still working to make parents less reverent of children than they have since become. Yet, even granting such mitigations of Mrs Swift's apparent coolness, nobody could argue that Swift's early years were suffused with a warm maternal glow.

If we assume a childhood to be natural when it is passed with a father and mother, in a secure family and a settled residence, Swift had to deal with shattering conditions. His father was gone before the son even appeared. Such a loss would give fatherhood unique meaning: missing it so deeply, Swift would expect much from those whom he set in his own father's place; and he would therefore feel repeatedly disappointed by these older men. On those whom he loved, he would bestow, as his best gift, a father-

[1] Forster, p. 40; although this fact is always assumed, it has not been proved; one might have expected the mother to wait until the son entered the university. Since Jane Swift was married in Dublin 1699 (though she settled at last in England), her youthful connection with Ireland could not have ended in the 1670's. Lyon says that she was at her uncle's (presumably William) in Bride Street, Dublin, when she wrote her letter of 26 May 1699 (Lyon, f. 7 of preliminaries; Ball I. 30 and n. 2).

[2] See *MLN.*, LXV (Apr. 1950), 256–7.

[3] None of his letters to her is extant; but the heading of one which he never completed is preserved on a leaf used for notes:

Moor Park—August the 5th 1698

Dear Mother.

(*Bulletin of the John Rylands Library*, XXXVII [1954–5], 372.)

liness too stern for their needs, or a father's direction where they looked for a lover's softness.

The early loss of his true mother; the loss, a few years later, of his nurse, or foster-mother; and the loss again of his own mother, would accustom him, as a natural pattern, to separation from women who loved him, to sudden partings with women whom he felt drawn to. We may speculate that he would therefore tend to forestall the misery of being thrown off by curtailing an attachment before the woman should do so. His sister's advantage in seniority, and in continuously enjoying their mother's presence while he lived among cousins or strangers, was complicated by the odd design of all their travels: for after a long separation during which he must have been reminded of them by his nurse, he rejoined the mother and daughter in circumstances which almost surely made an anti-climax; he then was sent away from them to the Kilkenny School, and finally found they had gone to England together. When he was in England alone, his mother and sister were together in Dublin; when he was in Ireland alone, his mother and sister were together in Leicester. It would seem normal to him (we may further speculate) that a woman he loved should move away as he approached, or that he should move away from one who approached him; it would seem normal that a child should cut himself off from his family and choose to live in another household. Finally, if we assume that he resented his mother's apparent neglect of him, but that he could not admit such a complaint openly (even to himself), an obvious question is what became of the feeling. Unless Swift was remarkably different from other children, he probably attached the resentment to the sister who had enjoyed his mother's attention while he was missing it. We should not feel puzzled if as an adult he acted coldly towards Jane, especially if his coldness should seem (to him) connected with her making a marriage as imprudent as their mother's.

Chapter Five

KILKENNY

Swift's knowing how to read at an early age need not imply that he was unduly precocious. The achievement was apparently a goal not infrequently set by eager parents or guardians. Aubrey reports that Katherine Phillips 'had read the Bible thorough before she was full four yeares old'. An early seventeenth-century writer on education was annoyed that grammar schools had to be troubled with the very young in the first place, and thought no child should enter until he could read the New Testament in English.[1] One may reasonably say that Swift would have learned at home how to read and write English, also a little arithmetic. He would have become familiar with his primer (or some equivalent), the psalms, and of course the New Testament. By the school statutes of 1684, the Kilkenny students had to know their Latin accidence before entering, and to be ready immediately for the study of grammar.[2]

At this school a high level of preparation was probably expected of the boys. Founded in the sixteenth century by the eighth Earl of Ormonde, here was certainly the finest institution of its kind in Ireland. The best of the 'old English' gentry of the Pale sent their sons to it; and among the students had been Richard Stanyhurst, the Elizabethan historian and translator of Virgil; Peter Lombard, historian and Roman Catholic Archbishop of Armagh; and Luke Wadding, a Franciscan scholar and a fervent organizer-in-exile of Irish Catholic patriotism.

[1] Foster Watson, 'The Curriculum and Textbooks of English Schools in the First Half of the Seventeenth Century', *Transactions of the Bibliographical Society*, VI, pt. I (Oct. 1900–Mar. 1901), 160.

[2] Edward Ledwich published the statutes in *History and Antiquities of Kilkenny*, in *Collectanea de Rebus Hibernicis*, IX (Dublin 1781), 509–17.

It was the normal training ground for the boys of Swift's family.

The town itself stretched mostly between the Ormondes' castle, high on a cliff overlooking a bend in the river, and the thirteenth-century cathedral, on a rise about a thousand yards north-west. We know what impression the town made upon a visitor in 1709:

> Kilkenny is a large straggling city with Irishtown. I think it has as much ground under it as any I have seen except Dublin. The houses are but ordinary. There are here several old abbeys and buildings, one of them the cathedral of St Kenny's [i.e., St Canice's], a fine old Gothick building. Kilkenny is finely watered by several excellent springs, by the noble river Nore and two others. From a bridge on the former you have a fine prospect of the castle belonging (as does most of the town) to the Duke of Ormond. 'Twas built [i.e., greatly rebuilt, at the Restoration] by the old duke. It is finely situated to the river but in no other respect answerable to the character it bears. There is not one handsome or noble apartment. The rooms are dark and the stairs mighty ugly.[1]

The school stood in the west of the cathedral churchyard[2] and accommodated from fifty to sixty boys, most of them between nine and fifteen years old. Some, Swift was to know in later life: his cousin Thomas, William Congreve (admitted only half a year before Swift left), Francis Stratford, who as merchant and speculator was to make and lose a hundred thousand pounds.[3]

At the head of the school stood men who provided these boys not only with a stern set of moral principles but also with immedi-

[1] Thomas Molyneux, in T.C.D. MS. I. I. 3 (*Natural History of Ireland*, pp. 91–2). I have freely made deletions and altered spelling and punctuation.

[2] It is sometimes said that the school in Swift's time was already on its present site, across the river from the old town. But all the references to the new site seem to date from 1684, except for one dated 1666 which I take to be a misreading of 1686. The date on the entrance gateway, on the register, and on the statutes is 1684. But see John Browne, 'Kilkenny College', *Transactions of the Kilkenny Archaeological Society*, I (1849–51), 221–9 (Dublin 1853).

[3] See Burtschaell. Stratford is entered at T.C.D. as coming from a 'Mr. Wilson', and not Ryder; however, Swift twice says they were at 'school and university' together (*Journal*, 14 Sept. 1710, 1 Mar. 1711/12).

ate examples of how well-directed talent, elevated by responsive patronage, could climb to power and dignity in the established church. In addition, one of the men eventually provided a showpiece of how little integrity of character might underlie both the expressions of morality and the happy career. A prudent use of hypocrisy and a wise choice of sponsorship were effective, if not essential, factors of ecclesiastical prosperity.

During Swift's stay, the Kilkenny School was under two successive masters of extraordinary abilities: Edward Jones and Henry Ryder. Jones (1641–1703), who came from Wales, had been educated at Westminster School and at Trinity College, Cambridge, winning scholarships at both. He took his B.A. degree in 1664 and was elected a fellow of his college three years later. Going to Ireland as domestic chaplain to the Duke of Ormonde (then lord lieutenant), Jones became master of the school at Kilkenny in 1670. After ten years, during which his church preferments steadily mounted, he left; and in 1683 he was made Bishop of Cloyne. Returning to England during the troubles of 1688–90, he never again settled in Ireland. In 1692 he was made Bishop of St Asaph, a charge which he distinguished by 'corruption, negligence, and oppression'.[1] After considerable litigation he was suspended for eleven months (1701–2) and died a year after resuming his function.

The nature of Jones's crimes, though not directly relevant to Swift's career, is worth noticing as a specimen of what could be accomplished by a thoroughly unscrupulous prelate—a specimen about which Swift could not have missed hearing:

> By his own confession he had promoted to a canonry one who had been accused to him of crimes and excesses; he had permitted laymen to perform the office of curates; he had been guilty of a simoniacal contract in the disposal of some of his preferments, and had allowed his wife to receive money, by way of earnest, for certain promotions. Besides which, he had been in the habit of appropriating to himself a year's profits of vacant livings, on the plea of carrying

[1] *DNB*.

on the lawsuit for the recovery of an advowson—a plea, it is almost needless to add, never put into practice.[1]

Swift's other master enjoyed both a speedier rise and a deeper integrity. Born of a Bedfordshire family, Henry Ryder (*c.* 1646–96) had also been a scholar at Westminster School as well as Trinity College, Cambridge. He took his B.A. degree in 1666/7 and went to Ireland in 1672 to be master of the Free School in Dublin. About eight years later, Ormonde persuaded him to leave that post and come to Kilkenny. Ambitious, like Jones, for ecclesiastical preferment, Ryder did not long remain a schoolmaster. He managed to accept a prebend of Ossory (1681) without giving up his work in Kilkenny; but in 1683 he was collated to a prebend of St Patrick's Cathedral, and he moved back to Dublin soon after. His progress in the church lasted until he became Bishop of Killaloe, 1693.[2]

For fourteen years, therefore, the Kilkenny School was headed by men from Trinity College, Cambridge. Thomas Cartwright, a founder of the Puritan party in England, had been a fellow of Trinity, where his influence was powerful. The tradition of Calvinism was a Cambridge tradition, and the movement was almost as strong in Trinity as in Emmanuel College, from which came the fathers of Puritan New England. In the selection of a schoolmaster, theology was a high consideration; and Jones and Ryder may well have brought to Kilkenny some of the austerity and intensity which they had met as undergraduates.

In neither the curriculum nor the pupil discipline of Anglican schools at this period was there much variety. Clothing, games, buildings, the government of masters or ushers might indeed differ widely. But the studies and the moral training of the boys did not. By combining what we know of Restoration pedagogy in general with the details of a Kilkenny School charter given only

[1] Condensed, with omissions, from D. R. Thomas, *The History of the Diocese of St Asaph*, 1908, I. 137.

[2] Venn; G. F. R. Barker and A. H. Stenning, *Record of Old Westminsters*, 1928, II, 811; H. J. Lawlor, *Fasti of St Patrick's* (Dundalk 1930), pp. 139, 254.

two years after Swift left, we can deduce the elements of his education.

We may, on all grounds, assume, therefore, that the pupils at Kilkenny underwent a solid course of education. It would probably have started in the fifth form with the reading, writing, and speaking of Latin. When they reached the fourth form, the children would learn syntax, parsing, and construing, while continuing to improve their earlier accomplishments. A book commonly read at this point was *Aesop's Fables*. Greek was often added in the third form, where the readings might include the New Testament in Latin and Greek; students would learn to write letters and to make double translations (English–Latin and Latin–English); they would be embarking upon such standard authors as Caesar, Cicero, and Terence. The second form would probably include oratory, the composition of Greek verses, Greek–Latin double translation, and more difficult authors. In the first form Hebrew might be introduced. The study of rhetoric in the upper forms was particularly important because of the value, in adult life, of effective writing and public oratory. In fact, the highest product of the written exercises was the formal theme; and the goal of the spoken exercises was the oration—both, of course, in Latin.

Throughout the curriculum, naturally, a fundamental aim was the inculcation of Anglican doctrine and morality.[1] 'The teaching a little Latin and Greek . . . would not deserve the name of Christian education; were not at the same time the greatest regard had to the subduing of *disorderly passions*, the rectifying of *perverse inclinations*, the implanting of *virtuous habits*, and the securing of them by *religious principles*, which are attainments far beyond all the most *curious arts* and *profoundest sciences* in the world.'[2] The sort of character-training which accompanied formal instruction at home and in school may be gathered from one of the numerous 'advice' books of the period, implicitly designed—many of them—to instruct those newly come to the heights of society in the elegant exercise of their increasing power. It was,

[1] Foster Watson, *op. cit.*, pp. 162–6. [2] *The Royal Grammar* (1695), f. A4^{v}.

of course, ordinary that students should be punished for bad manners or indecent deportment; and school statutes can be quoted penalizing foul language, cursing, gambling, physical violence, infringement of the sabbath, disobedience, and slovenly dress.[1] For more elusive principles of conduct and morality, we may generalize from a work like *The Whole Duty of Man*. While this presents ideals, rather than actual conditions, its popularity indicates that the doctrines set forth were commonplaces of counsel if not of behaviour.

The *Whole Duty*, though its authorship is still uncertain, comes obviously from a setting of pious, royalist Anglicanism. The prefatory letter to the first edition (1658) was by the Rev. Dr Henry Hammond, brother-in-law to Sir John Temple and favourite uncle of Sir William Temple. This gracious gentleman, like Swift's grandfather, devoted himself to the cause of Charles I, and similarly died just too soon for the Restoration to compensate him. The book which he introduced was a manual of religious conduct for middle-class and humbler families, adapted 'to the very meanest readers'.[2] If we ponder the number of parsons to whom Swift was related, through both his mother and his father, as well as the nature of his own career, we must assume that the outlook of such a book was congenial to his family circle.

Apart from the need of enforcing active piety in each part of the daily routine—we are recommended to think of Judgment Day while dressing[3]—the *Whole Duty* has a specific and significant tendency. Overpowering all other teachings is the attack on pride. Part of man is spirit, but part is flesh, a lump of corruption, subject to illness, pains, and at last to death—when it is 'laid to rot in the earth'.[4] The soul itself is a battleground where the passions and the will have it out with the understanding. Unless God should step in, the contest will lean toward evil. Let any man look into his heart, says the author, and he will see that his soul is diseased. The understanding is dark; the will is crooked; and the passions are 'disordered and rebellious, even against the voice of

[1] Foster Watson, *The English Grammar Schools to 1660* (1908), pp. 135–6.
[2] *The Whole Duty of Man* (1728), p. i. [3] P. 404. [4] P. i.

his own reason'.[1] So treacherous is man's depravity that marriage has only two purposes: 'the begetting of children, and the avoiding of fornication'.[2] The method of the *Whole Duty* is to deny: it teaches us to shun sin. Nowhere is man safe from the Enemy. Sleep itself, if not severely limited, can be 'many sins in one': waste of time, injury to body, deprivation of the soul, and violation of God's command to labour.[3] The individual is cautioned ceaselessly to examine himself, to upbraid himself, to repent. Today of course the prayer book still keeps these injunctions; but they hardly underprop those manuals of 'life adjustment' which seem our nearest equivalent to the *Whole Duty*.

Exactly how the school was managed while Swift was there we are uncertain. However, the statutes laid down in 1684 have been preserved, and they should be in the same spirit as the earlier conduct.[4] The pupils' morality was strengthened by attendance at the cathedral on Sundays and holy days. Prayers with scripture readings were held every morning and evening. For these, all the boys assembled at seven in the morning during the autumn and winter, six in the spring and summer. Lessons lasted until eleven (or ten), when the pupils went through the catechism for half an hour. Four more hours of classwork followed in the afternoon, beginning at one during the winter, twelve in the spring and summer. On Thursday and Saturday, which were half-days, the routine ended with the catechism; and the afternoons were free for recreation. Otherwise, the twelve-month school year was interrupted only by short vacations at Easter, Whitsuntide, and Christmas, too short for a journey to England.

The little time allowed for play outside might be spent along the river Nore, where Swift probably suffered the tragedy which he was to recall forty or fifty years later: 'When I was a little boy, I felt a great fish at the end of my line which I drew up almost on the ground, but it dropped in, and the disappointment vexes me to this very day.'[5] There is also a credible tradition that the pre-

[1] P. vi. [2] P. 173; cf. the marriage service in the prayer book. [3] Pp. 204–5.

[4] The outline of the school schedule is borrowed from John C. Hodges, *William Congreve* (New York 1941), p. 18.

[5] Ball IV. 76–7.

occupation which he was later to show with Anglo-Latin word games was conceived here, since they were an ancient and universal pastime of schoolboys. 'He said', Lyon writes, 'he first learned, soon after he entered the school, these words which he termed—*Latino-Anglice*, "Mi dux et amasti cum". This kind of writing was afterwards one of those whimsical amusements that he sometimes entertained himself with.'[1] Swift's most important comrade was his cousin, also fatherless and separated from a mother in England. Thomas bore the name of the family hero; he was about the same age as Swift's sister Jane. Although born in Oxfordshire, Thomas apparently fell upon his Irish uncles' charity when he was five years old, because his father died and the widow was left very poor. With such striking parallels to Swift's circumstances, he must have been an effective substitute for an elder brother; and as they were not only to go on through school and university together, but to embark as well upon the same career, the relationship could (for a while) only grow deeper.

What impression did the school make upon Swift? According to his comment more than a quarter-century after he left, it was the usual combination of drudgery and release; certainly these memories are less bitter than the reflections on his Trinity College years:

> I formerly used to envy my own happiness when I was a schoolboy, the delicious holidays, the Saterday afternoon, and the charming custards in a blind alley; I never considered the confinement ten hours a day, to nouns and verbs, the terror of the rod, the bloddy noses, and broken shins.[2]

I have suggested that Swift's relatives trained him in an austere religion and a harsh morality. Against the crazy shifts of material circumstance during the Commonwealth and Restoration in

[1] Lyon, pp. 12–13: the translation is, 'My ducks eat a masticum'. The tradition of Swift's carving his name on the sideboard of a seat is too weak to be worth refuting (John Browne, 'Kilkenny College', *Transactions of the Kilkenny Archaeological Society*, I, 1849–51 [1853], p. 229). Yet Lyon says, 'In the school-room his name still remains, as he cut it on the side board of the seat of his class with his knife, after the custom of boys' (p. 13).

[2] Ford, 12 Nov. 1708.

Ireland, one may assume that such rigorous principles came to seem the more attractive and absolute to those who held them. In a school established on the same principles and managed by masters themselves imbued with the spirit of Trinity College, Cambridge, we can only suppose that the corruption of the human heart became plainer to the young eye. Hard industry was necessary to occupy the errant attention; constant self-amendment was needed to put down pride; and the power of the rational will had constantly to be employed against the disorders of the passions. If Swift does not mention such lessons, it was probably because he took them for granted. Yet to a child born fatherless and cut off from his mother, his teachers should have seemed parents indeed, especially when they inculcated the historical prejudices, the political dogmas, the stern faith, and stern morals of his family. Contrariwise, in a more elusive process, through knowing cousin Thomas, rather than sister Jane, as an elder comrade, by living among schoolmates and masters who were exclusively masculine, and following a regime that allowed only a few quick interruptions of the school year, Swift would probably have found the remote femininity of his mother and sister to be a deepening enigma, with associations of danger, allurement and jealousy.

Chapter Six

TRINITY COLLEGE

Many but not most of the boys leaving the Kilkenny School went on to the university: from April 1685 to March 1687 less than a third did so. Almost as many returned home 'to their father', whatever might be his occupation. Some were apprenticed to attorneys, surgeons, or merchants; one to a sadler (in London). One left 'to be a gardiner'. Some became ill; one 'left the 5 class sicke of a consumption'. Swift's cousin Godwin left (July 1686) 'to be a merchant in Spaine'; his cousin Deane left (August 1688) 'to be a merchant in Portugall'.[1] Swift and his cousin Thomas proceeded to Trinity College, the University of Dublin. Under the date 24 April 1682—April was the usual month for boys to go from this school to the university—they were both admitted as pensioners, or paying, boarding undergraduates.[2]

In making this passage, Swift did not leave the province of the Butler family. Ormonde looked after the interests of Trinity College as carefully as he guarded those of the lower school which he had refounded. He considered T.C.D. to be first a nursery of clergymen, and thought the Church of Ireland should be staffed with its graduates.[3] He saw to it that the College recovered its lands in Kerry (which had been claimed by others), and he obtained additional grants to improve its revenues.[4] Carte's praise of Ormonde's devotion to 'that learned society' is not excessive: 'He was a vigilant overseer of their discipline and conduct, a powerful encourager of their studies, a generous patron to such

[1] MS. register of Kilkenny College, in T.C.D. Library. [2] Burtschaell.

[3] Carte IV. 279–80.

[4] E.g., the 'Munster lands' of Bodl. MS. Carte 45, f. 65, and the petition concerning T.C.D. property, mentioned *ibid.*, f. 77.

as were educated in that college.'[1] Before entering, Swift may possibly have visited his mother in Leicester (or, less probably, he may have done so later in his six-year stay at the College): his one voyage to England which we cannot with certainty account for would fit most conveniently here.[2]

There were then over three hundred students in the College,[3] which had been founded at the end of the sixteenth century. The buildings, on the grounds of an Augustinian priory, were set among green fields east of town, about a mile and a half from the castle. Before Swift took his B.A. degree, however, the city, now about 60,000 in population, had expanded to include the College itself.[4]

The grounds lay roughly half a mile south of the Liffey, and were enclosed by an uneven oblong of a wall, the longer sides running parallel with the river. In the west front—one of the narrower sides—stood the gate-house. For the college architecture, the models had obviously been the English university quadrangles. Centred within the whole walled area, like a picture in a large frame, was the original and regular block, erected in 1593. Made of thin red Dutch brick, the houses looked more like Cambridge than Oxford; they were two full stories high, with large dormer windows above in the pointed roofs. The walks edging the inner faces of these buildings surrounded a court which was divided into four plots by a pair of intersecting walks. The space was not much larger than 'two tennis courts stretching side by side'.[5]

In the east and west wings, students were lodged. The south side was for the fellows and perhaps some students; it also housed the library. In the centre of the remaining, north side rose the turreted hall, with the kitchen to the east of it and the chapel to the west. Built on to the south-west corner of the quadrangle, the provost's residence abutted against the west wing. On the north side of the chapel stood a steeple, sole vestige of the Augustinian

[1] Carte IV. 18. [2] See *MLN.*, LXV, 256–7. [3] Maxwell, p. 74

[4] *Ibid.*, p. 102; cf. Luce, *Berkeley*, p. 31, and Stubbs, p. 143; also Ogg II. 11.

[5] Maxwell, p. 11.

priory, kept as a landmark for ships passing up the river. To some restive students, the modest, conventual effect of the block could not have seemed liberating. But tangible marks of encouraging, if erratic, growth stood about. Between the west façade of the quadrangle and the west wall of the entire College, extended a 'Great Court', bordered on the north-west by three L-shaped stories of imposing chambers—'Sir Jerome Alexander's Buildings'—erected in the 1670's. During Swift's residence, additional college chambers were built in the same area by other benefactors.[1] A new hall and chapel, projected by Narcissus Marsh—provost, 1679–83—were under way (on the same sites as the old) when Swift entered. The account of them given by Marsh pictures scenes which Swift often watched, and reminds one that, even in the seventeenth century, scaffolding was a normal feature of the academic landscape:

> Whilst I was Provost of the College, both the hall and the chapel being too little and straight to receive the number of scholars that was then increasing very much each year, I resolved upon building a new hall and chapel. I thought it most proper to begin with the house of God, and thereupon caused the foundation of a new chapel to be laid, and before the structure was half finished I was removed, and Dr. Huntingdon compleated the work. In the meantime the scholars were forced to attend prayers in the College hall. When the chapel was finished, the next work was to build a larger hall, and because the old one could not be conveniently enlarged as it stood, it was necessary to pull that down and to build a larger in its place, both in length and breadth, which was the work of some years. Whilst this was doing the scholars having no place to eat in, they were forced to make use of the library for that purpose, and because the books were not chained, 'twas necessary that they should remove them into some other place. They laid them in heaps in some void rooms.[2]

The constitution of the College possessed a history more complex than that of its fabric. In its early years, the community had,

[1] Stubbs, p. 125.

[2] Condensed from Stubbs, pp. 116–17. I have not indicated my many omissions and changes in spelling and punctuation.

like most Irish institutions, suffered violent alternations of backsliding and reform. Through the reign of James I, moreover, it had retained a close bond with Cambridge; its teachers had been predominantly Puritan; and its religious policy tolerant. When Laud became chancellor of the university (1633), a new charter was procured from the king, less democratic than the original and less tolerant in religion. But a series of ineffectual provosts, the earthquake of the 1641 Rebellion, and the alterations of the Commonwealth radically undermined both the discipline and the finances. At the Restoration, Ormonde resumed his place as chancellor, with Jeremy Taylor (then Bishop of Down and Connor) as vice-chancellor, and Thomas Seele as provost. The reorganization which followed established the College as it stood when Swift entered. Although Taylor died the year of Swift's birth, Seele continued to be provost, and secured the new order.

Besides openly grounding him in the fading traditions, humanistic and scholastic, which made the staple of European university studies, Trinity College re-enforced some moral or social doctrines already familiar to Swift and at the same time introduced him to intellectual currents which were new to him and the world. Thus in its own recent history, as well as in changes made while Swift was a student, the College illustrated again the peculiar mutability of property in Ireland and the dependence of Irish policy upon English events. It also revealed once more both the difficulty and the overwhelming desirability of preserving any stable order in the troubled nation. The heads of the College embodied yet again the assortment of contradictory ingredients which might contribute to advancement in the church: genuine piety and erudition, practised hypocrisy, consistent adherence to the schemes of superiors, private asceticism. But through them and other senior members of the College, Swift also met for the first time the little cloud which was to float eventually over the whole world and toward which his mature attitude is among the problems that the modern reader of his works has most trouble in comprehending: this is the natural philosophy, the new experimental philosophy, inspiring the Royal Society and producing in the end our own idea of science. Contrary to the arguments of many scholars, Swift originally encountered the new philosophy not as in any way subversive of the humanistic or religious orthodoxy of his elders but as embedded in the same groundmass: if he judged by his masters and teachers, it appeared subversive only of those scholastic speculations which came early to disgust Swift himself. Scholars have often connected Swift's mockery of virtuoso experiments with men and books which he came upon as an adult. Yet we will discover the themes of his satire of 'science', including several leit-motivs of both *A Tale of a Tub* and *Gulliver's Travels*, not merely in the general intellectual life of Dublin or Trinity College, but above all in the opinions and researches of his beloved tutor and lifelong friend, Dr Ashe. Finally, if, apart from such factors in the milieu, another kind of token is wanted of what the College came ultimately to signify to Swift, we may look ahead into his middle age and foresee that one of the methods he would most earnestly contemplate for the disposition of his estate would be to leave it to the institution of Jeremy Taylor and St George Ashe.[1]

Under the statutes, as recast by Taylor, the presiding officer of the College still had the title of provost. (As a university—consisting of a single college—the corporate body also owned a chancellor and vice-chancellor.) Besides him, there were seven senior fellows—with power of election—and nine junior fellows. As to their pupils, in addition to the two hundred or more pensioners, provision was made for seventy scholarship students, of whom thirty had to be natives of Ireland—'chosen out of the poorest, if they be deserving'.[2] In a society so narrow, with rather a small gathering of students, the head of the institution must have had a direct influence upon the undergraduates. While Swift was in residence, there were two provosts, Narcissus Marsh (1679–83) and Robert Huntingdon (1683–92). Both men were extraordinary for their piety and scholarship; and in their lives will be seen

[1] G. P. Mayhew, 'Swift's First Will and the First Use of the Provost's Negative at T.C.D.', *Huntington Library Quarterly*, XXI (Aug. 1958), 295–322.

[2] Robert Bolton, *A Translation of the Charter and Statutes of Trinity-College* (Dublin 1749), pp. 31–3.

some of the patterns set most conspicuously before the adolescent Swift.

As an undergraduate at Magdalen Hall, Oxford, Marsh (1638–1713) had been used to fasting every week from six o'clock Thursday evening until eleven Saturday morning. He was ordained even before the canonical age, having been elected a fellow of Exeter College less than five months after taking his B.A. degree. From the principalship of St Alban Hall, Oxford, he came to his Trinity College post (1679) through an appointment arranged by the great Duke of Ormonde.

As a provost, Marsh was more conscientious than serene; and he welcomed his elevation to the bishopric of Ferns and Leighlin (1683). Concerning his resignation from the College, there appears in his diary a famous utterance which should speak to the heart of a modern university administrator:

> Finding this place very troublesome, partly by reason of the multitude of business and impertinent visits the Provost is obliged to, and partly by reason of the ill education that the young scholars have before they come to the College, whereby they are both rude and ignorant; I was quickly weary of 340 young men and boys in this lewd and debauch'd town; and the more so because I had no time to follow my always dearly beloved studies.[1]

Apart from religion, Marsh found his absorbing interests in music, oriental languages, and the new experimental philosophy of nature. In the words of his epitaph, he 'dedicated his leisure hours to the study of mathematics and natural philosophy; and above all was highly skilled in the knowledge of languages, especially the Oriental'.[2]

Marsh was associated with William Petty and William Molyneux in the founding of the Dublin Philosophical Society. On becoming Bishop of Ferns (which did not involve abandoning the capital), he by no means gave up this connection; and among his letters from the country to his fellow philosophers, one of Marsh's characteristic regrets is that he has done little toward his 'history

[1] Maxwell, p. 74. [2] *Biographia Britannica*, v (1760), 3050, n.

of the generation of insects, on which subject I have meditated and made observations for many years': unfortunately, he writes, there are few insects in his present neighbourhood (Staplestown)—'and especially of flies the fewest that I ever saw in any place and of those not one rare or unusual'.[1] This gap between hope and fruition marks his other contributions to the Society's transactions—a catalogue of experiments to be performed with magnets,[2] and a critique of a fellow member's hygroscope.[3]

Though Swift's character of Marsh was composed at least two decades after their academic relationship ended, the unremitting severity of the analysis might suggest a reaction against an adolescent awe of apparent saintliness and erudition:

> His disposition to study is the very same with that of an usurer to hoard up money, or of a vicious young fellow to a wench; nothing but avarice and evil concupiscence, to which his constitution has fortunately given a more innocent turn. He is sordid and suspicious in his domestics, without love or hatred; which is but reasonable, since he has neither friend nor enemy. . . That which relishes best with him, is mixed liquor and mixed company; and he is seldom unprovided with very bad of both. He is so wise to value his own health more than other men's noses, so that the most honourable place at his table is much the worst, especially in summer. It has been affirmed that originally he was not altogether devoid of wit, till it was extruded from his head to make room for other men's thoughts. He will admit a governor, provided it be one who is very officious and diligent, outwardly pious, and one that knows how to manage and make the most of his fear.[4]

Nevertheless, Marsh had one abiding influence upon the young genius which Swift may never have suspected. For it was in the *Institutiones logicæ* written by the provost 'in usum iuventutis academicae Dubliniensis' that he studied those commonplace examples and ancient truisms which he was to manipulate in his most brilliant satires: 'homo est animal rationale'; 'nullus equus est rationale'; 'si simia non sit irrationalis, est homo';

[1] T.C.D. MS. Molyneux I. 1. 2, ff. 75–75^{v}, letter of 30 Jan. 1684.
[2] B.M. MS. Ad. 4811, ff. 160^{v}, 162^{v}–3. [3] *Ibid.*, f. 174^{v}.
[4] T. Scott XI. 189–90.

'solum animal rationale est disciplinae capax'; and those apostolic names 'Johannes, Petrus, Thomas' used as examples of individual men.[1]

After the usual withdrawal to England during the 'troubles' of 1689–90, Marsh returned to stay in Ireland, becoming in turn Archbishop of Cashel, of Dublin, and of Armagh (1703), and therefore Primate of all Ireland. He died a bachelor and was buried in St Patrick's Cathedral.

Robert Huntingdon (or 'Huntington', 1637–1701), Marsh's successor as provost, was the son of a curate. He went up to Merton College, Oxford (1652), and was elected a fellow the same year he took his B.A. degree (1658). Huntingdon's interest in biblical studies and oriental languages was so passionate that he accepted an appointment as chaplain to the English 'factory' (or trading settlement) at Aleppo in order to satisfy it. Arriving there in 1671, he continued to live and travel in the East for ten years. During this time his main occupation, in addition to study and worship, was collecting manuscripts, for himself as well as others. Narcissus Marsh, then for the most part in Oxford, was one of his constant correspondents; others were John Fell, Edward Pocock, and Edward Bernard. When Huntingdon came home (1681), he took up his Merton fellowship again. But when Marsh resigned from the provostship of T.C.D., Huntingdon was urged to accept it, and finally, reluctantly, did so. To close friends, he complained—as Swift was to do in middle age—that his residence in Ireland seemed an exile.[2]

Like Marsh, Huntingdon admired the new natural philosophy, and the first formal meeting of what became the Dublin Philosophical Society was held in his lodgings. The significant aspect of his participation seems to have been lending his authority to the membership. His more direct contributions are not dazzling: he

[1] Dublin, 1681, pp. 116, 185, sig. A5, pp. 175, 42. The Bodleian Library's copy of Marsh's book is endorsed on the title page 'donatū à Rev^{do} Authore D. Narcisso Marsh, S.T.P.' (8° A. 138 Art). The important discovery of Swift's allusions to the commonplaces of the old logic was made by Professor R. S. Crane; all but the third of my Latin sentences are examples suggested by him.

[2] Stubbs, p. 118.

read the group an account of porphyry pillars in Egypt, and gave them two bottles of Connaught mineral waters to be experimented upon.[1]

In 1688 Huntingdon fled from Ireland. Although he returned for a short stay after the Battle of the Boyne, he soon gave up the provostship (1692) and re-established himself in England. Untempted by a bishopric at this point, he refused a see and took an English benefice instead. But in the year of his death, he did accept the bishopric of Raphoe in Ireland (1701).

If such men guided the young Swift indirectly, the person who most intimately affected his evolving character was his tutor and lifelong friend, St George Ashe. Twenty students of Swift's class were under this one scholar's tuition.[2] Though Ashe's family came from Wiltshire, his father's estate lay in county Meath, Ireland, and he himself was born in Roscommon. An older brother, Thomas, inherited the family property, worth about a thousand pounds a year; a younger, Dillon, took orders and was made vicar of Finglas: Swift went to college with Dillon and made fast friends of both.

Ashe received his B.A. degree from T.C.D. in 1676, and was elected a fellow of the College three years before Swift's admission. Mathematics and the new, experimental philosophy were his peculiar interests: he was chosen professor of mathematics (1685)[3] and a fellow of the Royal Society, and he followed William Molyneux as secretary of the Dublin Philosophical Society. To the *Philosophical Transactions* of the Royal Society, Ashe contributed a number of papers, some while Swift was an undergraduate. One may, alas, estimate the depth and virtuosity of these researches from their subjects, which include a solar eclipse, a man whose fingertip bled periodically, and 'a girl in Ireland, who has several horns growing on her body'.[4]

It was while Swift lived under his guidance that Ashe worked most actively for the Dublin Society. During the icy winter of 1683–4, he compared the effects of freezing upon eggs, urine, and

[1] B.M. MS. Ad. 4811, ff. 162, 163v. [2] Stubbs, p. 143, n. [3] *Ibid.*, p. 115.
[4] *Philosophical Transactions*, abridged ed., 1809, III, 86, 156–7, 229–30.

other substances.[1] Soon after, he read a paper arguing that mathematics can give more certainty than any other form of reasoning; in its echoes of Descartes and its contempt for scholasticism, his argument seems perhaps more earnest than original. But if we think of how such themes were to scatter themselves over Swift's fantasy of Laputa (not to mention other works), we shall find the reasonings of Ashe to be of peculiar interest. Mathematics, he writes, is supreme,

> because quantity, the object about which it is conversant, is a sensible obvious thing, and consequently the ideas we form thereof are clear and distinct and daily represented to us in most familiar instances; because it makes use of terms which are proper, adequate, and unchangeable; its axioms and postulata also are very few and rational; it assigns such causes and generations of magnitudes as are easily apprehended and readily admitted; it rejects all trifling in words and rethoricall [*sic*] schemes, all conjectures, authority, prejudices, and passions; lastly, so exquisite an order and method in demonstrating is observed, that no proposition is pretended to be proved, which does not plainly follow from what was before demonstrated.[2]

In the summer of 1684, Ashe reported his detailed observations of a solar eclipse; in the autumn, he tried to demonstrate that it was possible to square the circle.[3] He gave regular reports on the weather and described a spiral barometric glass which would 'express all variations minutely enough'.[4] He produced a discourse on air which curiously foreshadows the 'Aeolism' of Swift's *Tale of a Tub*—though Boyle's experiments are probably Ashe's inspiration:

> No one is ignorant how necessary a part of natural history it is to consider the various affections, properties, and alterations of air since its influence is so universal, that no portion of matter is exempt from this ubiquitarian, like an anima mundi it permeates all; even the most solid metals possess it, if their sound may be ascrib'd to the motion of the included air; and the hardest gems have a con-

[1] B.M. MS. Ad. 4811, f. 1.
[2] *Ibid.*, ff. 21^{v}–2.
[3] *Ibid.*, ff. 148–9, 154, 156.
[4] *Ibid.*, ff. 187–8 and *passim*.

siderable proportion thereof; their transparency being allow'd to proceed from the abundance of their pores; plants seem to owe their very life and being to the air they include, which does as it were supply the defect of a heart, in asmuch as . . . it is moderately comprest and dilated reciprocally, and begets a kind of systole and diastole.

When Ashe contemplates the new experimental philosophy and judges the traditional forms of natural science against it, his tone rises to rhapsody:

> Natural philosophy (as it is generally managed) is little else than a learned romance, which may amuse and divert, but can never satisfy the mind of man, which is fed only by experiment and demonstration, and not with gay empty speculations, or spruce hypotheses. . . All the search of inquisitive men for so many ages, has not been able to fasten upon this Proteus the air, but these few following affections, (viz.) heat and cold, dryness and moisture, different degrees of gravity, and its spring or elasticity; for the happy discovery of some of which, and the improvement of 'em all we are obliged to the age we live in, and most of all to our own countrymen.[1]

Even when Ashe travelled, he did not forget the Dublin society, but sent home such descriptions as the following of Cassini's telescope:

> He has a telescope of above two hundred feet long, by which he made his late discoveries, this he manages by a tower built on purpose, and has a contrivance of clock work which governs the telescope so, that it keeps pace with any star or planet.[2]

Later, when he was a bishop, Ashe preserved his hunger to learn about new advances in the arts and sciences: in a characteristic message to a prospective visitor, he writes, 'Do not forget to bring your latest Mercuries both French and English, and other new books.'[3] However, the fullest and most naïve statement of his faith in the experimental philosophy belongs to a speech in which

[1] B.M. MS. Ad. 4811, ff. 135ᵛ–6. [2] *Ibid.*, f. 140.
[3] T.C.D. MS. Lyons, no. 749: letter of 18 Jan. 1700/1, to William King.

he asked Lord Clarendon, as lord lieutenant of Ireland, to be patron of the Society (January 1686). Here, although he recalls the phrases of Bacon, Hobbes, and Sprat, the young don directly expresses his own principles. In a series of historical ironies, the man who was to be remembered above all as Swift's teacher, not only eulogized the institutions which his pupil would ridicule, but also reproached those who were already making fun of them:

> 'Tis true, knowledge was of old for the most part only the study of the sullen and the poor, who thought it the gravest peice of science to contemn the use of man-kind, and to differ in habit and manners from all others; It was heretofore condemn'd to melancholy retirements, kept as a minor under the tuition of ambitious and arrogant guardians, buried in cloysters, or the more dark obscurity of affected jargon and unintelligable cant; Antiquity too was ador'd with such superstitious reverence, as if the beauty of truth, like that of a picture, cou'd not be known or perceived but at a distance, as if theire eyes, like the praepostrus [*sic*] animalls, were behind them, and their intellectuall motions retrograde; No wonder then that knowledge did not outgrow the dwarfishness of its pristine stature, and that the intellectuall world did continue such a microcosm: for while they were slaves to the dictiates of their forefathers, their discoveries, like water, cou'd never rise higher then [*sic*] the fountains, from whence they were derived. . . [But when, through the founding of] the Royall Society; captive truth was rescued from its former bondage, and clouded knowledge began to shine more bright; when instead of words and empty speculations were introduc'd things and experiments, and the beautiful bosome of nature was exposed to veiw, where we might enter into its guarden, tast of its fruits, satisfy our selves with its plenty, instead of idle talking and wandering under its fruitless shadows; Then philosophy was admitted into our palaces and our courts, began to keep the best company, to refine its fashion and appearance, and to become the employment of the rich and of the great.

Having thus exemplified several commonplaces which were to be satirized in *A Tale of a Tub*,[1] Ashe went on to reproach the mockers of the great enterprise:

[1] Compare especially the *Epistle Dedicatory* and the *Preface*. (Of course, I do not believe that Swift was directing his satire against Ashe.)

> Even in our cradle, like Hercules, we have suffer'd persecution, and been fircely oppos'd by a loud and numerous; though (God be thanked) an impudent sort of adversaries, the railleurs and the witts . . . we are told by them that our time is spent in vulgar experiments, in empty useless speculations, which (suppose true) is it not necessary that many loads of unprofitable earth shou'd be thrown by, before we come at a vain of gold, yet certainly the contemplation even of flies and shells and the most trifling works of nature (which they so much ridicule) is more manly then downright idleness and ignorance, and the extreams of raillery are more offensive then those of stupidity; They should reflect that all things are capable of abuse from the same topicks by which they may be commended,[1] that (besides the ill manners in discountenancing such studies as our great master has declared himself the founder and promoter[2]) burlasque [*sic*] and laughter is the easiest and the slenderest fruit of witt, that it proceeds from the observation of the deformity of things, whereas there is a nobler and more masculin pleasure which is rais'd from beholding their orders and beauty.[3]

Yet in his boldest praise of mathematics and experimental philosophy, Ashe never meant to weaken the reputation of the church. Of his orthodox piety and his ecclesiastical energy, there is solid evidence. During a parochial visitation as Bishop of Clogher, for example, he boasted of having 'set five or six churches a building'[4]; little over a week later, he had 'confirmed near two thousand persons', given orders to repair 'all the ruined churches in the diocese', and placed curates 'wherever they were wanting'.[5] Ashe's letters to a fellow bishop regularly end with a sober request for his friend's prayers. He deeply, chronically resented the growth of nonconformity, complained of the dissenting ministers' 'crowds at communions', and pressed for an end of their freedom to perform marriages.[6] As a token of the steady eye which he kept on his own clergy, we may just remark him prose-

[1] The reference is to the practice in manuals of rhetoric of arranging under the same headings parallel exercises in praise and blame.

[2] Charles II, in the charter of the Royal Society.

[3] T.C.D. MS. Molyneux I. 4. 17, no. 2. For the complete text, see Appendix D.

[4] T.C.D. MS. Lyons, no. 714: 21 Aug. 1700.

[5] *Ibid.*, no. 717: 30 Aug. 1700.

[6] *Loc. cit.* and *passim.*

cuting a lamentable Mr Kirkwood who, in addition to worse vices, had 'sat two nights and three days drinking at Eniskilliny, without ever going to bed'.[1]

During the Revolution, Ashe went to England and became chaplain to Lord Paget, English ambassador at Vienna. Afterwards he was for three years provost of T.C.D. (1692–5), then Bishop of Cloyne, Bishop of Clogher, vice-chancellor of T.C.D., and Bishop of Derry. In Swift's circle, we shall find Ashe close to several persons: he acted as Congreve's college tutor, he ordained George Berkeley, and he became a friend of Swift's dearest companion, Esther Johnson. (In the fabulous scenario of Swift's 'marriage' to her, Ashe is commonly named as the priest.) Upon his death, Addison wrote, '[He] has scarce left behind him his equal in humanity, agreeable conversation, and all kinds of learning.'[2] The possibility that Swift made Ashe the target of his satires upon virtuosi must be explicitly dismissed, not only because the same ideas appear so commonly and in so many other places, but as well because Swift's tone toward Ashe is so uniformly affectionate and respectful: the connection between teacher and pupil only reveals how early and in how orthodox a setting Swift first came up against the ideas.

[1] T.C.D. MS. Lyons, no. 720: 9 Sept. 1700. [2] Ball III. 3.

Chapter Seven

STUDIES

i

So pervasive and ancient are the misrepresentations of Swift's career as an undergraduate that the first blame for the errors must fall upon Swift himself; for he originated the tradition of his own disgraceful academic record. On the other hand, the parallel report that his discipline was as regrettable as his scholarship belongs to a later authority. Both these stories are misleading. However, to arrive at a more reliable account, one must examine in some detail the programme of the college, the behaviour of Swift's classmates, and a few statistics relating to academic marks and disciplinary fines. Since the evidence remains fragmentary, it is only by such an examination that one can either understand what sort of degree Swift finally took, or have a glimpse of the sort of student he actually was.

Swift's schooling was mapped in well-defined areas.[1] Nearly all instruction at the College was verbal, and Latin was generally the medium of study. At dinner and supper, if the young men conversed at all, they had to use Latin. For the B.A. course the statutory subjects comprised little besides languages—Latin, Greek, and Hebrew—and Aristotelian philosophy as inherited from the Middle Ages by way of Renaissance commentators. On the quarterly examinations the undergraduates received marks in Latin and Greek, the 'theme', and the department of Aristotle which they were studying. *Bene*, *mediocriter*, *negligenter*, *male*, *pessime* represent the range of marks, and *haud* or *vix* was available as a kind of minus sign.[2]

[1] Most of my material on curriculum and pedagogy is paraphrased from Maxwell, pp. 49–53. [2] Forster, pp. 38–40. See Appendix E.

Undergraduates were assigned to tutors—fellows of the College—who saw them frequently (sometimes daily) as individuals or in small groups, to test them on what they had learned and to assign further work. Earlier in the century, the pupils (who were commonly adolescent) had often lived in their tutor's rooms. Specialists among the fellows lectured (in Latin) on the separate subjects. Normally the lecturer in a course would read to the students and then question them to be sure they understood what they had heard. This method did not satisfy everybody. When Thomas Molyneux (B.A., T.C.D., 1680) was at the University of Leyden in 1683, he wrote home to his brother in Dublin,

> The professor of mathematicks and astronomy reads every Wednesday in the schools, though none of the rest of the professors do. Their lectures are usually three quarters of an hour long; not read out of a book, as the way is with us and at Oxford, but spoke off hand, on such subjects which suppose they have well read and considered before they ascend their pulpits.[1]

The Dublin undergraduates had to take notes as they listened, and to expand them every week into a Latin commentary on the lectures, which was shown to the lecturer. They had also to prepare a theme, or version of English into Latin, every week, upon special subjects. All undergraduates went to lectures on Greek. They all had to declaim, two a week in turn, on a subject taken from morality or politics.[2] These declamations were held in the hall on Saturday or Friday after morning prayers.

To each class was given a different name: first year, junior freshman; second year, senior freshman; third year, junior sophister; fourth year, senior sophister. In the first year the concentration was on logic, probably as expounded in Boethius' sixth-century Latin version—with exhaustive commentary—of Porphyry's already bulky Greek *Introduction* to the *Categories* of Aristotle. In Swift's time, the undergraduates probably used Narcissus Marsh's manual of logic as a guide.

[1] 'Sir Thomas Molyneux', *Dublin University Magazine*, XVIII (1841), 474.
[2] Bolton, p. 69.

Aristotle himself was reached in the second year, when the lecturer took up some part of the *Organon*—or body of Aristotle's writings on logic—'as briefly as possible, not going from the context after commentators'.[1] The *Physics* followed in the third year and the *Metaphysics* and *Nichomachean Ethics* (during Lent!) in the last. For the M.A. course the added subjects were mathematics and politics.

To demonstrate their mastery of the material, the students engaged in strict syllogistic disputations, lasting no more than an hour apiece and involving at least four disputants. These were scheduled in the afternoons, between two and four. In each class there were three disputations every week on a question drawn from the lectures. It was essential, therefore, that the entering freshmen learn logic before anything else (a little as elementary composition is used in American universities today).

> The most distinctive feature of the academic course at this period was the disputation. This the universities had inherited from the Schoolmen. The mediaeval conception of the degree was that of a licence to teach. Hence these trials in argument. At the lectures there were disputations upon the present or preceding lecture: sometimes the students were ordered to dispute *more Socratico*. Disputations were also held in public, especially for candidates for degrees. The Respondent opened his thesis in logical form; others attacked with the aid of syllogisms; the Moderator presided and judged. The topics discussed were usually selected from the classical authors, the Scriptures, or the works of the Fathers. And, as thought became more secularised, such subjects, as 'The comparative value of hereditary and elective princes', or 'The influence of the moon upon the tides', were included.[2]

Of course, an odour of sanctity permeated the curriculum. The commonest product of a seventeenth-century university was clergymen. At six in the morning, students began their day with a short chapel service; the first lectures were at seven. Morning prayers followed at ten, evening prayers at four. By the statutes, undergraduates were required to attend all three services daily;

[1] Bolton, p. 71. [2] Maxwell, p. 52.

but the fine for absence was only a penny, and in Swift's class even Thomas Wilson, who was to become the saintly Bishop of Sodor and Man, missed chapel 'some fifty or sixty times' in less than a year (1685–6).[1]

These rites were the responsibility of the masters of arts in holy orders (except for lawyers and physicians, all fellows had to enter into holy orders within three years of their commencing M.A.). They had also, on Sunday and Friday after prayers, to discuss a biblical text 'in the manner of a sermon', a practice known as 'commonplacing'. There were special services for Fridays and holy days; on Sunday mornings a sermon, delivered by a resident Master, accompanied the prayers. Undergraduates and bachelors of arts had the exercise of giving the blessing before meals, the thanks afterward, and the Bible-reading at dinner. Once a week the younger undergraduates were also rehearsed in the catechism.

Swift's description of how he himself fit into this milieu is well known:

> At fourteen he was admitted into the university at Dublin, where by the ill treatment of his nearest relations, he was so discouraged and sunk in his spirits, that he too much neglected some parts of his academick studyes, for which he had no great relish by nature, and turned himself to reading history and poetry. So that when the time came for taking his degree of batchlor, although he had lived with great regularity and due observance of the statutes, he was stopped of his degree for dullness and insufficiency, and at last hardly admitted in a manner little to his credit, which is called in that college speciali gratia. And this discreditable mark, as I am told, stands upon record in their college registry.[2]

This is the voice of an elderly man, past his three score and ten. With the frailties of adolescence he has only a restrained sympathy. Although fourteen was not an amazing age for one coming up to a university, it was recognized to be distinctly early. Richard Sherlock regretted having entered Oxford at fourteen, and said, 'To send raw and green youths thither before the tongues be learned and understood . . . proves often such a defect, that will

[1] Keble I. 14. [2] *Autob.*, ff. 7v–8.

hardly after be made good without double diligence.'[1] 'Double diligence', no doubt, was precisely what Swift lacked. In his college class he was either the youngest or very nearly so; yet if he had seemed precocious enough at school to go along with his elder cousin when Thomas moved to Dublin, the shock of the new standard and the new, adult society of Trinity College may have troubled him so that he could not demonstrate his true powers until much later.[2]

To qualify for a degree, a candidate for the B.A. performed a scholastic disputation. But before he was admitted to this final and perfunctory ritual, he had to complete twelve terms of residence. At the beginning of each term examinations were held in the subjects lectured on the term before; and no term counted toward a degree until the candidate passed the corresponding examinations *haud male* or better.[3] Of Swift's academic attainments there is useful documentation in a list of the marks given to 119 students on the Easter term examinations 1685.[4] This was one of the last examinations before he took his B.A. degree the following February. In 'physics' (i.e., the third-year course of Aristotle), he received *male*, in Greek and Latin *bene*, in Latin theme *negligenter*. By far the most common mark on this examination was *mediocriter*; about as many *male*'s appear as *bene*'s, which is not very many, and about the same number of *negligenter*'s. Cousin Thomas (Swift's elder and a scholar) received *mediocriter* in everything. The rarest and severest mark on the roll, *pessime* (apparently failure), was applied to neither. Besides Swift, only six of the students examined received *bene* in Greek and Latin, and only eight received *bene* in more than one subject. Edward Chandler, described by Leslie Stephen as 'a man of more learning than capacity',[5] received *mediocriter* in all three divisions. The famous Thomas Wilson received *male* in physics, *male* in Greek and Latin, and *mediocriter* in theme.

If the Easter 1685 results were typical of Swift's academic

[1] Keble I. 12 (quoting Sherlock).

[2] His age on admission was about 14·5, against an average that year of 16·2 (Stubbs, p. 143, n.).

[3] *N. & Q.*, 21 Aug. 1875, p. 151. [4] See Appendix E. [5] *DNB*.

standing, he clearly exaggerated his own 'dullness and insufficiency'. While he did take his B.A. degree *speciali gratia*, or by special grace, this favour was not uncommon: four other students graduating with him—all older than Swift—received the same dispensation, out of a total class of thirty-eight. The year before, two out of thirty-eight took B.A. degrees *ex speciali gratia* (February 1685); the year after, seven out of thirty-one (February 1687); a year later, three out of thirty-three (February 1688).[1] It is true that the fellows once described *speciali gratia* as a 'mark of unworthiness and disgrace' (February 1688); but this was in denigration of a papist upon whom Tyrconnel had forced them to confer the M.A. degree, and whom he now wished them to elect as a junior fellow.[2] In the mid-nineteenth century the special grace was invoked when a 'merely technical or purely formal' exercise was dispensed with.[3]

In other words, the young Swift did passably well in college, but not so well as the septuagenarian Swift could have wished. He excelled in those pursuits in which he was himself to be distinguished—language and literature; he did poorly in what he would always dislike—abstract philosophy and formal rhetoric. The story is hardly unusual. In Anthony Wood, for example, there is a similar note on Samuel Daniel, and Wood obviously approves of the poet's taste for 'easier and smoother studies' than 'pecking and hewing at logic'. Bacon, Milton, and Hobbes showed the same resentment of university scholasticism. William Wake, Swift's contemporary, who became Archbishop of Canterbury, also gives such an account: 'Running too fast through the systems of logic and metaphysics, I took a sort of distaste to both; and neglecting those studies, applied myself more to the classic authors, which were much more easy to be understood and more

[1] T.C.D. MS. *General Registry*, pp. 238, 249, 257, 271.

[2] Barrett, pp. 5–6.

[3] *N. & Q.*, 21 Aug. 1875, p. 151. George Salmon gives another account in *Non-Miraculous Christianity*, 1881, pp. 224–5, n. He seems wrong, however, first in assuming that *male* meant failure, and secondly in assuming that the 1685 Easter term examinations would have been the only ones on which Swift received such a mark.

pleasing to me.'[1] Neither Swift's lack of zeal for the college exercises nor the fellows' willingness to excuse him from some of them will puzzle anyone acquainted with merely that part of the procedure which survived into the nineteenth century:

> The proctor on the candidate's visit hands a paper to him containing four quartettes of questions; the first quartette comprising questions in ethics, the second in metaphysics, the third in casuistry, and the fourth in physics; and [here] is the first question of each of these four quartettes:
>
> An omnia peccata paria sint?
> An sensibus sit fidendum?
> An bellum possit esse utrinque justum?
> An terra sit immobilis?
>
> Upon questions of which these are fair specimens, each candidate is required to write *twenty-four* syllogisms on the *wrong* side, and *twelve* on the *right*. When three candidates are thus prepared, each with a batch of syllogisms and two theses, viz., one in Greek, upon *anything at all*, and one in Latin, *in laudem philosophiae*, they proceed to the Examination Hall, accompanied by a proctor and a moderator, whose presence is rendered necessary, lest the disputants in the heat of debate should attempt to convince one another by any less harmless method than a syllogism.[2]

As for Swift's attitude toward those relatives who maintained him at the university, that censure may be due to several circumstances. His uncle Godwin may have been Swift's main support, but it was during the boy's undergraduate years that Godwin's fortunes went into a decline. Deane Swift says that 'about two years' after Swift had been admitted to Trinity College, Godwin's prosperity began to fail.[3] He reports that although Godwin's income during the reign of Charles II rose as high as three thousand pounds a year, he ruined himself by foolish schemes of investment, the silliest being an iron-works in which he was cheated by his three partners. Swift's own disgust with this project happens to be on record; explaining the origin of the name of

[1] Sykes, *William Wake* I. 10.
[2] *N. & Q.*, 21 Aug. 1875, p. 151.
[3] D. Swift, Appendix, p. 41.

Swandlingbar, 'a famous town, where the worst iron in the kingdom is made', he says,

> It was a most witty conceit of four gentlemen, who ruined themselves with this iron project. *Sw.* stands for *Swift*, *And.* for *Sanders*, *Ling.* for *Darling*, and *Bar.* for *Barry*. Methinks I see the four loggerheads sitting in consult, like Smectimnius, each gravely contributing a part of his own name, to make up one for their place in the iron-work; and could wish they had been hanged, as well as undone, for their wit.[1]

Possibly, the family felt no need to give Swift an account of the case in detail; so the reduction in his stipend, which would naturally have followed Godwin's losses, may have seemed like a slighting of the poor cousin. Furthermore, Swift could not have helped transferring to his other guardians some of the resentment which he did not apparently like to admit against his own father and mother.

Since Godwin married four times, had eight children, and from them received at least fifteen grandchildren, his assistance to Jonathan must have been an act of disinterested kindness. Though the tradition of his nephew's bitterness toward him is strong, the evidence is all secondary. In fact, there is no conclusive proof that Godwin *was* the boy's mainstay through school and university; the early biographers propagate the story, and no argument has been advanced against it. Uncles William and Adam may well have shared the expense of both Jonathan and their other fatherless nephew, Thomas. The first-hand evidence all points at William as the most helpful uncle. It was he who helped Mrs Swift collect the arrears due her husband at the King's Inns; it was he to whom Swift apologized for having 'always been but too troublesome'; it was he who obtained a testimonium from T.C.D. for Swift when he went up to Oxford.[2]

The source of Swift's low spirits remains complex. Poverty seems not enough of a reason. When William King was an under-

[1] Davis IV. 282. It is just possible, alas, that Deane Swift's own account (pp. 18–20) is based on this source.

[2] Ball I. 8–10.

graduate, he found himself far worse off than Swift—'contending with straitened means and almost overwhelmed, relatives and friends neglecting me, as they themselves were struggling with poverty; so that I had scarcely twenty pounds, through the whole space of six years in which I stayed at college, from any other source than from the college itself'.[1] Nevertheless, King's temper was unaffected; and if he had any emotional crises, they were due to theological qualms rather than shabby clothes. Certainly Swift had respect for the university itself; he considered the scholarly discipline there to be 'much stricter . . . than either in Oxford or Cambridge'.[2] Yet he obviously felt that as a student he had been unappreciated: after receiving his Oxford M.A. by incorporation, he wrote (1692), 'I am ashamed to have been more obliged in a few weeks to strangers, than ever I was in seven years to Dublin College.'[3]

ii

But while Swift's academic standing too has revealed little cause for despair or bitterness, there are signs that his deportment was a spot where the harness rubbed. Records are available for only a little of the time before he took his B.A., when, in his own words, he lived 'with great regularity and due observance of the statutes'.[4] Later, when we do have records, the case is complicated by the upheavals throughout the kingdom as James II's policies revived memories of 1641: Protestants were fleeing, and the government was tampering with the college constitution as well as the municipal corporations and similar bodies. Every level of society felt the demoralizing effect of sudden remodelling. In January 1687 the appointment of Tyrconnel as lord lieutenant meant the 'signal for a general exodus of all such Protestants as could by any means remove themselves and their goods to England and Scotland'.[5] In the spring Trinity College men heard how the vice-chancellor of Cambridge University was deprived

[1] C. S. King, *A Great Archbishop of Dublin*, 1906, pp. 7–8.
[2] Ball III. 309. [3] *Ibid.* I. 10. [4] *Autob.*, f. 8. [5] Dunlop, p. 123.

of his office for refusing to admit a Benedictine monk as master of arts.

Still, a connoisseur of undergraduate mischief would hardly be shocked by the range of cases which the senior fellows of Trinity College handled in these years (1686–8). We find one Mosse ordered 'to be admonished for climbing the walls, and tampering with the locks'. Two scholars, Kieff and Griffith, were accused 'of indecent conversation with two women in Stephen's Green; and of unseasonable walking in the night'; Kieff was found guilty of fornication and expelled. Another pair of students were ordered to be expelled for fighting in town at night—'having formerly been guilty of bilking of taverns, and other irregularities'; and a third, a scholar, who had joined in this fracas was to be whipped and admonished. Half a dozen were admonished 'for bilking a tavern'. Another was expelled 'for frequenting the town, and almost totall neglect of duties'. A scholar named Spencer wounded the porter; it was ordered that he 'be publickly admonisht and make a confession on his knees in the hall . . . and be suspended of his scholarship; the profits of his scholarship during his suspension are to be paid the porter'. Another student was expelled 'for writing, and publishing a scandalous libell on ladies of quality'. Several scholars were punished for 'a tumult raisd by them in ye town'. Four other students received various penalties—whipping, suspension from degree, admonishment—'for lying out of ye college and riotous behaviour at an unseasonable time of night'. On all these selected instances, a desperate comment may be heard in an order of the house, July 1688, that the walls of the College should be built three feet higher.[1]

Of all Swift's contemporaries, the liveliest college history belongs to John Jones, who later took degrees in divinity but did not become a parson. Three years older than Swift, Jones came into the College only a week after him, sat under the same tutor, and was graduated B.A. at the same time. Having started out as a sizar, he won a scholarship in his third year; yet he needed a

[1] T.C.D. MS. *General Registry*, pp. 249, 252, 258, 261, 265, 266, 267, 272, 273, 275.

special grace to admit him to the degree. This in turn leads us to the episode of unique interest here; for, two and a half years after achieving the B.A., Jones was briefly deprived of it for a scandal which illustrates in cheerful detail one style of discipline maintained in Swift's class.

At Trinity College, as at other British universities, it was customary each year for a chosen student to deliver a mocking speech called the *tripos*. The orator bore the title *terrae filius* and spoke a macaronic mixture of English and bad Latin. It was Jones who performed the tripos at the commencement of July 1688, ridiculing—as was the custom—the eccentricities of other members of the university, particularly the officers and fellows. The wit of the production reveals more ingenuity than refinement; one section, for example, relates to the fleasome breeches of the rake whom Tyrconnel tried to foist upon the College as a fellow:

> 'Tis almost incredible so many cattle should thrive on so bare a pasture. Every night he dares venture them off, he's in danger of losing them. Once when he lay without them, they crept from the garret to the street-door.

And so forth. Another scene is a tavern conversation between this man and a whore. Jones's special object of attack was the amateur scientist, like Ashe—who himself speaks in a dialogue on eclipses: 'I conclude, we are all like to be in the dark.'

Because Jones went too far in his libels, he lost his degree two days after his performance, 'for false and scandalous reflections in his tripos'. At the end of the week he was allowed to apply for restoration of the degree but was suspended instead from the benefits of his scholarship—probably for a month.[1] Although there have been attempts to father Jones's tripos upon Swift, the evidence is insignificant. He later became a famous schoolmaster and safely grew into a D.D. Many of Swift's relatives were sent to him; and one of his pupils, Thomas Sheridan, was to be for many years Swift's closest friend.

For several kinds of common offences, the college authorities

[1] This was the usual period. See Barrett, pp. 20, 66–9.

imposed simple fines: a penny for absence from chapel (6 a.m., 10 a.m., 4 p.m.); half-a-crown for failure to appear at nightly roll-call in hall (9 p.m.); twopence for absence from chapel when a surplice had to be worn; twopence for missing catechism; a penny for not attending disputations, declamations, or lectures. Missing chapel was Swift's (like most students') commonest offence; the lectures which he cut most often—the record is only for broken stretches over two years, largely after he took his B.A. degree—were on mathematics.[1]

In all categories, however, Swift shows up rather badly, whether we compare him with Congreve, three years his junior; Thomas Swift, a scholar; Dillon Ashe, the brother of Swift's tutor; or with the two bishops-to-be of the English establishment, Thomas Wilson and Edward Chandler. Except for Congreve and Ashe, these men all graduated with Swift. Cousin Thomas's fines are, with fair (but not perfect) consistency, lighter than Jonathan's. For example, during eight weeks in the summer and autumn of 1687, Swift paid 4s. 9d. (not counting 12s. 2d. cancelled) to Thomas's 2s. 7d. (not counting 2s. cancelled). During one week in the summer of 1686, only a single other student was fined as heavily as Swift for missing chapel. Still, we may find some comfort in Swift's friend Stratford (the future merchant), who sometimes matched and sometimes outdid him. Over three weeks in the autumn of 1686, for example, Stratford was fined 4s. 10d. (not counting 5s. cancelled, for missing roll-call) against Swift's 2s. 11d. (not counting 1s. cancelled, for missing services requiring a surplice); while Thomas Swift paid merely 1s. 3d. (not counting half-a-crown cancelled, for missing roll-call).[2]

Such comparative figures can be fairly reckoned for only limited periods; so the evidence remains inconclusive. Over a three-week space soon after he was made B.A., Swift was fined 6s. (not counting 4d. cancelled) to Stratford's 2s. (not counting 2s. 6d. cancelled). During a similar period in the spring, Swift's fines were 3s. 10d.; his scholar cousin's 3s. 8d.; Congreve's 1s. 9d.;

[1] For a description of the available records, see Barrett, p. 8.

[2] 13 Aug.–7 Oct. 1687; 10–16 Jul. 1686; 16 Oct.–5 Nov. 1686.

and Thomas Wilson's 1s. 11d. During two weeks in the summer, Swift was fined 1s. 1d. (not counting 7s. 6d. cancelled, for missing roll-call); Thomas Swift, 9d. (not counting 7s. 6d. similarly cancelled); Congreve, 11d.; Thomas Wilson, 7d. (not counting 5s. cancelled, for missing roll-call). Compared with Swift's accounts, the fines of Dillon Ashe, Thomas Wilson, and Edward Chandler seem negligible.[1]

On even this fragmentary record, we should not be surprised by outbursts of grosser misconduct, especially with the thunders of Revolution approaching. In March 1687 Swift was admonished for 'neglect of duties and frequenting the town'; however, six others, including his cousin (and possibly his room-mate) were censured with him. This was in a period when the government was pressing the fellows to admit as one of their number the unqualified Bernard Doyle, who would not take the oaths. Soon came word that the fellows of Magdalen College, Oxford, were under pressure to elect a papist as president—the beginning of a process which ended, early the next year, with the turning out of all but one of the fellows of Magdalen and their replacement by Roman Catholics. Meanwhile, Tyrconnel went so far as to transmit to England a bill for repealing the whole Act of Settlement in Ireland; but the Privy Council rejected this in Westminster. At the end of June 1688 news arrived of the trial and acquittal of the Seven Bishops at Westminster Hall.

If Swift chose this season to break discipline again, he was suiting his mood to the times. On his birthday, over three weeks after the Prince of Orange landed at Torbay, he was found guilty of new crimes: he had, with five others, started tumults in the College and insulted the junior dean. The whole half-dozen were suspended from their degrees. Swift and another boy were singled out for carrying themselves even more unbearably—'adhuc intolerabilius'—than the rest; and both were ordered to beg the junior dean's pardon publicly, on bended knees.[2] After a month,

[1] 6–26 Mar. 1686; 1–21 May; 19 June–2 Jul. For further comparisons, see Appendix F. My dating may be a week out, since it is not clear, in the MSS., whether the date which appears on each recto applies to the leaf or to the opening.

[2] Barrett, pp. 14–15. While only Swift's surname is mentioned in the sentence, I

the degrees were restored, though by then all the culprits may not have been in residence.

We may notice here that if Deane Swift was right, Uncle Godwin suffered a stroke, or 'a lethargy', about 1688, and lost his speech and memory.[1] The repercussions of such an event could only have added to a dependent nephew's anxieties. But with the national crisis moving so fast and so close, undergraduate unrest would inevitably mount. Among the senior members of the College, too, there was trouble, as Tyrconnel continued to intimidate them and tried to win possession of the college silver.

Not that escapades bolder than Swift's would be out of character for a twenty-year-old university student of any century. They suggest that he was more than a drudge and less than an angel. If he felt 'discouraged and sunk in his spirits', he did not show it by hangdog behaviour. Thomas Wilson, who was to be practically canonized by John Keble, was not only fined about once a week for missing chapel; but for other misconduct, 'chiefly non-attendance at disputations and lectures', he was fined more than seventy times in less than a year; and within the same period he was on four occasions charged five shillings for being out after hours: yet Wilson, a remarkably pious young man, was on the verge of ordination—Keble's apologies for him make a pretty exercise in casuistry.[2] On Swift's side, we should reflect that it would be an ordinary human pattern for a boy who

---

agree with Barrett that the reference is to him, and not to his cousin Thomas. This cannot be proved, as Barrett supposes, by the omission of 'Se^{r}' (for 'senior') from Thomas Swift's name and the retention of 'D' (used in the buttery books for 'dominus' or graduate) during the period of Jonathan's suspension from his degree; first, because 'Se^{r}' does not appear consistently, and secondly because another student who was once suspended—John Jones—kept his title of 'D' even during his suspension. (In September 1684 a student was similarly suspended from his degree for a month because he had affronted the junior dean [T.C.D. MS. *General Registry*, p. 241].) However, Barrett's third argument is convincing—that one of the admittedly less culpable boys, holding a scholarship, was suspended from it; so if 'Swift', judged more guilty, received no such suspension, we may assume he held no scholarship. In the *Senior Buttery Books* for these weeks, Thomas appears to have paid almost no fines, and one assumes therefore that he conducted himself exemplarily. Sometimes disciplinary judgments were noted in the buttery books; no such note appears beside Thomas's name.

[1] D. Swift, p. 36. [2] Keble I. 13–14.

felt resentful against his family to spite them (not of course deliberately) by making a poor showing at the university. Perhaps the old Dean Swift of 1738 felt embarrassed by his college record but remembered the dreariness of his student budget and justified one fact by the other.

iii

Since the administrative class, to which Swift belonged, was to be numbered in the hundreds, there could be few of them whom he would not meet sooner or later; and since a university degree appears among the normal accomplishments of this class, he was bound to find at Trinity College many people who would remain his acquaintances in later years. It could hardly be otherwise, for in Ireland any Protestant of Swift's generation who did take a university degree was more likely to choose T.C.D. than Oxford or Cambridge. Among the names which reappear, most became clergymen, several rising to the episcopal bench; but other careers are also found: soldier, merchant, author, politician, schoolmaster. A sampling is worth tracing—two or three in detail; for from a prospect of the fates of Swift's acquaintances, we may judge what paths lay open to the young student. Though the church did absorb the bulk of the manufacture of the college, and other learned professions took most of the remainder, Swift need not have considered his ultimate fate to be predetermined.

The non-cleric whose early career shone most brilliantly in Swift's eyes was probably Congreve. But he left the Kilkenny School only in April 1686,[1] moving on to Dublin four years later than Swift. There, however, he shared the same tutor and bought six times as much beer and wine, at least in the College. After the first days of 1687 Congreve is not listed on the books (though he may have returned at the end of the year); and he left without collecting a degree.[2]

Henry Tenison went into parliament. He was the eldest son of

[1] MS. register of the Kilkenny College, in the T.C.D. library.
[2] Hodges, pp. 22–6.

the Bishop of Killala, entered Trinity College two and a half months after Swift, and took his B.A. degree in 1687. Afterwards, Tenison moved on to complete his legal training in London, at the Middle Temple. In the Irish House of Commons his career began when he accepted the election for county Monaghan 1695. Later, he was also chosen M.P. for Louth; and there Swift—to whom he was 'Harry'—paid him a visit.[1] Soon, he obtained an appointment as commissioner of the revenue, and seemed handsomely launched on the way of public life. But the tale was cut short in 1709, when he died. For the sake of 'Harry's' memory, Swift once gave assistance to a jobless servant of Tenison's.[2]

Francis Stratford, though five years Swift's elder, was admitted less than a fortnight before him, came under the same tutor, and graduated B.A. at the same time. A quarter-century later, when Stratford was the wealthy merchant, he and Swift were, according to dubious tradition, coupled in a *Spectator* story about two schoolmates, one 'an impenetrable block-head' and the other 'the pride of his master': 'The man of genius is at present buried in a country parsonage of eight-score pounds a year; while the other, with the bare abilities of a common scrivener, has got an estate of above an hundred thousand pounds.'[3] Although the theme may indeed be based on the contrast of Swift with Stratford, it gives an unfair impression of their performances, since Swift was undistinguished at T.C.D., and Stratford at least graduated without the need of a special grace. On the quarterly examination for the Easter term 1685, their marks averaged out to something very similar.[4]

The clerics of course came nearer to Swift's road; and we shall see that while family influence could do much for them, it could not insure success. Dillon Ashe, for example, though addicted to puns, claret, and philandering, was brother to a bishop; and his brother made Dilly the archdeacon of his diocese.

Yet Jeremiah Marsh, the son of an archbishop, is a surprising case of mediocre achievement. The father was Francis (not Nar-

[1] Ball IV. 454. [2] *Journal*, 28 May 1711.
[3] 15 Apr. 1712, by Eustace Budgell. [4] See Appendix E.

cissus), Archbishop of Dublin. The son, about Swift's age, came up to Trinity College (from St Paul's, London), a few months after him; but they took their B.A. degrees at the same time. Though Marsh followed his father as treasurer of St Patrick's Cathedral, and also became Dean of Kilmore, he rose no higher. Swift, in December 1713—when he still had some power—wrote that Marsh was 'one I always loved, and have shown it lately, by doing everything he could desire from a brother'[1] (meaning to suggest, not very truthfully, that he was trying to help Marsh to the bishopric of Kilmore). Archbishop King in 1714 described him to the Archbishop of Canterbury as 'a grave, sober, discreet man, and would make a very honest bishop'.[2] But Marsh remained a dean.

Talent too could not guarantee distinction. John Richardson (B.A., 1686), though a gifted scholar, deeply religious, and energetic in the pursuit of his ends, chose to devote himself to the conversion of the Irish-speaking natives. His cause found small favour with those irresistible powers who desired no weakening of the 'English interest'; and the summit of his preferments was an impoverished deanship.[3]

Neither, as another classmate shows, were political ties infallible. John Travers, though four years Swift's senior, entered Trinity College less than a year ahead of him. In his adult years, he apparently made friends both with Swift's beloved Esther Johnson and with the family of Bartholomew Vanhomrigh, whose daughter was to provoke Swift's gravest indiscretions. For many years, Travers was chaplain to the Irish House of Commons, who successfully demanded a D.D. for him. Nevertheless, his highest preferments were a city vicarage and the chancellorship of Christ Church Cathedral.

None of these classmates enjoyed the career to which Swift eventually aspired. Among those who did were Peter Browne, Ralph Lambert, Thomas Wilson, and Edward Chandler. Browne became Bishop of Cork; Lambert, Bishop of Meath;

[1] Ball II. 103. [2] C. S. King, *A Great Archbishop of Dublin*, 1906, p. 172.
[3] *DNB*.

Wilson, Bishop of Sodor and Man; and Chandler, Bishop of Durham. In this quartet of fortunates, the one whose eminence Swift found hardest to digest was the Bishop of Meath; for Lambert pulled himself up by unswerving submission to a Whig junto whose programme depended upon weakening the church: climbing, Swift once said, is performed in the same posture as creeping.

Wilson and Chandler pursued their hopes in the English establishment, outside Swift's orbit. It is Browne whose story ran closest to Swift's; and by peering ahead at his utterly conventional success, we may judge the depth of Swift's unorthodoxy. Admitted to Trinity College less than two months after Swift, Browne took his B.A. degree at the same time. In 1692 he was elected a fellow and seven years later provost of the College. Here the 'austere, retired, and mortified man'[1] enforced discipline upon students and fellows alike. When Browne met one of his subordinates gownless in London, he did not conceal his displeasure; and he was further displeased when the same gentleman (the bon vivant Benjamin Pratt, a classmate of Swift's and Browne's, who later became provost himself) failed to raise his cap to Browne in the college hall. Browne executed the T.C.D. statute obliging celibacy, and deprived a man of his fellowship for getting married. Once a pair of undergraduates tried to stop the dean of the College from pronouncing judgment on a friend, by snatching the paper from the dean's hand; Browne immediately expelled them. Nevertheless, he gained something of the reputation Swift was to acquire, for 'austere and simple habits, lavish and secret . . . charities'.[2] Patrick Delany (who in Swift's middle age became his friend and later his biographer) was a disciple of Browne's, but apparently emulated his master's quirks with his virtues.

Browne's success was due to a course which Swift was to hear ineffectually recommended by his own archbishop—the composition of substantial works upon respectable, theological subjects. 'Say not, that most subjects in divinity are exhausted,' William King helpfully advised Swift (1711); 'for, if you look into

[1] Ware II. 296. [2] *DNB.*

Dr. Wilkins's heads of matters . . . you will be surprised to find so many necessary and useful heads, that no authors have meddled with.'[1] While Swift never so wildly mistook his talents as to attempt such a project, Browne (who judged King's *De origine mali* to be fundamentally misconceived) first established himself as a prospect for ecclesiastical elevation by the systematic rebuttal which he wrote of Toland's deism.

Browne's book, *A Letter in Answer to . . . Christianity Not Mysterious*, was published in 1697, two years before he became provost. Narcissus Marsh (then Archbishop of Dublin) supposedly asked him to write it, and valued the finished work so highly that he recommended the author's promotion. Toland allegedly boasted, thereupon, that it was he who had made Browne a bishop. Browne crusaded against toasts to the dead; and Swift once warned a parson of the Cork diocese 'not to drink or pledge any health in his company, for you know his weak side in that matter'.[2] Even while counting him as a friend, Swift did not spare his character:

> He is a capricious gentleman; but you must flatter him monstrously upon his learning and his writings; that you have read his book against Toland a hundred times, and his sermons, if he has printed any, have been always your model, etc.[3]

Nevertheless, though Swift ridiculed his productions, Browne's achievement in metaphysics is genuine; A. A. Luce calls him 'a subtle thinker with decided views of his own'.[4] Sober volumes of clerical erudition continued to flow from him throughout his life, and he also won a shining reputation as a preacher. 'The most speculative writer of his age', Swift was to label him—'and as scholars tell me, excellent in his way, but I never read much of his works'[5]: yet in 1710 it would be he, not Swift, who became Bishop of Cork.

From such a prospect of Swift's elders and contemporaries, one need not have had his genius to realize that no way to preferment

[1] Ball I. 286. [2] *Ibid.* III. 246. [3] *Ibid.*, p. 244. [4] Luce, p. 31.
[5] Sherburn V. 17.

was secure. Yet there were honourable steps that aspirants normally took. For a person comparatively unsponsored, as Swift was to be, a studious college record, marked by a scholarship, would be followed by holy orders, a fellowship, and industrious publications on aspects of divinity. Within the church, he would support the labours of those superiors to whose principles he felt he could adhere. He would also tie himself to the policies of those statesmen who seemed aligned with his superiors. If he could deliver a sermon or write a pamphlet to advance the aims of his patrons, he would carefully do so.

If one did not make an early choice of an ecclesiastical calling, or if the gradual route of modest industry disgusted him, he might risk the heavier gamble of a tutorship, chaplaincy, or secretary's post in a great house, with the hope that the head of the family would graciously reward him for services rendered, by fixing up a comfortable benefice after a reasonable term of years. Since the church was almost an administrative department of the government, not only were bishops more regularly chosen on political than spiritual grounds (especially in Ireland, where the lay peers who troubled to attend the House of Lords were sometimes outnumbered by the more sedulous bench of bishops), but cathedral stalls and good livings generally were conferred for secular reasons. The number of chaplains was great, of bishoprics few; the supply of parsons manufactured at universities 'seems consistently to have exceeded the demand'. 'If you expect preferment', a prudent adviser told a harness-weary curate, 'you must bustle and try to peep after it, as most of the profession do in these days.'[1]

Now, consistently throughout his life, Swift was to execute some of the prescribed manœuvres. By pursuing them quite systematically, he could have risen, as Atterbury did, in the face of an alert opposition. But even in his college days, he seems to have split differences. Apparently, he exerted himself to keep the respect of St George Ashe and other distinguished men whom he admired; but he let his studies slide, even though scholarly oc-

[1] Dorothy Marshall, *English People in the Eighteenth Century*, 1956, p. 101.

cupations always interested and entertained him, and though he reverenced men of learning. Likewise, he could violate the college discipline even while his relatives, not his own parents, were maintaining him at T.C.D. If this impression is sound, he had already entered upon his policy of flirting with disaster while longing for success, of pretending to be indifferent to what he wanted most.

Nevertheless, the people whom Swift met during this period were a kind of social capital, on which he drew interest for the rest of his life. They were a second set of acquaintances, to be added to those relations among whom he had passed his infancy and childhood. Decade after decade, their names were to recur in his correspondence. Through William Waring (B.A., 1685) Swift probably met the only woman to whom we know he proposed marriage. Captain John Pratt (B.A., 1689) became Swift's financial guide and invested large sums for him. Pratt's older brother, Benjamin (B.A., 1689), another of Ashe's pupils, became Swift's friend and collaborated with him in church politics. The university studies which Swift followed were mostly traditional and hardly peculiar to Trinity College; basically, the prescribed work did not differ much at Oxford or Cambridge. However, the individuals after whose lives he was to shape his first hopes and ideals belonged to Dublin in the ninth decade of the seventeenth century.

Even so, for a serious, bright, ambitious young man of Swift's circumstances—with a modest immediate family, little financial underpinning, and few powerful friends apart from those on whom he had himself made an unusual impression—no career was more likely, in England or Ireland, than the ladder of preferment of the Established Church. To gain any distinction, if he should select this career, he would have to assert himself either by extraordinary services to the distributors of good things, or else by unusual genius.

Chapter Eight

THE DUBLIN PHILOSOPHICAL SOCIETY

It was while Swift was at Trinity College that the most fruitful intellectual tradition of his time found an establishment in Dublin—a natural philosophy built upon observation, experiment, and mathematics. Although Swift was not to give a deep and positive response to this development, it was to be his repeated theme; and his treatment of it is one focus of his work. Perhaps the first source of what will appear as his indifference or hostility to the modern tradition of natural science was his meeting it under the misleading though attractive auspices of the members of the Dublin Philosophical Society.[1]

To this group of learned men, like their equivalents in Oxford, London, or Amsterdam, divisions of knowledge which have since grown mutually exclusive seemed either indistinguishable or else mutually strengthening. Only by reading the problems of the nineteenth century into the events of the seventeenth century have historians been led to think otherwise.[2] During Swift's

[1] A careful history of the Dublin Philosophical Society is needed. In my notes below I use the following sources, giving the references in the square brackets: B.M. MS. Ad. 4811–12, of which I quote from only the first [Ad. 4811]; 'Sir Thomas Molyneux', four articles in the *Dublin University Magazine*, XVIII (1841) [*D.U.M.*]; *Correspondence of the Philosophical Society of Dublin with the Philosophical Society of Oxford*, in R. T. Gunther, *Early Science in Oxford*, XII (1939), 128–208 [Gunther]. Further materials will be found in the following: T.C.D., Molyneux papers (MS. I. 4. 17, 18); Southampton Civic Centre, Archives, Molyneux papers; Thomas Birch, *History of the Royal Society*, 1756–7.

[2] Ogg II. 523–30 is thoroughly misleading, though many scholars share his confusions. In England during the seventeenth century, there was no essential conflict between religion and what we now call science, or between humanistic studies and experimental research, or between the universities and the new philosophy of nature; there was no essential tie between Puritanism and experimental science;

youth, keen philologists were eager experimenters; pious divines practised mathematics. The 'illuminati' of Dublin possessed what today would be a rare combination of aesthetic, scholarly, and scientific energies; and in the service of the state they might be high commissioners, privy councillors, or, as bishops, members of the House of Lords: too many jobs were chasing too few people. These men saw no conflict between physics and faith, imaginative writing and scholarship, music and mathematics, or classical poetry and experimental science. Humanistic values, as well as the Established Church, they took for granted. To them, astronomy was a way to demonstrate morality, and Christianity was an inspiration for algebra. 'After great study', Narcissus Marsh wrote in his diary, 'I had a good invention in conical sections, for which God's holy name be praised' (7 February 1690/1).

Surveying the composition of the Society, we shall first observe what a variety of occupations were pursued by the comparatively few members of the governing or intellectual class of the kingdom, and secondly what an intimate alliance this particular body of them had with Swift's university. Surveying the operations of the Society, we shall discover a remarkable range of subjects foreshadowing episodes or images in Swift's writing: astronomical researches which anticipate Laputa, excremental or animal experiments like those at the Academy of Lagado, a toy fleet like the one Gulliver would steal from Blefuscu, a study of spittle such as Swift was to deride in *A Tale of a Tub*, and even a flying island. These and other instruments of Swift's ridicule were already commonplaces—though not yet of belles-lettres—and they existed in what to him would seem a framework of absurdity. That he need not have learned of them in Dublin, we must insist; but that they were available to him many years before he embarked upon his great literary enterprises is certain.

Although Sir William Petty and William Molyneux were the

---

and seventeenth-century science had little influence upon technology: see A. R. Hall, *Ballistics in the Seventeenth Century*, Cambridge 1952; R. L. Colie, *Light and Enlightenment* (Cambridge 1957), p. 4 and *passim*.

most knowledgeable researchers of the group, it was centred in the dons of Trinity College and supported by clergymen connected with them. Besides Ashe, Marsh, and Huntingdon, the earliest members included Edward Smyth, a fellow of the College; Samuel Foley, still a fellow but later to be Bishop of Connor and Down; and William King, formerly a fellow but now rector of St Werburgh's and eventually to become Archbishop of Dublin. Behind the conception of the Society, however, the most important agent was of course Molyneux.

A Dubliner by birth (1656), he had been educated at Trinity College and in the Middle Temple, London. But having no taste for the law, he devoted himself to mathematics, architecture, engineering, optics, and other scientific or philosophical pursuits. His translation of Descartes's *Meditations* was published in 1680, when he also began a correspondence with the great astronomer Flamsteed. He became a friend of Locke's as well; in fact, both William Molyneux and his younger brother Thomas seem to have sought out or written to as many famous scientists as they could. In Dublin he promoted regular gatherings of men who shared his interests.

During Swift's second year at Trinity College, the earliest steps were taken toward setting up a 'philosophical' society like the one at Oxford. Soon Huntingdon offered the hospitality of the provost's residence to the group which Molyneux assembled; and the first formal meeting was held there in October 1683. Marsh, who was still Bishop of Ferns, read a paper; so did St George Ashe and Molyneux himself. At the end of the month Molyneux wrote to his brother (who was studying medicine in Leyden) that he had, in imitation of the Royal Society,

> promoted the rudiments of a society, for which I have drawn up rules, and called it *Conventio Philosophica*. About half a score or a dozen of us have met about twelve or fifteen times, and we have very regular discourses concerning philosophical, methodical, and mathematical matters. Our convention is regulated by one chief, who is chosen by the votes of the rest, and is called *Arbiter Conventionis*, at present Dr. [Charles] Willoughby (the name president

being yet a little too great for us)... Sir [William] Petty and all the virtuosi of this place favour it much; and have at some times given us their company.[1]

Petty was one of the most extraordinary Englishmen of the seventeenth century. Born in 1623, son of a London clothier or weaver, he claimed to have mastered, before he was sixteen, arithmetic, navigation, French, Latin, and Greek. After studying medicine in Holland and France, and being a fellow-student of Hobbes at Paris, he returned to England. In 1650 he was made a fellow of Brasenose College, Oxford. Petty became famous the following year by an achievement of which Swift must have heard: a hanged murderess was cut down too soon; and Petty, instead of dissecting her body as planned, brought her back to life with the help of another doctor. Shortly afterwards, he was made professor of anatomy in Oxford and vice-principal of Brasenose College. But in 1652, when he was appointed physician-general to the Parliamentary army in Ireland, he entered upon a thirty-five-year period of alternating his residence between England and Ireland.

His friend, the great Robert Boyle, was already in that kingdom, on a visit (1652–3) to his Irish estates. Boyle described it as 'a barbarous country, where chemical spirits were so misunderstood and chemical instruments so unprocurable, that it was hard to have any Hermetic thoughts in it'.[2] Together, he and Petty carried on experiments in anatomy. However, the scheme which established both Petty's main reputation and his private fortune was a survey of the lands, forfeited by the Roman Catholics, which were to be divided between the 'adventurers' and the Parliamentary soldiers. Not only did he carry this out by an ingenious method which was remarkably efficient; but through the opportunities afforded him by the project, he managed to obtain a great deal of land for himself. After the Restoration, confirmed in the estates which he had acquired, Petty gave up much of his administrative work and extended his scientific pursuits. He was

[1] *D.U.M.*, p. 472. [2] *DNB*.

a charter member of the Royal Society, and received his knighthood on the occasion of its establishment. When Molyneux was planning the Philosophical Society, Petty was in Dublin. He helped draft the original rules and constitution of the Society, and compiled for it a list of simple experiments which could be easily performed. For the year beginning November 1684, he was elected president.

Meanwhile, the Society had been active from its inception. Even the hard winter of 1683–4 did not impede events. Ashe and Marsh used the intense cold for experiments in freezing liquids; and though the surface of the Liffey was solid for more than six weeks, the philosophers met every Monday. Encouraged by the Oxford and Royal Societies, they soon decided to give themselves a 'better form'. Marsh, Petty, Willoughby, and Molyneux 'were pitched upon to draw up rules', and quickly presented a set modelled upon those of the Royal Society. These were accepted of course, and at the end of January the first officers were elected—Willoughby as president and Molyneux as secretary-treasurer. In April 1684 they began meeting in a room of their own, 'in [the] Crows-nest'. By May of the following year, Molyneux could tell his brother that they had a fixed place in a house in Dame Street, 'where we have a fair garden for plants, and a laboratory erected for us'.[1] When Clarendon arrived as lord lieutenant (1685–6), they tried to interest him in their work; he encouraged them to seek a charter, and he came to a meeting.[2]

In the researches carried on by the members, no man showed more energy than Swift's tutor. Ashe's devotion to geometry and meteorology has already been noticed. He read papers on mathematical problems; gave accounts of the barometric pressures, winds, rainfall, etc., at Trinity College; brought in curiously shaped stones and fossils (including one 'taken out of the bladder of a noble man's cook in the country who lately dyed of it'[3]); and described a horse 'whose yard was fix'd about two inches below the anus', with 'two teats under the belly'.[4] John Jones's ridicule

[1] *D.U.M.*, pp. 477, 481. [2] Ad. 4811, ff. 178v, 180–80v. [3] *Ibid.*, f. 165v.
[4] *Ibid.*, f. 170v.

of Ashe as a virtuoso obsessed with eclipses had some justification. To calculate the eclipse of the sun in July 1684, he and Molyneux drew up tables; but the observations were almost completely obscured by poor weather. The following December, an eclipse of the moon was due, and again Ashe laid plans. Again the sky was overcast, and nothing could be seen. In November 1685 the moon obliged him with another eclipse; Ashe reported that a cloudy sky had made precise observations impossible.[1]

Molyneux discussed telescopes and dioptrics. He showed how a telescope could be used to examine a miniature portrait in detail: it 'makes all the features appear most strong', he said, 'and likewise hereby the faults of such a peice of painting are most apparent, which otherwise are apt to escape the unarmed eye'; it represents 'the small face of a curious peice of miniature with all the advantage imaginable, and as big if not bigger then the life'.[2] He dissected a newt and showed the circulation of its blood with a microscope.[3] He talked on the petrifying properties of Lough Neagh and on hydrostatics.[4]

Allen Mullen, M.D. of Trinity College, was famous for his *Anatomical Account* (1682) of an elephant which had been accidentally burned in Dublin. He performed experiments on dogs, usually filling them with odd substances. He pumped eighteen ounces of water into the thorax of one, and found that it grew short-winded. Into the jugular vein of another, he injected an infusion of opium mixed with brandy and water; the dog died. He cut off a piece of another's lungs, and tied up the surrounding tissue to prevent bleeding; the dog lived.[5] Mullen fed a die to a dog: 'he kept it in his body twenty-four hours, when it came out it had lost half its weight, but retain'd its cubical figure most accurately, and every point on each side.'[6]

Petty was good at giving advice. He proposed experiments on land carriages and on mineral waters, made a list of instruments needed by the Society, and suggested general rules of procedure.[7]

[1] Gunther, pp. 148–9, 157–8, 180. [2] Ad. 4811, ff. 13^{v}–14.
[3] *Ibid.*, ff. 163–3^{v}. [4] *Ibid.*, ff. 9^{v}–10, 166^{v}.
[5] Gunther, pp. 140–1, 145, 184; Ad. 4811, ff. 176–6^{v}. [6] Gunther, p. 143.
[7] Ad. 4811, ff. 11^{v}–12, 27, 48^{v}, 62.

He liked to design models. For the road-haulage experiments, he displayed a 'land carriage' of Lilliputian dimensions, 'a solid parallelopiped of five inches thick, and ten inches long, weighing ninety-nine ounces: being so ordered that it may be put on wheels, either one sett or two setts, of equal or unequal diameters, or it may be made a sled, or to be drawn on four or two dragging wheels, or on the ful flat'.[1] Even before the Society had been formed, in May 1683, he had demonstrated a toy navy: 'He has a fleet of ships in little modells of about one and a half and two foot long, of all kinds, more than the King of France, and with these in a great broad trough of water he performs wonders.'[2]

Other topics came up often and from many sources: magnetism, the calculation of the longitude, methods of softening wood or of petrifying it, the 'formation of letters and an universall character',[3] water pumps and other devices to raise water. Often the research is plainly misguided, such as an almost Laputan attempt to show that water does not move 'naturally': 'The figure of the particles that do compose water are the most unfit for motion; for it has been long demonstrated that round bodys are the most fit; but the parts of water are generally agreed to be oblong.' Hence, argues the philosopher, 'its first and chief motion proceeds from the elastick power of the air containd in it', and it moves fast or slow 'from the different pressure of the externall air upon it'.[4] Some of the research is excremental, such as a report on the worms found in a dog's intestines,[5] or details of the spherical little 'bladders' voided by a sick man instead of faeces: 'Some containd a hard substance of a consistence like a greene plum and some a harder: they were of very different colors and bignesses, some nigh as big as a pidgeons egg.'[6]

Many of the experiments were copied from those of the Oxford and Royal Societies; and what the members did not perform themselves, they might learn about through correspondence with these or with various philosophically disposed individuals. Their London correspondent could tell them, 'The spot in the

[1] Ad. 4811, f. 161v. [2] *D.U.M.*, p. 482. [3] Ad. 4811, f. 175.
[4] *Ibid.*, f. 41v. [5] *Ibid.*, ff. 177–7v. [6] Gunther, p. 197.

sun is disappeard. Monsr. Mariotte at Paris is dead.'[1] Their Oxford correspondent could report, 'Human spittle, clarified by standing, being mixt with syrup of violets, turn'd to a delicate green color.'[2] Petty might read them the account sent to him of a new satellite around Saturn.[3] Similarly, they learned at second hand about an 'odd meteor' (obviously a mirage) occurring in hot weather over Rhegium, Italy, which made cities appear among the clouds, and men walking.[4]

As the troubles closing James II's reign upset any sort of orderly business, the meetings of the Society grew irregular; and the group was finally dispersed. When it came to be re-formed, in the spring of 1693,[5] Swift was living in England.

Meanwhile, without estimating how much he heard of the Society's business, we can be sure that he had an acquaintance with most if not all of the members. In Jones's tripos alone, is sufficient evidence that the students were aware of their seniors' researches; and both there and in Ashe's address to Clarendon, is evidence that outsiders used to ridicule these occupations. For personal and historical reasons, though Swift might respect or even admire the men themselves, he would be likely to treat their scientific pursuits as outmoded hobby-horses, no more worth while than the logic and metaphysics which the same men handled at the university. In humanistic studies, the College programme had a rational articulation; the purpose of each exercise seemed clear. But to a nature as order-loving as Swift's, the miscellaneous enthusiasms of half-baked experimenters would by contrast seem a jungle.

Furthermore, in defending the philosophy of systematic experiment and observation, it had been common for zealous propagandists (not usually the real scientists themselves) to appeal to the usefulness of the inventions which would come out of the research: there was a note of panacea in most of the recommendations. By the end of the seventeenth century this note was turning sour. To many younger men, the Royal Society appeared

[1] Ad. 4811, f. 27v. [2] *Ibid.*, f. 48. [3] *Ibid.*, f. 165v.
[4] *Ibid.*, ff. 170v–1. [5] *Ibid.*, f. 182.

to have belied Sprat's promises and to represent a decaying fad, as specious as alchemy or astrology. It was one thing to believe that scholasticism had been overthrown by Bacon, or to see Descartes's mechanical philosophy defeated (as it was soon to be) by Locke: these could be interpreted as victories of empiricists over system-builders, of simple facts over wild speculation. It was another thing to espouse yet another universal system just as its sun seemed to be put out.

> The question at issue is not whether there was a feeling in society that philosophers should study 'things of use' instead of weighing the air and magnifying the flea, but whether the philosopher himself yielded to such an opinion. The evidence seems to show that he did not; he clung to his old name and status and resisted the attempt to make natural philosophy a sort of superior technology restricted to the problems of cider-making and navigation. Theoretical studies held the field—the scientist could be a Gimcrack if he chose—so that by the end of the century the interest aroused by publicists like Samuel Hartlib had waned because the promised miracles had not occurred.[1]

Most of the discussions held by the Society were ill informed or amateurish when they were not absurd. Though a sympathetic historian can recognize the deep issues underlying the grotesque experiments, an undergraduate would feel less patient. He would not know that behind the collecting of petrifications, for example, lay problems like the origin of life, the difference between animate and inanimate, and the validity of the biblical story of creation. Or if he did, he would assume not that these grand inquiries were premature, and the investigators wrestling with tasks for which their instruments were not yet adequate, but that the mysteries were essentially unfathomable and the labour spent on them wasted.

Did he also think this labour tended directly to undermine the Established Church? Hardly—since no one ever accused Ashe, King, or Marsh of impiety; and since the first became Bishop of Clogher, the second, Archbishop of Dublin, and the third, Pri-

[1] A. R. Hall, *Ballistics in the Seventeenth Century* (Cambridge 1952), pp. 163–4.

mate of all Ireland, Swift would hardly have associated their interests with Puritanism. If he ever considered, as a group, the savants who dominated the Society, his judgment must have been one of unusual esteem, however sadly he may have regretted their foibles. Indeed, it would be just because he thought he understood these men, or appreciated their virtues, that he could freely dismiss as folly the labours which absorbed them.[1]

Naturally, the forces which broke up the Society also shook the College; for by the time William of Orange landed in England, Tyrconnel had done his work in Ireland. He had swamped the corporations with Roman Catholics, and his threatening attitude toward the Act of Settlement was well known. Prudent families of Protestants began to dispose of their property and to leave the country. In some districts the Irish Catholics, believing their sun had risen at last, simply seized various belongings of the Protestants.

The idea of 1641 was sharp in every Protestant imagination. Those who had no fear for themselves were anxious about their families, and the departures grew into an exodus. 'All combine to leave the state,/Who hate the tyrant, or who fear his hate.'[2] Robert Huntingdon and Edward Jones fled to England in 1688. Narcissus Marsh was driven from his bishopric early in 1689, and after a brief stay in Dublin went to England. William Molyneux moved to Chester at the end of January 1689.

By this time Trinity College was in an impossible situation. In the summer of 1687 Tyrconnel had tried to intimidate the provost and senior fellows into appointing a Roman Catholic to a lectureship for which there was no proper endowment. They managed to defeat him; but early the following year the king ordered them to admit a Roman Catholic to a fellowship. They

[1] I do not accept the theses argued by either Robert Merton, in 'Puritanism, Pietism, and Science', in his *Social Theory and Social Structure* (Glencoe, Illinois, 1957), pp. 574–606; or R. F. Jones, in 'The Background of the Attack on Science', in *Pope and His Contemporaries*, ed. J. L. Clifford and Louis Landa (Oxford 1949), pp. 96–113. See Colie, pp. 49–65, and *passim*.

[2] Dryden, *Aeneid* I. 498.

showed evidence that the candidate had committed thefts and had fathered bastards. The king did not press them further, but Tyrconnel withdrew the annual grant of money which the College had been accustomed to receive from the Exchequer. Meanwhile, one of Tyrconnel's judges was trying to 'discover' a plot by some of the students to murder the lord deputy. His honour at last admitted that this was 'a very ridiculous business'; but when the provost and fellows tried to sell some of the college silver (a conventional method of raising money), Tyrconnel intervened and would not let them.[1]

By the beginning of 1689, none of the tenants of the college properties were paying rent, and supplies fell so low that 'but one meal a-day' was ordered to be provided in hall, 'and that a dinner, because supper is the more expensive meal'. Most of the students must have left about this stage. Early in March ten fellows, including Ashe, embarked for England; and another died. In September the four who remained were simply turned out, and a regiment of foot was quartered in the College. Though the refugee fellows only began to return after the Battle of the Boyne, a tiny skeleton crew of senior members stayed in Dublin all through the troubles.[2]

Swift and his cousin Thomas were probably gone by the end of January 1689.[3] Although they had arrived together, worked under the same tutor, and no doubt left together, they had begun already to move apart. The elder boy had won his scholarship after two years as an undergraduate, had behaved himself rather more decorously than his cousin, and now paused a while before the correct next step. This was to resume his studies for the M.A. at his father's college, Balliol, Oxford, which he entered in November 1690. (Dillon Ashe had gone up to Magdalen Hall in May.) But Jonathan took another route, starting from Leicester.

[1] Stubbs, pp. 119–27. [2] *Ibid.*, pp. 127–33.

[3] Barrett, p. 13. In a letter of 1692, Swift said he had spent seven years at Trinity College, a figure which would set his departure in the spring of 1689, or probably earlier—since his emphasis is on the length, rather than brevity, of the period (Ball I. 10); Temple, in May 1690, says Swift 'was near seven years in the College of Dublin, and ready to take his degree of master of arts, when he was forced away by the desertion of that College upon the calamities of the country' (Ball I. 2).

Part II

Chapter One

TEMPLE

i

'The troubles then breaking out', Swift wrote of himself, 'he went to his mother, who lived in Leicester, and after continuing there some months, he was received by Sir William Temple, whose father had been a great friend to the family and who was now retired to his house called Moorpark near Farnham in Surry.'[1] Leicester, of course, he never meant to be more than a halting-place. Swift and his mother must immediately have considered what career he might follow. With his ancestry, his schooling, and his poverty, the most sensible direction was ecclesiastical, except that he had, in his own words, 'a scruple of entring into the church meerly for support'.[2]

While the future remained unsettled, Swift did not limit his conversation to his mother; for his conduct with one young woman stirred up unnecessary anxieties. The girl was Elizabeth Jones, daughter of the Rev. John Jones, vicar of Wanlip, Leicestershire[3]; and it was Mrs Swift herself who brought him 'to a knowledge' of the family, for Miss Jones was her cousin.[4] The friendship reached a stage where his 'prudent mother' began to feel alarmed that he might be in love with her. However, the end of Swift's visit was the end of the affair, unless the 'letters to Eliza' which he later asked a friend to burn, were written to her.[5] A few years after he left, she married an innkeeper[6]; and in an-

[1] *Autob.*, f. 8. [2] *Ibid.*, f. 9. [3] Near Belgrave. [4] Ball IV. 55–6.

[5] *Ibid.* I. 29–30.

[6] Theophilus Perkins of Loughborough, married at Thurcaston 1692; Josiah Birkhead was the surety.

other trip to Leicester, Jonathan was soon involved with another young woman.

From his mother's house he went to Surrey as a sort of secretary, writing, reading aloud, and keeping accounts for the son of the Swifts' benefactor in Ireland. 'His whole family', Temple wrote, 'having been long known to me obliged me . . . to take care of him.'[1] Of all Swift's conscious decisions, this was to be the most far-reaching; and of all Sir William Temple's decisions, none was to give him a larger share of immortality. It was too late for the host to be much altered in character by his protégé, but Swift's nature underwent, from Temple's example, the deepest changes it could suffer after adolescence. From an appreciation of the older man's attitudes and values, we can come to understand what the younger man purposed and worked for.

The profundity of Temple's effect on Swift has always been underestimated. During a period of twenty years Swift was to transcribe, edit, and see through the press almost the whole body of Temple's literary works, including three volumes of correspondence and two of memoirs. Having come straight from the university, he was to live for a decade (with two long breaks) in the Temple family. From that household he was to take the woman who as a child of eight met him on his arrival, as a girl of eighteen saw him finally depart, and as a woman of twenty followed him to his native city, there to remain his most intimate companion until she died. Swift obtained a most minute knowledge of Temple's career, drew parallels between it and his own, and sometimes acted on these parallels. He felt directly the effects of Temple's experiences as a son and a father. He admired Temple's character and his mind. Temple's literary style, political philosophy, moral outlook, and aesthetic judgment became either models or points of departure for Swift's own.

It was not alone the man Temple had become that formed Swift: it was also the man he had been. If Swift had not possessed a comprehensive familiarity with this history and background, he could neither have bathed Temple's memory in the

[1] Ball I. 2.

superlatives which he devoted to it, nor have identified himself, again and again, with the patterns of his master's life. The migrations of various Temples between England and Ireland; the domestic arrangement of a single Sir William usually attended by two ladies (his sister and his wife) but often cut off from his beloved Dorothy; Temple's repeated efforts to reform national policy, which were repeatedly and treacherously frustrated; his utter lack of material reward for a career of distinguished public service—these were some of the points at which Swift was either to find or to make his own life run parallel with Temple's.

ii

Temple was the same age as Swift's uncle Godwin. He had been half-orphaned at eleven, when his mother died; and much of his early education was supervised by her brother, Dr Henry Hammond, author of the introduction to *The Whole Duty of Man*. Afterwards, as dean of Christ Church, Oxford, Hammond had a reputation for 'shaming the vicious to sobriety, encouraging the ingenuous to diligence, and finding stratagems to ensnare the idle to a love of study'.[1] When the saintly man died, Temple showed the power of his attachment by falling 'quite sick' at the news.[2] Hammond was the main instiller of those virtues which were to make Temple appear to Swift as a Christian hero.

The college selected for the boy by his father was not, however, royalist and Anglican, like his uncle's, but markedly Puritan: Emmanuel, Cambridge.[3] Here, though his tutor was the great Platonist and liberal thinker, Ralph Cudworth, the effect of the two opposing Christianities was to give Temple a cool disposition toward all churches. Even at twenty-four he could write, 'Faith must be purely an inspiration of heaven or an operation of custom, not a work either of force or reason'[4]; neither Hammond nor Cudworth would have smiled at this maxim. Like Swift,

[1] John Fell, *Life of Hammond*, 1661, p. 49.
[2] Lady Giffard, in Temple's *Early Essays*, p. 9.
[3] Lemuel Gulliver's college. [4] Woodbridge, p. 27.

Temple found the exercises of scholasticism unappetizing; and although Cudworth pressed him to study logic and philosophy, his 'humour' was too 'lively' to pursue them.

> Entertainments which agreed better with that [humour] and his age, especially tennis, passed most of his time there [i.e., at the university], so that he used to say, if it had been possible to forget all he had learned there, he must certainly have done it.[1]

The fact that he was remarkably handsome probably contributed to his delinquency.

After Cambridge there were the conventional (but unusually extensive) travels on the Continent, and the very unconventional six-year courtship of Dorothy Osborne—happily concluded by their marriage. The tenacious opposition of Temple's father to his choice of wife did not weaken the intimacy of parent and child. Temple set great store by filial obedience, and at later critical points in his career, he submitted to his father's judgment.[2]

Five months after the birth (1655) of their first child, John, the Temples established themselves in Ireland, where they lived quietly until the eve of the Restoration. But Temple was obviously waiting to be called into the service of the state. Meanwhile, though they divided their time pleasantly enough between a place built for them in the country and old Sir John's house in Dublin, they were made regularly miserable by the successive deaths of their numerous children; for during this period only John survived.

iii

With Temple's election to the Irish convention of 1660, his public life got under way; and he was a member of the parliament at Dublin the next year. Working on important committees, he journeyed between England and Ireland, and met the king for the first time. His moderateness and his powers of conciliation

[1] Lady Giffard, quoted by Woodbridge, pp. 10–11.

[2] E.g., in his refusal to be ambassador to Spain and his refusal to buy the office of secretary of state.

were so successful that later, when he sat in the English parliament, another member said, 'he was glad [Temple] was not a woman, because he was sure he might have perswaded him to any thing'.[1] This tribute is reported by Temple's sister, Martha, whose distinction it was to have been widowed almost immediately after her marriage to Sir Thomas Giffard (1662).[2] Lady Giffard stuck closer to her brother than even Lady Temple, whose authority in the family seems at times to have been weaker than that of her sister-in-law. In 1665, the whole family—Sir William, Lady Temple, Lady Giffard, and John Temple—moved to England, where they went to live in Sheen, Surrey (near London), while Temple pursued his ambitions among the court circle.

At last, in the middle of the year, the court sent him to Munster; his charge was to keep the prince-bishop to a promise of invading the United Provinces, with whom England was at war. Although the larger purposes of this project were shattered, Temple saved the pieces so well that in 1666 he was made a baronet. In his next, and most spectacular, feat, Temple revealed a candour, and a faith in the efficacy of candour, rarely found among the huddled notions of diplomacy. (To Swift, this was to seem one of Temple's most admirable traits, and one of those most worthy of emulation.) From observations during his travels, from recent events on the Continent, and from talks with John De Witt, Grand Pensionary of Holland, he had formulated the central principle of his diplomacy: that the English must join with the Dutch to prevent Louis XIV from overwhelming Europe. Temple's optimism about the possibility of consummating this wish is as characteristic as his misguided confidence in Arlington—the secretary of state—and Charles II, both of whom were busy undoing his web quite as fast as he pulled the threads into place. Nevertheless, the Triple Alliance (of England, Sweden, and the United Provinces) was arranged, and arranged

[1] Temple, *Early Essays*, p. 9.

[2] In a letter to Ormonde 13 May 1662 Sir George Wentworth says his nephew, Sir Thomas 'Gifford', died when he had 'not beene aboue a weeke a married man' (Bodl. MS. Carte 31, f. 517).

so quickly that Temple received amazed congratulations on having 'in five days' concluded a treaty which the French ambassador had thought would be still under discussion after six weeks.[1] Swift of dispatch and easy of access, Temple disposed of all the ramifications by June 1668. He now innocently trusted that 'the general interests of Christendom [were] secured against the power and attempts of France'.[2] Macaulay, echoing Pepys, calls the Triple Alliance 'the single eminently good act performed by the government during the interval between the Restoration and the Revolution'.[3] Even Burnet admitted it was 'the masterpiece of king Charles's life' and said that if the king had stuck to the treaty, it would have been 'both the strength and the glory of his reign'.[4] Thanks, however, to the tortuous manœuvres of Arlington and the king, the Alliance—though popular enough in both Holland and England—achieved practically nothing.

Nevertheless, when Temple arrived home, he seemed to have killed the minotaur, and might have claimed a peerage or a pension. That he chose to do neither, and that he hesitated several weeks before accepting a new post as ambassador to Holland are signs of another trait which impressed Swift: Temple's deliberate indifference to visible rewards. Temple apparently was guileless enough to believe that by requesting no preferment he would deepen Charles's reliance upon him. He also credited himself with sufficient magnanimity to enjoy the pure kudos of patriotic service for its own sake without regretting the lack of negotiable benefits. But he was more transparent and less saintly than he imagined. In politics as in crime nothing binds men closer than reciprocal profits. Charles sold his powers to whoever would give the services he required, and Temple, by not pressing his own advancement, lost both the ability to enforce his policies and the one consolation which might have softened his failure; for he found himself ruefully out of pocket through the demands of his public career.

[1] Woodbridge, p. 85. [2] *Ibid.*, p. 91.
[3] 'Sir William Temple', in *Constitutional Essays*, World's Classics edition, p. 346.
[4] Burnet I. 440.

iv

During his first service in Holland, 1668–71, Temple learned to allay a bit 'that frankness of my heart which made me think everybody meant as well as I did'.[1] Although he conceived of his function as to shore up 'the Triple Bond', he was actually a blind of integrity behind which a new war with the Dutch was projected. While Charles and Arlington secretly arranged the Treaty of Dover (by which England joined with France against the Dutch and against Protestantism), Temple was assuring the anxious Pensionary that no crown would 'enter into counsels so destructive to their honour and safety as those he suspected'.[2] In September 1670 he was recalled, ostensibly for brief consultation, but really to keep him out of the way without alarming the Dutch. Not until the following August, after almost a year's loitering in a chilly court, was he released from his mission and permitted to rejoin Lady Temple, John, and Diana—a daughter born in 1665—all of whom the king had forced him to leave in Holland.

Even now he had not learned, Lady Giffard writes, 'the lessen . . . one should alwayes be perfect in, before one comes to court, to swallow every thing'.[3] For a few years he took care of his family and improved the estate at Sheen, without, however, ceasing to watch closely the developments in foreign and domestic policy. He refused to accept the high offices which were offered to him until he could take up the negotiations to end the very unpopular war.

After concluding a separate peace with the Dutch representatives in England, he went to Holland as 'mediator' between France and her opponents, the United Provinces, Spain, and the Empire. Since Charles II was secretly co-operating with the French, Temple had to endure four years' worth of mock bargaining which took him back and forth, from England to Holland to Flanders; and although nobody got out of the miry slough less bedaubed than he, the treaty finally signed at Nimeguen (Feb-

[1] Woodbridge, p. 106. [2] *Ibid.*, p. 107. [3] Temple, *Early Essays*, p. 16.

ruary 1679) was a joke, which only postponed the judgment to come.

In explaining why Charles did at last turn against Louis XIV and allow peace to be made, Temple nicely illustrates another of his elementary principles which Swift was to adopt. This is the assumption that the ultimate spring of national policy is the character of the executive or ruler who enunciates it:

> Though the wise reflections of the best historians, as well as the common reasonings of private men, are apt to ascribe the actions and councils of princes to interests or reasons of state, yet whoever can trace them to their true spring, will often be forced to derive them from the same passions and personal dispositions which govern the affairs of private lives.[1]

Not that Swift had to learn the principle from Temple; it was a commonplace, and it fitted in with Swift's intuitive conception of society. In the reign of Louis XIV, moreover, there seemed to be irresistible proof of it, if anyone should raise a doubt. But Temple's authority, and the many examples he supplied, fixed the doctrine so that even when the evidence led a different way, Swift would account for political decisions by the character of the man making them. In the following anecdote, retailed by Swift himself as a precious revelation from Temple, no mention is made of the widespread popular discontent with the court's pro-French policy, but all the weight is laid upon the private feelings of the king. Yet the 'article' which Temple and Swift treat as crucial has no basis in fact.[2]

> The secret of the king and the dukes [i.e., the Duke of York's] being so eager and hearty in their resolution to break with France at this juncture, was as follows.
>
> France in order to break the force of the confederacy, and elude all just conditions of a general peace, resolved by any means to enter into separate measures with Holland; to which end it was absolutely necessary to engage the good offices of the King of England, who was look'd upon to be master of the peace whenever he pleas'd. The

[1] *Introduction to the History of England*, p. 284. [2] Cf. Ogg I. 556–8.

bargain was struck for either 3 or 400 thousand pounds. But when all was agreed, Monsieur Barillon the French ambassador, told the king; That he had orders from his master, before payment, to add a private article; by which his majesty should be engaged, never to keep above eight thousand men of standing troops in his three kingdoms. This unexpected proposal put the king in a rage, and made him say, —'d's fish, does my brother of France think to serve me thus? Are all his promises to make me absolute master of my —— come to this? Or, does he think that a thing to be done with eight thousand men.

'Tis possible I may be a little mistaken as to the sums of money, and number of men; but the main of the story is exactly as I had it from the author.[1]

While the close of the histrionic enterprise at Nimeguen hardly purchased Temple everlasting honour and renown, he did get to know William of Orange so intimately that the young prince often dined with the Temples and came to place complete confidence in Sir William. In April 1676 the prince asked his opinion about a marriage between himself and Princess Mary, daughter of the Duke of York—a match which Temple wished to encourage. After hearing the hopeful answer, the prince decided to 'enter upon this pursuit'.[2] The wedding, which took place a year and a half later, tilted the balance of European power: without it, the Glorious Revolution and the War of the Spanish Succession might not have occurred.

V

The reversals and irresolutions of Charles II began now to tell upon Temple, giving him—as his sister says—'a distast to the thoughts of all publick imployments'.[3] He returned to England in March 1679 and never went abroad again. For almost two years more he did carry on a political career of sorts. Though unwilling to reach for the office of secretary of state (which several times was dangled before him), he directed the unsuccessful re-

[1] Swift's note to pp. 355–6 of Temple's *Letters* III.
[2] Temple, *Memoirs* II. 155. [3] Temple, *Early Essays*, p. 20.

organization of the privy council, represented Cambridge University in parliament, opposed the Exclusion Bill, and dodged the Popish Plot. This was, however, no time for moderation; and his attempts to keep peace between the king and the commons were as futile as the pilgrims' words at Vanity Fair. Temple withdrew to Sheen in January 1681, and (through his son John) promised Charles that he 'would never meddle any more with any publick affairs'.[1]

The life of action which he renounced for himself, Temple felt eager to open to his son. When John was only nineteen, Sir William wrote from The Hague to Lord Arlington,

> I hope [after this mission], to go and sleep at home, and leave my son in the busy world, which requires men spirited with some other heats, than I have about me. If upon his coming over you can find any thing you would have said to me, though he be young, yet I am pretty confident he may be trusted with it; for he has a plain steddy head, and is desirous to do well.[2]

When John did deliver a letter from Danby, the lord treasurer, Temple told Danby he hoped the boy would 'live to deserve some place in your service'.[3] Temple seemed as well to wish to involve his son in his literary occupations; for when he dedicated a volume of memoirs to John, he wrote, 'Whatever I leave of this or any other kind, will be in your disposal.'[4] In general, he seems to have felt the same close identification with John's destiny that his own father had felt with Temple's. That attitude was intensified by the fact that no other child of his was living. The charming Diana had died of smallpox in 1679—'a child he was infinitely fond off; & none ever deserv'd it more from a father'.[5] Temple had not taken the event easily. 'My heart is so broken', he wrote, 'that I have done nothing since as I should do, and I fear never shall again.'[6]

But not even John was to outlive his father. He had been married in 1685, and a year later Sir William gave him the Sheen

[1] Temple, *Memoirs* III. 139. [2] Temple, *Letters* III. 39. [3] *Ibid.*, p. 62.
[4] *Memoirs* II, sig. A4^{v}. [5] Lady Giffard, in Temple, *Early Essays*, p. 21.
[6] Woodbridge, p. 207.

property. The parents moved with Lady Giffard farther into the country, near Farnham, Surrey, where they took over a small estate which Temple named Moor Park, after the place in Hertfordshire where he had spent his honeymoon. As this neighbourhood threatened to become a battleground for the Jacobite and Williamite troops, the elder Temples moved back to Sheen, and there both families remained until the end of 1689. When William of Orange came over in 1688, Temple—exercising the sort of prerogative which his own father had been used to—would not let his son go to meet the prince at the landing. The day after the coronation, however, the king made John Temple secretary at war (12 April 1689). Advising William on the Irish situation, the new minister apparently persuaded him to set free Richard Hamilton (a brigadier-general in the Irish army, imprisoned in the Tower) so he might go to Ireland and argue Tyrconnel into giving up. Instead of doing what he had promised, Hamilton joined the rebels himself. Out of shame for his costly mistake, John Temple drowned himself. Within a week of his appointment, he took a boat on the Thames, and leaped out near London Bridge.[1]

His son's death at the age of thirty-two stunned Temple and added a final darkness to his retirement. '[It] brought a cloud upon ye remainder of his life & a damp upon ye good humor so natural to him & so often observ'd yt nothing could ever recover.'[2]

When Swift arrived as a fatherless refugee, it was this childless great gentleman that he met, one who, after the deepest experience of court life and diplomacy, had retired to the compensations of a disillusioned domesticity.

[1] See Ogg II. 247; *MLN.*, LXII (Mar. 1947), 145–54.
[2] Lady Giffard, in Temple, *Early Essays*, p. xii.

Chapter Two

MOOR PARK

The troubles which dispossessed the Temples were of course the same that drove Swift to England. He was in the household at Sheen or Moor Park at least by the close of the year, and probably before the summer.[1] Swift came to his new home as to delectable mountains, although the excitement of the young student hardly shines through the words of the old dean—recording only that he 'continued for about two years' there. Temple had not lost touch with kings and states. He was host and guest to William III and to the Duke and Duchess of Somerset. The closest of his friends, Henry Sidney, was still busied with the 'airy visions' which he himself had left behind. To Swift's public career, however, both Sidney and the Duchess of Somerset were to make extraordinary, if negative, contributions.

All the clan of Sidneys were familiar to Temple from Penshurst and Dr Hammond. As a boy he had adored Henry's beautiful elder sister, Dorothy—the fair Sacharissa of Waller's lyrics. Her son, the second Earl of Sunderland, was (unfortunately) a trusted old acquaintance until Temple achieved enough sagacity to

[1] In the autobiographical fragment Swift says first that he was received by Temple 'who was now retired to his house called Moorpark near Farnham' (f. 8); but farther on, that Temple, getting tired of Sheen, 'bought an estate near Farnham . . . where Mr Swift accompanied him' (f. 9). In a letter of 1727 he speaks of having eaten too many apples at Richmond (i.e., Sheen) when he was about twenty, and then mentions Moor Park as belonging to a later era (Ball III. 413–14). It is possible to explain away the implicit references to Sheen as the place where he originally joined the Temples, but easier—I think—to assume that he did begin to live with them there, toward the middle of 1689, after William III was secure on his throne. Of course, Swift's memory was remarkably fallible, especially as to dates: the Pindaric ode to Temple which Swift headed 'June 1689' was certainly written later, Woodbridge (p. 219, n.) and Pons (p. 143, n.) notwithstanding; but the date he gave it may still be significant. Lyon, supporting the notion that Swift lived with Temple at Sheen, writes, 'The Dean often said so himself' (p. 18).

realize that the earl—then secretary of state—was feeding him lies and using him as a tool. With Algernon, a brother of Henry, Temple had a friendly correspondence which came to an end when the republican views of the exile made letters to him dangerous. At Sheen another brother, Robert, later Earl of Leicester, was a much-liked neighbour.

Henry Sidney had tremendously good looks and winning manners to recommend him, also a shrewdness for pushing his own chance. As a politician he could not, said Swift, 'turn a wheel for a mouse'; but he had the invaluable foresight to realize, almost before everybody else, how probable it was that William of Orange would succeed James II. While living in Holland, Sidney made so much a friend of the prince that the scheme of inviting William to England in 1688 might be said to owe its success more to him than to any other person. Apart from a triumphant career of philandering, this was his most illustrious achievement. Sidney's term as secretary of state was an avowed receivership; his brief lord lieutenancy of Ireland was remarkable for the chaos it engendered; and his title of Earl of Romney (1694) was less a token of the king's esteem than of his affection.

If proof were lacking of Temple's inability to judge character, his respect for Sidney would be enough. Nevertheless, at one time or another during Temple's eighteen years of retirement, Sidney not only took the titles already mentioned but served as a member of parliament and as a privy councillor, held high military offices, and acted as a lord justice both of Ireland and of the realm. He kept up influential connections in France, Holland, and Ireland; he was with King William at the Boyne. Into Moor Park's quiet garden-state he brought constant reminders of the renowned metropolis, with glistering spires and pinnacles adorned. The young Swift could not foresee that a crisis in his own development would some day evince the earl's inadequacies.

Other members of the household were to count for much more in Swift's life than either Temple's relatives or his guests. Rebecca Dingley, a spinster of the Hammond connection, stayed on as a waiting woman to Lady Giffard.[1] Temple's steward was Ralph Mose. Bridget Johnson, a widow, held the post of housekeeper.[2] She had been married to Edward Johnson, who had been Temple's steward in his time; and to him she had borne three children. Esther,[3] the eldest of these, was a sickly girl of eight when Swift arrived. This first-born, frail, and now fatherless child, who was to inspire Swift with his deepest love, learned penmanship from him, and her writing as an adult was sometimes taken for his. In addition, he recommended books for her to read, and 'perpetually instruct[ed] her in the principles of honour and virtue'.[4] He found himself, no doubt, more comfortable with Dingley, Mrs Johnson, and little Hetty than with the two old ladies and the baronet.

At the moment, however, Swift's chief of men was Temple, whose way, though it seemed glorious, had apparently been ploughed by patience, temperance, and deeds of peace. Lady Giffard's picture of him in 1690 brings out the ageing statesman's affability and love of intimate society. His mood, she said, was naturally gay, but occasionally soured by fits of gloom. 'His conversation was easy and familiar with all people, from the greatest princes to the meanest servant.' His keenest pleasures were domestic: talking with friends and enjoying the house and garden.[5] An intelligent Swiss visitor, seeing Temple about four years later, was struck by his health and serenity: 'He is free from business, and to all appearances free from ambition . . . and though he is gouty and getting on in years, he tired me in walking.'[6]

Lady Temple was no passionate, moody girl with an epistolary flair. Smallpox had long since spoiled her beauty; nine children born and buried had darkened her temperament. She

[1] Her grandmother was a sister of Temple's mother.

[2] The first wife of Ralph Mose was still alive; there is a bill for her clothes among Mr James Osborn's collection of Temple family papers (no. 21). According to the Farnham parish register, Bridget Johnson did not marry Mose until 1711.

[3] Though christened Hester, she used the other form.

[4] T. Scott XI. 127.

[5] Temple, *Early Essays*, pp. 28–9.

[6] Woodbridge, p. 232.

had learned—in her own words upon her son's suicide—'what this world is':

> It seems it was necessary that I should have a near example of the uncertainty of all human blessings, that so having no tie to the world I may the better prepare myself to leave it; and that this correction may suffice to teach me my duty must be [my] prayer.[1]

For Lady Giffard, on the other hand, the family woes were vicarious; and she far outlived both her sister-in-law and her brother. Widowed at twenty-four, within a fortnight of her marriage, but ten years younger than Temple, she relished the high and secure station made for her at his side. During his travels she was with him more often than his wife; she copied her studies from his and became something of a bluestocking. While gracious and cordial to Lady Temple or others of her own rank, she does not seem to have unbent much toward inferiors. Swift shows no sign of having felt or returned any great fondness on her part. She was no doubt happier endearing herself to her magnificent young friend at Petworth, the Duchess of Somerset.

Not that the intimacy between Moor Park and Petworth was unnatural. The duchess, Elizabeth Percy, daughter of the fifth Earl of Northumberland, was a cousin of the Sidneys. Temple had corresponded with her father and had admired her grandfather. Before she was fifteen, her avaricious guardian (the dowager countess) had pushed her into two disgraceful marriages. But she was released from the one by widowhood and from the other by a combination of flight and murder; for a jealous rival of her second husband had him killed after she had already run away from home. According to a strong tradition, her flight, which ended in Holland, was assisted by the Temples. In the spring of 1682, about four months after the murder, she married Charles Seymour, the shallow, arrogant sixth Duke of Somerset. Red-headed, stubborn, and shrewd, she still continued to be notorious, less however for private than for public intrigue. Whatever Swift's first impressions of the duchess may have been,

[1] Woodbridge, p. 218.

they did not teach him to avoid the grossest slanders when he came to attack her character in print two decades after his earliest opportunities to observe her.

Swift mingled eventually with even the most exalted visitors; but his duties that first year were defined rather modestly by Temple: 'He has lived in my house, read to me, writ for me, and kept all accounts as far as my small occasions required.'[1] The work seems light enough, and the milieu afforded advantages that were hardly conceivable in Dublin or Leicester. Unfortunately, however, Swift now suffered for the first time the illness which never left him and which grew irregularly in severity: Ménière's disease, a disturbance of the inner ear, causing vertigo, deafness, or both. Swift mistakenly distinguished between the effects of the disorder upon his hearing and upon his equilibrium, not understanding that the various symptoms were all due to the same evil. His giddiness and 'coldness of stomach' he traced to an over-indulgence in apples, and therefore worried all his life about eating fruit, which he loved; the deafness, he traced to a cold.

> I got my giddiness, by eating a hundred golden pippins at a time at Richmond [i.e., Sheen] . . . four years and a quarter [later], having made a fine seat about twenty miles farther in Surrey [i.e., at Moor Park], where I used to read and sleep, there I got my deafness.[2]

When Swift consulted physicians, they suggested the climate might be to blame, and 'weakly imagined that his native air might be of some use to recover his health'[3]; so he returned to Ireland. Temple wrote him a letter of recommendation to Sir Robert Southwell, who was going with the king on the Irish expedition; Southwell was to be principal secretary of state for Ireland, and would have abundant patronage to dispense:

[1] Ball I. 2. [2] *Ibid.* III. 413–14.

[3] *Autob.*, ff. 8–8[v], where he gives a slightly variant account of the disease: 'For he happened before twenty years old, by a surfeit of fruit to contract a giddyness and coldness of stomach, that almost brought him to his grave; and this disorder pursued him with intermissions of two or [three] years to the end of his life.'

> He has Latin and Greek, some French, writes a very good and current hand, is very honest and diligent, and has good friends, though they have for the present lost their fortunes.[1]

Temple suggested that Southwell find a place for Swift either in his own service or as a fellow of Trinity College, Dublin.

If Swift travelled by his usual route, he stopped off at Leicester on the way and saw his mother. But whether his patron's recommendation did him any good or not has never been discovered, except that he certainly received no fellowship. This was an unhappy moment for such an aspiration, because the College was still trying to repair the injuries of the Revolution, and no new fellows were appointed until the spring of 1692. As for the Hibernian air, his health actually grew worse in it; and at Temple's invitation he decided to come back. Returning to England about August 1691, he again visited his mother, staying with her through the autumn.[2]

A new amorous adventure gave rise now to fresh scandal; we have an account of the episode in the answer which Swift delivered to an inquiry from the Rev. John Kendall, who had married Swift's cousin, Jane Errick. Though Swift told Kendall, 'I could remember twenty women in my life, to whom I behaved myself just the same way', this case must have had a special glow about it. Again the family feared marriage. Jonathan's excellent prospects with Sir William Temple should be cultivated by prudence, not spoiled through impetuosity. No, answered Swift, if anything was going to block his advancement, it was only his 'own cold temper, and unconfined humor'. Even at twenty-four he was alert to the perils of carnality: 'a thousand household thoughts . . . always drive matrimony out of my mind whenever it chances to come there', he said; 'besides that I am naturally temperate, and never engaged in the contrary, which usually produces those effects.' Through the dubious syntax the truth of

[1] Ball I. 2.

[2] On 14 Feb. 1692 he says he returned from Ireland 'about half a year ago' (*ibid.*, p. 7).

his character emerges: Swift was so sure of his own caution, so untempted by misconduct, that he could sneer at gossip-mongers:

> I should not have behaved myself after the manner I did in Leicester, if I had not valued my own entertainment beyond the obloquy of a parcel of very wretched fools, which I solemnly pronounce the inhabitants of Leicester to be.[1]

And so, quite unmarried, he went from Leicester to Oxford, where he visited his cousin. Dillon Ashe had taken his Oxford M.A., *ad eundem*, in December 1690. Thomas Swift was still in Balliol College, having been incorporated in November 1690. Jonathan saw him toward the middle of December and reached Moor Park about Christmas 1691.[2] With Thomas he must have discussed his own intention of entering Oxford University; for on June 14 following, he was incorporated from Hart Hall. Both cousins now petitioned to be admitted as candidates for the M.A. degree with a dispensation from one of the exercises, all others having been performed.[3] The favour was granted; and on July 5 (two days before Thomas), Jonathan received the degree.

[1] Ball I. 4–6.

[2] On 11 Feb. 1692 he says he has been back at Moor Park 'seven weeks' (*ibid.*, p. 4).

[3] Nichols II. 108.

Chapter Three

EARLY POEMS (I)

i

Literary aspirations were beginning to haunt Swift's breast. Soon after returning to Moor Park, he said, 'In these seven weeks I have been here, I have writ, and burnt and writ again, upon almost all manner of subjects, more perhaps than any man in England.'[1] The renewed contact with Temple must have strengthened these ambitions, since the diplomatist turned in retirement to the writing of essays and verses, the preparation of memoirs, and the editing of his own letters for publication. Copying out, during more than a decade, his patron's various works, set Swift a model of the highest value. Yet his own earliest known compositions are not prose but six poems, produced over four years (1690 to 1694); and their manner is not Temple's. The first four are 'pindaric' odes like those of Abraham Cowley; and the remaining two are in the newer fashion of Waller's or Dryden's heroic couplets.

If Swift's later and enduring style is to be considered 'characteristic' of him as a poet, these pieces suggest that he began by working against the grain. Eulogy was always to be his talent, but it would be best expressed ironically, through mock-insults, as when he would sneer at Lord Carteret for 'adher[ing] so obstinately to his old *unfashionable* academick education'.[2] In the early pindarics and couplets, however, he uses straightforward panegyric. Since his themes and values are blamelessly conventional, he is, in his search for freshness of effect, flung upon ingenious hyperbole; and since his language is too weak for the extravagance of his feelings, the outcome is bathos.

[1] Ball I. 4. [2] Davis XII. 160.

We may assume that he was sent in this false direction by Temple. When Swift as a young man said that he found a 'likeness of humours'[1] between himself and his patron, he was less stating a fact than voicing a hope. If Temple derided Halifax for possessing a 'humour; which he own'd always must have business to employ it, or would else be uneasy',[2] he could hardly have admired what Swift found in a famous piece of self-analysis: that (according to a 'person of honour in Ireland') his own mind was like 'a conjured spirit, that would do mischief if I would not give it employment'.[3]

Certainly Temple's literary preferences were opposed to those of Swift's maturity. Swift never felt Temple's distrust of the comic and satirical; and although Temple made a shining exception of *Don Quixote* (which he valued quite as highly as Swift did), his judgment of Swift's adored Rabelais was harsh and narrow.[4] Temple mentions La Rochefoucauld to oppose him;[5] Swift, to praise him. Mock-epic, of which Swift was to write the finest example in English prose, Temple judged as pernicious to poetry and virtue alike.[6] Though both Temple and Swift esteemed conversation as the most deeply satisfying kind of recreation, Temple detested the raillery and witticisms in which Swift rejoiced. 'Those squeez'd or forc'd strains of wit', Temple called them, 'that are in some places so much in request, tho' I think commonly men that affect them are themselves much fonder of them than any of the company.'[7] 'Raillery is the finest part of conversation', said Swift[8]; wit and ridicule are 'the meaner parts' of conversation, said Temple.[9]

Similarly, the puns and word games which Swift loved held small appeal for Temple; in fact, his difficulties as a diplomatist

[1] Ball I. 365. [2] *Memoirs* III. 67.

[3] Ball I. 4. (Cf. Swift's 'fatal bent of mind, / Still to unhappy restless thoughts inclin'd'—*Poems* I. 55.) The similarity between Temple's and Swift's expressions suggests that the 'person' may have been Temple; there are several methods of explaining away 'in Ireland'. In his letter to the Athenian Society the 'person of . . . honour' is probably Temple (Ball I. 7).

[4] *Of Poetry*, pp. 328–9. [5] *Miscellanea* III. 292. [6] *Of Poetry*, pp. 329–30.

[7] *Memoirs* II. 358; cf. *Miscellanea* III. 325–6, 335–6. [8] T. Scott XI. 71.

[9] *Miscellanea* III. 326.

were sometimes aggravated by his distaste for codes: 'God almighty has given it to other men to make cyphers and to flie, but to me only to walk upon plain ground and to read plain hands.'[1] Yet while Temple's tolerance for coarse words and coarse images falls well below Swift's, his relish for sexual innuendo appears far stronger. When Swift, for example, wrote biographies of the Norman kings, he suppressed most of the references to their illicit passions; Temple, however, devoted almost two pages of his *Introduction to the History of England* to the probable superiority of fornication over lawful procreation as a means of conceiving heroes[2]; and Temple's letters not uncommonly include risqué gallantries of a sort that Swift never permitted himself.

These contrarieties do not affect the strength of Swift's early reverence for Temple and his desire to imitate him. 'I never read his writings', Swift said at twenty-five, 'but I prefer him to all others at present in England.'[3] Eight years later, he could still declare that Temple had 'advanced our English tongue, to as great a perfection as it can well bear'.[4] We may then suppose that Swift tried at first to meet the requirements which Temple set up for poets—i.e., that they should

> raise up the esteem of some qualities, above their real value, rather than bring every thing to *burlesque*, which if it be allowed at all, should be so only to wise men in their closets, and not to *witts*, in their common mirth and company. . . All the wit, [which Waller] and his company spent, in heightning love and friendship, was better employ'd, than what is laid out so prodigally, by the modern wits, in the mockery of all sorts of religion and government.[5]

That Swift's dear teacher, St George Ashe, had made similar pronouncements, should have heightened his will to reach a standard so remote from the gifts we remember him for.

While such tendencies undermine the literary interest of the juvenile poems, they establish their documentary importance. As expressions of Swift's positive values, they are unique. Never

[1] *Select Letters*, 1701, p. 11; see also Woodbridge, pp. 87–8; *Letters* III. 305.
[2] Pp. 85–7. [3] Ball I. 365. [4] Davis I. 258.
[5] Letter of August 1667 to Lord Lisle (*Works*, 1720, II. 40).

was he to give such unequivocal, simple, direct embodiment to his ideals. And as one might expect from a man who made satire his employment, these ideals are more remarkable for their intensity than their originality. One effect of setting up a dead grandfather or an absent mother as models of conduct, was evidently to release Swift's notions of virtue from even the limits that a naïve child with visible parents can impose upon such notions. A man already in his middle twenties might well be excused from the celebration of such incandescent perfections as Swift lent to his subjects—which included the king, the Athenian Society, Archbishop Sancroft, and Temple.

ii

Charity ('doing good'), fortitude, and justice are the mainsprings of the ode 'To the King', which Swift wrote while he was in Ireland, between July 1690 and August 1691.[1] To set off the transcendent merits of William, Swift opposes him both to James II and Louis XIV; it is obvious that now, as throughout his life, the Revolution appeared to Swift a blessing. The seven stanzas of the poem are focused upon the benevolence of William III and his courageous generalship at the Battle of the Boyne. Swift denounces the sloth of the English people and the bigotry of the Scottish, who opposed William. He makes much play with the stereotype antithesis between 'great' and 'good': Louis XIV may seem great, but is not, because he is bad and tyrannical; William is truly great because he uses his power for good.

In this poem, Swift takes himself seriously, and is rather a moralist than an entertainer. While his conceits are not impenetrable, several of the allusions were difficult even at the time of composition, and a couple are annotated by Swift. The manner is pompous and rhetorical, with an excess of parentheses, apostrophes, exclamations, and other inflated figures; yet it is underpinned by an indignation which carries conviction. As a sibyl, the

[1] John Dunton quotes stanzas 1–2 in *The Dublin Scuffle*, 1699, p. 379. Swift may have attempted to publish the poem through Dunton.

young poet fails, but as a Juvenal he has some moments of success.

However, he also provides himself with a means of shifting the point of view from his own person, by dramatizing the constant presence of the muse, or spirit of poetry. It is significant that this device accords with the doctrine and practice of Cowley.[1] For Swift—not without irony—traced back his high estimation of Cowley as far as his own sixteenth year.[2] The much-praised poet, who had died about the time Swift was born, was now honoured chiefly for his odes and his love poetry (*The Mistress*); the unfinished epic, the *Davideis*, was no longer read; his ingratiating prose style had yet to be reassessed. Not only the metrical structure of Swift's ode but also its details echo Cowley.[3]

Certain themes which are common to all Swift's early poems appear first in this ode to the king. One is the representation of the poet as a seer, with powers of vision denied to common humans. Another is Swift's angry contempt for the mob, the vulgar mass of unthinking people. Another is the polar distinction between illusion and reality, also expressed as the contrast between true and meretricious virtue. Finally, there is Swift's patent eagerness to find and to acknowledge a genuinely heroic figure.

Certain recurrent images and oppositions also appear. The celestial is coupled with vision, reality, and virtue, and opposed to the earthly; similarly, the solid is opposed to the vaporous, the bright to the murky. William III, establishing himself over the giddy British populace, is like a bright-faced patrician god visiting Hades. In a parallel way, stars are opposed to earthly stenches, sudden flight upwards to sudden falls. William is like a true sun; Louis is like a false and falling meteor. With such motifs are associated violent, characteristic feelings, like profound awe of the hero, or revulsion from the crowd. But though there is a plethora of epithets, there is no relaxation of pose, no sign of humour.

Swift's actual development is foreshadowed, as one might expect, less in the praising than in the blaming. Here are some

[1] See Cowley's introduction to his *Second Olympic Ode* of Pindar.

[2] Davis II. 114.

[3] Cf. the last stanza of Swift's ode, and vi and x of Cowley's *Ode upon His Majesty's Restoration*.

points where the weak or erratic rhythms grow firm, and where the language grows expressive: the lines on James II's fate—

The remnant of a falling snuff,
Which hardly wants another puff,
And needs must stink *when e're it dies.*

Or the lines on Louis XIV's false 'meteor' (the parting attack on the Sun King is itself echoed in a paragraph of *A Tale of a Tub*[1]):

Stay but a little while and down again 'twill come,
And end as it began, in vapour, stink, and scum.

But these, alas, are probably the verses of which Temple would have least approved.

iii

Swift's ethical fervour is more outspoken in the ode to the Athenian Society. While revisiting Ireland and again at Oxford, he had heard about an extraordinary publication called the *Athenian Mercury*. It was professedly the journal of an anonymous group of learned men, comparable to the Royal Society. The members functioned mainly as a public information bureau, answering miscellaneous inquiries on a weird variety of topics. The ordinary run of questions was not absurd, but problems like 'Why are eunuchs never afflicted with the gout?' and 'How can witches contract their bodies into so narrow a compass, as to convey themselves through a key-hole?' were common.[2]

At Moor Park, Swift found that Temple himself approved of this periodical and had participated in its programme. The great man's naïveté and Swift's innocent trust in his opinion are measures of the muddle which characterized even the educated gentleman's attitude toward experimental science at the end of the seventeenth century. Out of timidity and diffidence, Swift dared not follow his own literary schemes but looked to Temple and Lady Giffard for hints. Yet he must have felt hot indeed for

[1] *Tale*, pp. 165–6. [2] Vol. II, nos. 20, 28.

fame if, even though assured of their respect for the Athenian Society, he bound one of his first literary ventures to the wheels of that 'crazy chariot'.[1]

The period of about a year and a half which had passed since Swift wrote his ode to the king had given him time to overcome his leanings toward clarity of expression; but while the new work is a distinct retreat from intelligibility, its argument can, with patience, be fathomed. Through twelve diffuse stanzas, composed in nine days,[2] Swift congratulates the nameless subjects of his adoration (actually a bookseller and some hack assistants) upon their great part in reviving learning after the wars of 1688–91, which are hopefully treated as though ended with a peace. He apologizes for the effusiveness of his own tribute, describing it as impetuous but well intentioned; and he urges them not to mind the 'sect' who cry them down. He praises their indifference to fame and the steadiness with which they maintain orthodox religion in the face of sniping doubters. But while he is delighted by their skill in refining philosophy and in removing its growths of pedantry or scholasticism, he reproves them for their compliments to women, which have turned the heads of the female sex. At the end he voices his anxiety about the future of the Athenian project, for he is afraid that 'censure and pedantry and pride' will break it down.

There is, as in the ode to the king, some conflict between the ostensible and the underlying themes of the poem, as Swift's own concerns shoulder aside the figures which he starts from. He cannot sustain an initial attempt at objectivity, and shifts awkwardly (though in the pindaric tradition) from the third or second person to the first. Instead of separating himself from the figure of the muse, he confuses himself with her; not only does the rhetorical value of the device thereby largely evaporate, but a grotesque, unnecessary ambivalence is introduced between her gender and his. She first appears as a dove; but that is displaced

[1] Craik I. 44. Yet Defoe, Motteux, Tate, and Richardson also contributed panegyrical odes to the *Athenian Mercury*.

[2] Ball I. 363.

by the spirit of philosophy, represented as a woman; the woman becomes suddenly a new embodiment of the muse; however, before one can take in the change of role, Swift makes her stand for womankind, and not poetry or philosophy. He now makes a comparison between the two sexes, and gives the advantage of course to 'nobler man', endowed with learning and wit. Through all these metamorphoses it grows obvious that Swift has not lost the preoccupation with young ladies that he revealed in his Leicester flirtation; and the freshest lines of the poem, as well as the freshest feelings, are those in ridicule of the picture which he finds so provocative:

> *With a huge fardingal to swell her fustian stuff,*
> *A new commode, a top-knot, and a ruff,*
> *Her face patch't o'er with modern pedantry.*

Another honest impulse breaks through the surface in Swift's longing for literary fame. Just as in his treatment of women, he here ridicules the object which allures him. Illusion versus reality, vapour versus substance—these motifs (employed with other functions in the ode to the king) are used to oppose apparent, popular fame to real virtue and piety. But the strength of his desire is evident from the intensity and minuteness with which he explores the hackneyed theme.

Just as, in the earlier ode, he had lavished celestial and divine qualities upon William, so here, though with even less propriety, he bestows the same attributes upon those invisible members of the Athenian Society who have replaced the king as protagonist and hero. Images which were stale enough before are reheated for the new poem: e.g., flies buzzing about the king reappear as flies buzzing about wit. The critics of the Society replace the rebels against the king. To abase himself before the honoured object, Swift associates himself with the despised 'blind and thoughtless croud'.

It is easy to see that Swift's point of departure has been Cowley's *Ode to the Royal Society*.[1] The quibbling over the sex of

[1] Pons, p. 177.

'Philosophy', however (in Cowley's first stanza and Swift's ninth and tenth), is a token of the degree to which Swift diverges from his predecessor. Where Cowley makes the word masculine, Swift makes it feminine, and even dwells on the resulting imagery. He also makes a more meaningful departure, in opposition to Cowley's praise of the natural philosophers' minute and experimental precision; for Swift welcomes the Athenians as being Christian humanists like himself, and resisting the Hobbesian 'new modish system of reducing all to sense'.[1] He shows his religious orthodoxy through a significant attack upon Epicurean atomism, a fashion which was now declining as it became associated with atheism. Richard Bentley, in the first Boyle lectures, ripped up the Epicureans by using the mathematical and experimental demonstrations of Newton's cosmology to disprove their mechanical determinism and their explanation of the origin of the universe by chance—as 'but a crowd of atoms justling in a heap', in Swift's phrase. Cowley had been eager to prove that Authority was a ghost dispelled by Bacon; Swift jeers at the wits who make Providence out to be an illusion, and he boasts, 'I believe in much, I ne're can hope to see.' Thus the ode to the Athenian Society, without parodying the ode to the Royal Society, does in some ways reply to it. Though Cowley died the year Swift was born, his philosophical outlook was less conservative: he hoped for an end of some mysteries which it was Swift's instinct to preserve. One cannot, after all, discover anything for science unless one believes it is 'there', ready to be found,[2] whereas for Swift the sublimest truths reach us neither through discovery nor demonstration but rather intuition or revelation.

iv

In another ode written about the same time, the old furniture reappears but with fresh elements and with renewed transparency of expression. Both changes are probably due to the same source,

[1] Cf. Hobbes, *English Works*, 1839, I. 389.
[2] Cf. Michael Polanyi, *The Study of Man* (Chicago 1959), p. 35.

the poem's subject; for it is addressed *To the Honble Sir William Temple*. This time, Swift has a hero both whom he sincerely admires and of whom he possesses direct knowledge: these facts no doubt account for his dropping the veil of obscurity. But furthermore, the imagery and the central ideas of the poem are largely derived from two of Temple's essays, *Upon Ancient and Modern Learning* and *Upon the Gardens of Epicurus*.

This is not to say that Cowley's influence has declined: it is pervasive still, but belongs rather to the framework of the poem than the core. The manner, diction, and imagery of Swift's opening recall Cowley's *To Mr. Hobbes* and his 'Leaving Me' (*The Mistress*, poem 11, lines 17–22). Swift's lines 50 and following echo the first lines of two odes by Cowley[1]; his eleventh stanza is close in part to the end of 'The Thraldom' (*The Mistress*, poem 2) and in part to the seventh stanza of *The Complaint*. Swift's concluding thirty lines are similar to the last two stanzas of Cowley's *Destiny*; the end of his last stanza echoes stanza 6 of *The Complaint*.

The typical aspects of Cowley's style, however, are least like that of Swift in maturity. Where one is expansive, the other is concise; where Cowley repeats an expression, Swift varies it; where Cowley loves to portray his own nature, Swift puts on a mask; where Cowley is a rhetorician, Swift is a moralist. Remove the posings from the ode to Temple, and what remains is Swift under Temple's instruction: the distrust of school logic, of speculation, and of pedantry; the delight in looking behind-stage and finding the trivial motives of great events; the eagerness to burn incense before true greatness; and a bitter, almost Hebraic anger at the jungle wrought by corrupt men in the lord's garden:

How plain I see thro' the deceit!
How shallow! and how gross the cheat!

Temple's values and moral ideals are in the poem. The 'pleasures of retreat' sung by Swift, though a common theme in

[1] Ode v (commending the reign of Charles II) and the second ode in the essay on Cromwell's government.

Cowley and in Restoration verse generally, meant more than a play on Horace's *secretum iter et fallentis semita vitae.* It is from Temple that Swift was learning to praise the 'private path of stealing life'; and when in later years the Dean bypassed his cathedral city to cultivate the gardens of his rural vicarage, he was indulging a taste fostered at Moor Park. The preferences of sincerity to dissimulation in political affairs, of peaceful to martial victories, of dilettantism to specialization, are other lasting ideals encouraged if not implanted in Swift by his master, and animated in this ode.

These public, explicit themes have a private, biographical significance. But before examining that in detail, we may briefly notice the formal structure of the poem. It is a series of rather disconnected stanzas, each of them a meditation upon some facet of Temple's character. In imagery and rhetoric this poem shares a great deal with the other odes. Its first stanza, for example, is a reworking of a motif from the ode to the Athenian Society (eleventh stanza). Similarly, the muse appears here as before, never acting as a genuine alternative to the poet's self-regarding point of view, but again dissolving, from the emblem of poetic inspiration into a rustic nymph, and then becoming a task-mistress. Swift's new subject, Temple, bows under as many superlatives as his old. This protagonist is not only 'good and great' but learned as well. The mob is now used to mark pedantry: the grubby accumulations of arrogant and vulgar university dons (Swift's residence in Oxford probably revived earlier feelings) are contrasted with the genteel learning of the hero.

A vital change is the casual treatment of the villain—a 'serpent' embodying the treachery which destroyed Temple's success at court. Swift seems so powerfully dazzled by his master's virtues that he merely glances at the enemy. Instead, the theme of his own comparative unworthiness (touched on in the ode to the Athenian Society, third stanza) grows loud; he ties himself to the 'barren earth', the antithesis of Temple's 'spirit so divine'.

The ode to Temple may even contain (perhaps not quite intentionally) some ironic squints at the ode to the king. In that earlier poem, Swift says that William is remarkable for at once 'doing good' and 'being great'. His bravery is of the order which is usually met 'only in romance'. In the later poem, Temple is 'learned, good, and great', a combination which 'we ne'er join'd before, but in romances meet'. Martial courage, however, is not Temple's distinction; he is crested with the superior 'laurel got by peace'. Instead of flaunting 'scepter, crown and ball', he has the wisdom to expose statecraft and court intrigues as 'juggler's tricks'.

V

If we now examine carefully the personal, non-literary aspects of the poem, it will be found to mirror the whole relationship between patron and pupil at the time when it was written. Temple's attitude toward Swift receives a special illumination from a younger diplomat's report of a session with Temple in 1677: 'He held me in discourse a great long hour, of things most relating to himself, which are never without vanity; but this most especially full of it, and some stories of his amours, and extraordinary abilities that way, which had once upon a time very nearly killed him.'[1] A man who enjoys such an indulgence at fifty does not sacrifice it at sixty-five. Since Temple had lost the most suitable vessel for his confidences when his son committed suicide, he could not have stood out long against the eager attentiveness of the impressionable young man who arrived so soon after that catastrophe. To the lonely refugee, who had never known his own father, and whose nearest substitute for one (Uncle Godwin) was dying or dead, the role of a son must have been all too easy to imagine.

The consequent relationship probably developed the more painlessly as Swift's diffidence was matched by Temple's one-sided conception of paternal dignity: for with both parties so reserved, there would be few overt gestures to make them conscious of what was happening: 'Constrained as we are in our demeanor toward [parents]', Temple had written,

[1] Woodbridge, p. 190.

> by our respect and an awful sense of their arbitrary power over us, which though first printed in us in our childish age, yet years of discretion seldom wholly wear out. Besides, a certain strangeness wrought between those relations by the disagreement of age and consequently of customs, which is hardly so far wrought out by the greatest kindness as to admit such a freedom and confidence as is common between friends of our own choice.[1]

For all Temple's boasts of simplicity, he displays, throughout his memoirs, a visible pride in the grace with which he managed points of ceremony.[2] He had a deep respect for his own presence and could hardly have avoided acting toward Swift with a condescension which at times injured his protégé's self-esteem.

By encouraging Swift's poetical beginnings, however, Temple further enriched the newcomer's filial role, since though Temple had intended his own son to act as his literary executor,[3] it was to Swift at last that he would do 'the honour, to leave and recommend . . . the care of his writings'.[4] Swift's longing for an author's fame, 'a mad reversion after death', is not only the theme of his final stanza but also—as he intimates—the element through which he establishes a real kinship with his master.

The ode to Temple proves that Swift in turn not only shared but correctly understood the ideals of the foster-parent from whom he differed so profoundly in character. Above all, the ode dramatizes the complexities of Temple's passion to retreat from the public life. For while the disenchanted diplomatist truly relished the garden retirement of his middle and old age, he wished also to enjoy in full the credit of his renunciations. Horace was not the only man Temple meant to praise when he wrote, 'It was no mean strain of his philosophy, to refuse being secretary to Augustus, when so great an emperor so much desired it.'[5] It is obvious who Temple thought had suffered the greater loss when he and the court parted; and it is obvious that he had not always felt indifferent to the prospect of becoming secretary of state.[6]

[1] Woodbridge, p. 21. [2] E.g., *Letters* III. 270–6. [3] *Memoirs* II, sig. A4ᵛ.
[4] Davis I. 259. Cf. Ball III. 301.
[5] *Miscellanea* II. 93 (*Upon the Gardens of Epicurus*).
[6] Cf. *Letters* II. 308, III. 334–7.

When he described in the *Memoirs* his refusals to take that post, he dwelt fulsomely upon the directness of the offers which had been made to him and the aplomb with which he had declined them.[1] He must have cultivated similar allusions in conversation: 'What a splutter', Swift later said, 'Sir William Temple [made] about being secretary of state.'[2] Nevertheless, although Swift was to hymn the charms of seclusion as loudly as his master, he would yield to them less single-mindedly at last—always, under a screen of indifference, informing himself of events, and usually trying, when he could, to have a hand in them.

Swift's attack—in both this ode and that to the Athenian Society—upon 'philosophy! the lumber of the schools' reflects the estimate which Temple had formed of natural, as distinct from moral, philosophy. For in this judgment he belonged to the opposite side from St George Ashe: 'I know no end', Temple wrote,

> [natural philosophy] can have, but that of either busying a man's brains to no purpose, or satisfying the vanity, so natural to most men, of distinguishing themselves by some way or other, from those that seem their equals in birth. . . I know no advantage mankind has gained by the progress of natural philosophy, during so many ages it has had vogue in the world, excepting always, and very justly, what we owe to the mathematicks.

While moral philosophers have always agreed (*sic*), Temple said, natural philosophers have always quarrelled:

> As, whether the world were eternal, or produced at some certain time? Whether if produced, it was by some eternal mind, and to some end, or by the fortuitous concourse of atoms, or some particles of eternal matter? Whether there was one world or many?. . . There were the same contentions about the motions of the heavens, the magnitude of the celestial bodies, the faculties of the mind, and the judgment of the senses. But all the different schemes of nature that have been drawn of old or of late by Plato, Aristotle, Epicurus, Des-Cartes, Hobs, or any other that I know of, seem to agree but

[1] *Memoirs* II. 14–15, 272–6, 385–7; *Memoirs* III. 1–8, 29, 57–8, 98–100.

[2] *Journal* 3 Nov. 1711; cf. 11 Nov. 1710.

> in one thing, which is, the want of demonstration or satisfaction, to any thinking and unpossessed man.[1]

This is the doctrine which Swift commends in his ode, which he was to paraphrase in *A Tale of a Tub*,[2] and which would remain his considered judgment throughout his life.

In the ode to Temple also appears the epitome of the grand view of history and politics which Swift inherited from his master. Like most historians and political theorists writing in the seventeenth and eighteenth centuries, Temple wished to trace public events not to their divine but to their human origins. He assumed, however, that the men to be examined were the heads of states, and that their separate, essential natures, rather than the circumstances of their people, determined the central line of history. In this assumption, to which Gibbon has given its most glorious illustration, Swift would be at one with him; and Swift would have repeated with perfect assurance Temple's declaration that 'all great actions in the world, and revolutions of states may be truly derived, from the genius of the persons, that conduct and govern them.'[3]

From such a standpoint, any political philosopher, but especially one with Temple's career behind him, would be bound to exaggerate the effect of intrigues upon history, and to be impressed by how much could proceed from how little—the doctrine of *maxima e minimis* once more. Swift's expression many years later need not be considered a paraphrase of Temple's, since the generalization was a natural outcome of both men's presuppositions, and it was also a commonplace of historians well into the era of Bolingbroke and Voltaire. But the parallel between teacher and pupil is worth a glance. 'Upon how small accidents the greatest councels and revolutions turn', is Temple's language; and again, 'How small shadows and accidents sometimes give a rise to great actions'.[4] Swift in maturity would put it as 'the greatest events depending upon slight and mean causes'.[5]

[1] *Miscellanea* II. 84–5 (*Upon the Gardens of Epicurus*). [2] Pp. 166–7.

[3] *Introduction to the History of England*, p. 301.

[4] *Memoirs* II. 334; *Letters* I. 11. [5] Davis VIII. 172, as varied on p. 229.

In his ode to Temple, Swift's tone has the excitement which one attaches to a discovery:

Methinks, when you expose the scene,
Down the ill-organ'd engines fall;
Off fly the vizards and discover all . . .
Great God! (said I) what have I seen!
On what poor engines move
The thoughts of monarchs, and designs of states.

On the contrary, Temple—as Swift after him—prided himself upon an aversion to secret political machinations and upon a devotion to simple, honest goodwill. They both had a way of reducing public affairs to questions of personal honour. Temple's success as an ambassador had hinged upon his knack of treating other ministers as private acquaintances whose faith he never doubted and whom he expected to trust him completely. Swift, in his later career, could not admire a statesman without believing that he told the truth to Dr Swift; and the great pamphleteer would rarely attack a statesman whom he did not call both a liar and an intriguer. The purity of their own motives, neither Temple nor Swift stopped to suspect: 'I can truly say', wrote Temple, 'that of all the paper I have blotted, which has been a great deal in my time; I have never written any thing for the publick without the intention of some publick good'[1]; and he would have made the same declaration with regard to his political activities. As Swift sings in the ode, Temple's armour was within himself, 'made up of virtue and transparent innocence'!

They could the more readily agree in this analysis as Temple's public career had been largely taken up with efforts to end or prevent wars, and Swift's first major campaign as a polemicist (1710–13) would be spent on similar aims. The supreme importance of civil and international peace has always been present to reflecting men, but in the seventeenth century it was an obsession of philosophers; and Hobbes had made it the overriding principle of his political and psychological systems. So it is

[1] *Miscellanea* III. 99.

not surprising that among the highest desiderata of human life, Temple placed peace second only to health.[1] On mercenary standing armies, both he and Swift were also agreed, for both connected them with violence and tyranny. 'Standing-forces or guards in constant pay', wrote Temple, 'were no where used by lawful princes in their native or hereditary countrys, but only by conquerors in subdued provinces, or usurpers at home; and were a defence only against subjects, not enemies.'[2] However, they differed in their estimates of generalship. Though Temple detested war, he could respect and admire military genius—as embodied for example in Prince Maurice of Nassau, or Turenne; he even admitted the glory of war.[3] Swift might admire the flair of a commander like Peterborough, or the courage displayed by Ormonde at Landen; but after writing his ode to the king, he would not again praise generalship. In the ode to Temple, of course, these ramifications do not appear; and the poet, with more paradox than coherence, can acclaim his hero's 'laurel got by peace' because

It melts the sword of war, yet keeps it in the sheath.

One final ideal which Temple incarnated for Swift, as only Bolingbroke would ever do again, was the vision of polite learning. After Trinity College and after Oxford, the great man's apparent familiarity with the languages, the arts, and the sciences not only awed but delighted Swift. Temple was, as a matter of fact, more 'modern' and comprehensive in his range than Swift; for he approached a unified conception of aesthetic taste such as was realized only in the nineteenth century. He displays a feeling for music and the plastic arts which Swift (for whom the sole interesting art besides literature was architecture) never dimly adumbrated.[4] Temple's contempt for specialized, speculative, or truly technical inquiries, and for those who pursued them, awoke Swift's eager sympathy. 'All that which we call scholastick or polemick', said Temple, with an eye on the academic, 'serves, I

[1] *Miscellanea* III. 104–5. [2] *Observations upon the U.P.*, p. 248.
[3] *Letters* II. 27. [4] E.g., *Miscellanea* III. 249–50.

fear, among us, for little more, than to raise doubts and disputes, heats and feuds, animosities and factions, in all controversies of religion or government.'[1] 'We have too long been led astray,' wrote the author-to-be of the *Battle of the Books*, addressing its inspirer:

> *'Tis you must put us in the way;*
> *Let us (for shame) no more be fed*
> *With antique reliques of the dead.*

vi

Swift did not agree with Temple in everything. When he failed to do so, instead of criticizing him, he found an embodiment elsewhere of the harmony which he sought. The severest lack in Temple, as Swift saw him, was probably religion. It is not that, like most men of the Restoration, Temple expressed an angry distrust of elaborate theological arguments[2]; for on this Swift was bound to agree with him. But Temple, in spite of his loyalty to the Established Church, approved the sort of religious toleration recommended by his tutor Cudworth and practised by the Dutch. While the young Swift may just possibly not have condemned this, his own tutor, Ashe, would certainly have taught him to do so; and the mature Swift would have abominated Temple's plan to encourage Protestant immigration into Ireland 'by some large degree of liberty in matters of religion'.[3] This is just the sort of proposal that Swift was to denounce (in 1710) as a contribution to atheism and a deliberate attack upon the national church:

> These men take it into their imagination, that trade can never flourish unless the country becomes a common receptacle for all nations, religions, and languages; a system only proper for small popular states, but altogether unworthy and below the dignity of an imperial crown. . . This pedantry of republican politicks hath done infinite mischief among us: To this we owe those noble

[1] *Miscellanea* II. 179. [2] *Miscellanea* III. 260–6.
[3] *Essay upon the Present State of Ireland*, published only in *Select Letters* (1701), p. 214.

> schemes of treating Christianity as a system of *speculative opinions*, which no man should be bound to believe; of making the *being* and the worship of God, a *creature* of the state.[1]

While Temple was a faithful communicant of the Church of England, he distrusted the material wealth of the church, and doubted the purity of ecclesiastical motivations, in a manner that was repugnant to Swift. Temple frowned on the granting of civil power to clergymen; Swift (in 1711) recommended it.[2] Swift, when he came to write on tithes, defended them as 'if not of divine original, yet at least of great antiquity'[3]; Temple said they were of late growth.[4] In the *Introduction to the History of England*, Temple went out of his way to argue that the medieval clergy, though pretending to pursue the 'greatness of the holy church', sought in fact the 'honours, power, and riches of the church-men'.[5] This sort of pronouncement, made in a particular digression, Swift must have contradicted. The rift which lay between the two men glares at us from the ode written by Swift upon William Sancroft.

One rarely mentions this saintly Archbishop of Canterbury without quoting Dryden's eulogy of him as the priest

> *whom, shunning power and place,*
> *His lowly mind advanced to David's grace.*

Consecrated primate in 1678, he was one of the seven bishops who, ten years later, went to the Tower sooner than obey those edicts of James II which seemed to undermine the Established Church. However, he refused either to ally himself, during the Revolution, with William of Orange, or, afterwards, to accept the new king. In February 1690/1, Sancroft—along with five other nonjuring bishops and about four hundred clergymen who lost their livings—was deprived of the primacy; in June he was ejected from the palace at Lambeth. A year after the deprivation,

[1] Davis III. 48–9; cf. also p. 169.
[2] *Journal* I. 347–8.
[3] Landa, p. 130; also pp. 123–35.
[4] *Observations upon the U.P.*, pp. 10–11.
[5] Pp. 130–1.

he sponsored and helped to arrange a succession of episcopal authority in the nonjurors; in November 1693 he died. He was, Swift wrote—a year and a half before Sancroft's death—'a gentleman I admire at a degree more than I can express'—

> partly by some experience of him, but more by an unhappy reverend gentleman my Lord the Bishop of Ely with whom I used to converse about two or three years ago, and very often upon that subject.[1]

While Sancroft was no Jacobite, Francis Turner, deprived, nonjuring Bishop of Ely, corresponded with James II not only in 1690 but later, and probably worked for his restoration. In 1694 he was almost invited to attend James at St Germains; in 1696 he was twice arrested. That Swift, so late as May 1692, should have boasted of Turner's acquaintance, both suggests something of the young man's ecclesiastical conservatism and indicates that he defied scandal in religious and political controversy as freely as he did in his private conduct. As Scott said, 'Whatever were [Swift's] principles in civil politics, he was uniformly a staunch high-churchman.'[2] Swift's attitude toward the nonjurors was probably like William Wake's judgment in 1689; though he himself had taken the oaths, Wake wrote to an acquaintance with other leanings, 'I am sure such as you cannot [refuse the oaths] for interest, and where men act and believe according to their conscience, though apparently against their interests, though I may differ from them in any opinion, I cannot but applaud their honesty, and wish them a satisfaction.'[3] The spectacle of the modest Sancroft martyring himself for the sake of noble but lost causes excited in Swift the special homage which he reserved for such defeated heroes as Charles XII after Poltava and the Earl of Oxford in the Tower. Unfortunately, Swift's movements from 1689 to 1692 are too intricate for one to be sure where he had occasion to meet either of the two bishops.

Partly to please Turner, Swift undertook to produce a large pindaric ode upon Sancroft. Beginning to compose it around

[1] Ball I. 363–4. [2] W. Scott XIV. 3. [3] Sykes, *William Wake* I. 45.

January 1692,[1] he confessed, five months later, that it was still on his hands:

> I cannot finish it for my life, and I have done nine stanzas and do not like half of them, nor am nigh finished, but there it lies and I sometimes add to it, and would wish it were done to my desire, I would send it to my bookseller and make him print it with my name and all; to show my respect and gratitude to that excellent person, and to perform half a promise I made his lordship of Ely upon it.[2]

Eleven whole stanzas and a twelfth incomplete are preserved. In the Miltonic opening lines,[3] Swift praises truth, of which he says Sancroft is the earthly image. Through the old man's stability Swift contrasts the wavering motion of the state and the mob with the firmness of the church. Drawing a parallel between the repudiation of Sancroft by the English and the treatment of Christ by the Jews, he condemns the viciousness of his own times. Above the impermanence of the many, Sancroft, a star of regularity in his retirement, is like the sun of *Paradise Lost*, Book III.[4] Swift asks for his guidance and complains about the hardships of the church, perhaps alluding to William III's indulgence of the dissenters. Treating the archbishop's withdrawal from office as an exaltation, Swift foresees his glory in heaven and hopes he will support his faltering brethren and help reform the nation.

The praise of Sancroft is, as one might expect, exaggerated; nevertheless, it is precise: he stands for religious truth, heaven-sent to show men the only rule of life, 'the way which leads to Christ'. The Anglican Church too receives more than perfunctory oblations, and Swift unequivocally gives it precedence over the state:

> *Why should the first be ruin'd . . .*
> *To mend dilapidations in the last?*

Similar exclamations toward the end, against those who 'tear

[1] Ball I. 364. [2] *Ibid.*

[3] Cf. stanza i and *Paradise Lost* III. 1–12; stanza ii and v. 95–113.

[4] Cf. ll. 149–53 and *Paradise Lost* III. 576–86. L. 116 is derived from Cowley's 'The Passions' (*The Mistress*, poem 16), ll. 1–2, 22–3.

religion's lovely face', while not trenchant, are not hollow. At twenty-four or five, Swift already possessed the temperament of a priest. His next step would be to mount the pulpit.

Apart from its value as a biographical document, the ode shows another stage in Swift's poetical evolution. Sancroft, though less remote than the king, was far less familiar than Temple; the style of the ode is correspondingly involved, tortured by conceits, and almost as dense as the ode to the Athenian Society. Although a new influence, that of Milton, has been added to that of Cowley, the rhetorical scheme has shifted only a little. A static hero, a rapt poet, and a mobile muse act out their usual confrontations; old phrases are reshuffled.[1] Just as William III had been opposed by a mob of English and Scots, so Sancroft is opposed to a herd of weak-faithed plebians. The archbishop takes his heavenly place among the stars; he is eulogized as both great and good—like the king—but his added virtues are rather holiness and justice than the learning attributed to Temple. Swift's scientific imagery is fuller here than before, and drawn more from Copernican astronomy and Cartesian optics than Epicurean physics (Hobbes could have supplied all the materials).

It would not be merely hindsight to suggest that Swift's inability to finish the poem was natural. He brings both Christ and the king in, and tries to exalt them both without reducing the intensity of his reverence for Sancroft. But one cannot treat a man as perfect who has refused to acknowledge a monarch, and then treat as perfect the monarch whom he has rejected. Contrariwise, Swift draws a lengthy but awkward analogy between Sancroft's ordeal and that of Christ: while the conceit is less grotesque than Origen's parallel of Christ on the cross and Ulysses tied to the mast, it is almost as distracting. Swift has been praising a man for divine virtues, and then brings in divinity itself; the effect can only be to dwarf Sancroft. The villains of the piece are the Puritans; yet one can hardly damn them for insubordinative religious zeal and in the next breath bless the founder of the nonjurors for

[1] E.g., cf. ll. 124–5 of the ode to Sancroft and l. 28 of the ode to Temple.

barely distinguishable conduct. Through a diffuse and vague employment of lofty epithets, Swift tries to blur the inconsistencies which he has created; but the longer the argument lasted, the deeper they were bound to sink. After a formal, convoluted introduction, however, he does speak briefly in his own voice, the effusion of an outraged prophet denouncing a poisoned age: 'Each line shall stab, shall blast, like daggers and like fire.' The poet's tone of invective was never to sound more violent; irony and humour were never to be more remote. Perhaps the source of the fury was exasperation at a poetical impasse.

Chapter Four

EARLY POEMS (II)

i

Further motives for Swift's becoming a priest begin to appear in his poem to William Congreve. In a letter of December 1693, evidently a long time after Swift originally decided to compose such verses, he described the finished work to his cousin Thomas and offered to submit it for criticism: 'They are almost two hundred and fifty lines not Pindaric.'[1] The poem was intended to go with any play by Congreve, and Swift hoped it would accompany the current one, *The Double-Dealer*, if that should prosper on the stage before going into print.

While Swift was only two years older than Congreve and had been to the same school and university, there is no other record of their intimacy before this poem. Now almost twenty-four, Congreve had been in England since 1689. After a spring and summer in Staffordshire, he had come up to London, where many of his relatives lived. In the spring of 1691 he began to study law in the Middle Temple, at a time when its routine 'was not one to disturb the pursuit of belles-lettres'.[2] At the inns of court, Etherege, Wycherley, and Shadwell had recently preceded Congreve, and he himself made little progress toward the bar. Conveniently situated for the Theatre Royal in Drury Lane and for Will's Coffeehouse near Covent Garden, the Middle Temple gave a student easy access to the world of the wits. Congreve's short novel, *Incognita*, appeared early in 1692, and he was one of Dryden's collaborators on the *Juvenal and Persius* of October the same year. When Dryden included several other poems and transla-

[1] Ball I. 368.

[2] Hodges, p. 35. My information on Congreve normally comes from Hodges.

tions by Congreve in *Examen Poeticum*, 1693, he singled out the young beginner as 'more capable than any man I know' of translating Homer. 'I am Mr. Congreve's true lover', he wrote to Jacob Tonson, and '[I] hope I shall never loose his affection.'[1] With this great patron's assistance, Congreve prepared his first play, *The Old Batchelour*, for the stage. Produced in January 1693, it had what was then the astonishing run of fourteen days; as a book it went into a third printing before April; and most connoisseurs clothed the young author in Dryden's mantle.

The Double-Dealer, which followed in October, had not the same reception. While judges of taste, led by Dryden, recognized the superiority of the new comedy over the earlier, the run of theatre-goers were displeased, perhaps because the satire was too harsh. In the dedication to the first edition (December 1693), Congreve put his 'illiterate criticks' in their place:

> The ignorance and malice of the greater part of the audience is such, that they would make a man turn herauld to his own play, and blazon every character. . . Some little snarling and barking there has been, but I don't know one well-mouth'd curr that has opened at all.[2]

This imprudent riposte was omitted from later editions. However, Swift, though writing his poem before he knew how the play was attacked or defended, hit upon the same theme:

> *What northern hive pour'd out these foes to wit?*
> *Whence came these Goths to overrun the pit?*

Though Swift adopted both the title and the heroic couplets of the complimentary poems prefacing *The Old Batchelour*, it is in fact he himself, and not either Congreve or the critics, that makes the underlying business of the poem. What spoils the shape of a panegyric is a covert struggle between Swift's eagerness to air his own feelings and his sense that the ostensible subject ought to be respected. Of the four irregular divisions into which the

[1] Dryden, *Letters*, ed. C. E. Ward (Durham, North Carolina, 1942), p. 59.
[2] *Works*, ed. M. Summers, 1923, II. 9–10.

whole poem falls, only the third is a convenient focus for both tendencies.

The beginning is a scene between the muse and Swift. She scolds him for treating her like a cast mistress when he sends her to praise Congreve. The present inspiration nevertheless bespeaks her divinity, since only a goddess could bridge the gulf between the dramatist and himself; and only Congreve's talent could extract such a tribute from the insulted spirit. 'Godlike', therefore, is

the force of my young Congreve's bays,
Soft'ning the muse's thunder into praise.

The figure and the ironies are anticipations of Swift's later style. By packing the conceits too closely, however, and changing his point of view faster than the reader can follow, he makes the composition dark and awkward. Swift half-boasted to his cousin, 'I cannot write anything easy to be understood though it were but in the praise of an old shoe'[1]; and here is sufficient proof.

In the next part (lines 49–108), he takes up the mob of bad poets and critics, who are separated from him as sharply as he from Congreve (though this parallel may be unconscious). The playwright's genius excites Swift's mercy toward them somewhat as the muse had established a link between Congreve and Swift. Two angles of attack are then used: first, that they pick up bits of Congreve's wit to supply their own defects; then that they find fault with Congreve in order to hide their own inferiority: the critic is thus a poet manqué. Who are the calumniators? asks Swift. Not London fops, as one might expect, but barely literate clods from the provinces, anxious to seem sophisticated.

Illustrating what he means, Swift tells, in his third part, of a Farnham boy who went from school to London and soon came back with all the manners of the town, showing off his familiarity with Dryden, Wycherley, and Congreve. At this point Swift is free not only to indulge a private discontent but at the same time to express admiration for a friend. As he describes and then flays

[1] Ball I. 366.

the boy, one cannot help suspecting that his irritation is stronger than the occasion calls for. The fury with the callow beardling for pretending to know men who don't know him may be genuine. Aggravating it, though, there must be almost a resentment against Congreve for seeing more of his new great friends than of his schoolmate, Swift. Still deeper, most readers would assume, is an involuntary comparison between his own position—so incommensurate with his ambitions and his felt gifts—and that of the younger Congreve. The bitterness, invidious or not, which seasons the poem, is more likely to come from these instincts than from fury over a stranger's boastfulness.

In the sixty lines remaining, Swift's tone is more evasive. On the surface he seems to tell how much luckier he is than Congreve. At Moor Park, in sight of Mother Ludwell's cave[1] and the stream which springs from it, Swift needs please only his Apollo, Sir William Temple. Congreve, in courting the multitude, exposes himself to arrogance and slander. This sentiment seems hollow. 'What's that . . . if mankind be a fool?' Swift asks. If it is nothing, the reader must wonder, why the fury on Swift's part? The praise of the Temple household as a bard's haven is neither intense nor concrete:

> *Happy beyond a private muse's fate,*
> *In pleasing all that's good among the great,*
> *Where tho' her elder sisters crowding throng,*
> *She* [*i.e., Swift's muse*] *still is welcome with her inn'cent song.*

Swift's following image of a country muse insulted by beaux, collides with the preceding story of the boor who went to town. In describing the suave aesthetes, moreover, Swift incongruously uses rustic metaphors: 'cattle . . . odious smell . . . offensive herd'. The four last lines are an unfortunate reference to the vision which persuaded St Peter to bring the gospel to the gentiles (Acts x. 11). Either Swift is unwarily striking a false note,

[1] G. C. Moore Smith would like to attribute a poem on this subject to Swift, but his argument, even when enlarged by Middleton Murry and Joseph Horrell, is to me unconvincing; see his edition of Temple's *Early Essays*, 1930, pp. xxvi–xxviii, 186–8, 206–7; also *Poems* III. 1068–9.

since he has just advised Congreve to despise the many; or he is again stating his hope that 'Congreve will reform the stage', i.e., preach to gentiles.

Swift, one infers, would cheerfully sustain the toils facing his friend; at least, more experience of the perils which he describes would give force to his contempt for them. Nevertheless, there is marked individuality in the poem. Cowley's influence is hardly absent,[1] but Swift also quotes from one of his own poems, now lost.[2] Some strokes, indeed, are as effective as a phrase from the pamphlets of his prime:

My hate, whose lash just heaven has long decreed
Shall on a day make sin and folly bleed.[3]

It seems that the feelings and topics toward which Swift turned in his first flights were to become in later years the staple not of his poetry but of his prose.

ii

With the poem to Congreve, Swift's versification undergoes its first important structural change in the direction of his eventual style: this change is the replacement of pindarics by couplets. While the metre is still pentameter and the rhythms conventional, Swift can begin to feel what his native gifts amount to. Already the rhymes, though not obtrusive, betray some of the ingenuity and the preoccupation with sound effects which were to mark his best-known manner: e.g., 'wit–counterfeit' (lines 55–6), 'since–impertinence' (lines 87–8). In tone a profound change is the almost (but not quite) wholehearted acceptance by Swift of the office of satirist; he refers to his 'old unvanquish'd pride' as what alone

suspends poor mortals fate,
Gets between them and my resentment's weight,
Stands in the gap 'twixt me and wretched men,
T'avert th'impending judgments of my pen.

[1] Cf. ll. 63–4 here and ll. 15–16 of Cowley's 'The Soule' (*The Mistress*, poem 15).

[2] Ll. 205–12.

[3] Cf., from *The Publick Spirit of the Whigs*, 'I will upon occasion, strip some of his insinuations . . . and drag them into the light' (Davis VIII. 39).

Rhetorically, there is an advance in that the muse draws apart from the poet, and either scolds or flirts with him. A wholly fresh element is the use of a fable (lines 115–46) and its exegesis (lines 147–74) to illustrate the central theme of the poem; the elaborate employment of animals as satirical parallels to humans is a similar first appearance of what was to become a permanent resource. (Temple also draws continual, conventional parallels between kinds of men and species of animals; but he means to be philosophical or 'scientific' in this habit, while Swift's way is emblematical.[1])

Nevertheless, the usual devices and motifs persist: mob versus hero, illusion versus reality, courtly vice versus country virtue, etc. There is imagery drawn from optics (lines 61–4), from Temple's writings,[2] and—most indecorously—from the Bible.[3] There are digs at amateurs of the new experimental philosophy (lines 93–4, 207–12). The mob in this poem is of Congreve's critics, who are also swarms of gnats (to match the flies of the odes to the king and to the Royal Society), or else who have (like Louis XIV) sprung from dung. The illusion is false wit, which is opposed to Congreve's true. Swift identifies himself and his muse with pastoral solitude; the critics and epigones of Congreve, with the urban society: unfortunately, the position of the urbane playwright himself is thus made equivocal.

Again Swift has the advantage of dealing with a hero whom he knows directly. However, there seems to be some conflict between the poet's conscious knowledge, his unconscious intentions, and his deliberate, rhetorical aims. Swift cannot apply as many superlatives to a junior school chum as to a fatherly king, patron, or archbishop. Surprisingly little of the poem therefore is devoted to direct eulogy. More than ever does the poet force his subject into the wings and manœuvre himself upstage. Swift's own yearning for reputation takes over; and since he can hardly claim that his own genius is superior to Congreve's, he praises instead

[1] E.g., Temple, *Miscellanea* I. 61–2.

[2] E.g., ll. 83–4 are drawn from the *Introduction to the History of England*, pp. 44, 70, or from *Miscellanea* II. 224; cf. also the ode to the *Athenian Society*, ll. 298–9.

[3] Cf. l. 32 and Luke xvi. 26; l. 231 and Acts x. 11.

the moral elevation of his rural seclusion as contrasted with the corruption of the playwright's milieu; he even brings in the figure of Temple—'all that's good among the great'—as guarantor of such elevation. The three figures clash grotesquely: the attributes which Swift praises in himself and Temple seem to negate the values represented by his friend.

To give power to his stifled admiration for Congreve, Swift must exalt its price: so he bestows upon himself the highest moral standards, the most exacting canons of taste; gone is the self-abasement of the earlier odes. Furthermore, to demonstrate his possession of such faculties, he must exercise them upon proper targets; so he denounces his friend's critics, plagiarists, and boasted, though fraudulent, intimates. While the resulting occasions do not in fact enhance the compliments, they perform the more useful function of giving adequate employment to Swift's spleen. Although, moreover, the victims of Swift's attacks had generally been, like the topics of his praise, outside his common experience, in this they are men of his own generation and environment. His satirical details are therefore vivid, if extravagant.

The muse has a full-bodied part in this poem; but as in the ode to the Athenian Society, she is made so womanly as to suggest that the poet is once more preoccupied with his own attitudes toward the opposite sex. This conjecture seems borne out by the wealth of clumsy similes drawn from courtship and seduction. Swift compares himself complimenting Congreve (instead of composing original works) with a rake sending to a comrade a cast mistress whom he has debauched. He compares fashionable, arty slang with bastards 'born between whores and fops'. He compares Congreve's name, bantered by pretended friends, with a 'fresh miss' whose favours 'the meanest coxcomb' makes believe he has enjoyed. He compares the muse among the critics with 'some bright country virgin' amid a chattering horde of beaux.

iii

The last of the early poems, *Occasioned by Sir W—— T——'s Late Illness and Recovery*, is still incompetent; but it is the shortest and the best. Though this piece is a fairly close imitation of Cowley's *The Complaint*, it is based upon an idea from Temple's essay *Of Poetry*: 'True poetry being dead, an apparition of it walked about.'[1] The form is again heroic couplets, and some of the lines open a new vein of earnest, powerful conceits:

Whether in time, deduction's broken chain
Meets, and salutes her sister link again;
Or hunted fancy, by a circling flight,
Comes back with joy to its own seat at night;
Or whether dead imagination's ghost
Oft hovers where alive it haunted most;
Or if thought's rolling globe her circle run,
Turns up old objects to the soul her sun.[2]

The design of the poem is—for Swift—rather simple, since it employs only two (though incompatible) arguments; and rhetorically it achieves remarkably sharp focus. The main reason for the improvement in definition and coherence is that the muse here not only stands quite apart from the poet but also takes on a function formerly assumed by an additional character; for she is the villain of the melodrama: she is the evil vapour, the false meteor, the optical illusion.

The poem is an odd sort of dialogue, made up of two speeches, each with its own framework. In the first half the muse appears and scolds Swift for not celebrating (in verse) Temple's return to health after a dangerous illness. Her speech rather ingeniously contains what might be called a poem-within-a-poem, or the true discussion of the avowed subject; for she recites the only lines directly relating to Temple's disease, which occupy no more than a fifth of the whole poem; and even these verses really describe

[1] *Miscellanea* II. 312; cf. also p. 313.

[2] To see how this style, when transfigured by irony and humour, becomes the characteristic style of *A Tale of a Tub*, cf. the parallel passage in the *Tale*, p. 158; cf. also K. Williams's contrast of Burton (pp. 15–16).

neither the siege nor the recovery, but the fears of Lady Temple, Lady Giffard, and the inferior members of the household (lines 37–66). The muse reproaches the poet. He is sad when he ought to sing. The time of fear is past. The grief feelingly displayed by 'Dorothea' and 'Dorinda' is no longer necessary. Temple has recovered. Swift should pile blessings on the occasion. Thus far the first half.

The poet's answer makes the rest of the poem. Rather than respond to her appeal, he confounds the muse. In his extraordinary reply he does not even mention Temple's illness; instead, he attacks the goddess for encouraging him to hope for fame and esteem where there was no chance of either. He lists the rules which she has urged him to use, and labels them madness. She has tricked him by pretending that virtue and talent will find their reward. A 'right woman' would waste no time upon one so doomed as he. Her advice has led to frustration; her hopes were delusive; she is herself a 'walking vapour'. All his efforts to please (i.e., one assumes, to please Temple) have met with 'contempt where thou hast hop'd esteem'. Finally, he points out that she herself is only an illusion; by renouncing her, therefore, he destroys her:

And since thy essence on my breath depends,
Thus with a puff the whole delusion ends.

Abandoning poetry, he therefore dismisses and annihilates the vision.

Here at last the figure of the muse has a significant relationship to the design of the poem. In fact, she foreshadows the brilliant effects which Swift was soon to achieve through the donning and doffing of masks or ironical poses. As one aspect of the poet's character, his literary ambitions, the muse confronts another, his fears of failure. By splitting himself in this way, Swift can pump his lines full of hot emotion without threatening the reader. Instead of denouncing the Jacobites, the Puritans, the university dons, or the critics, he points his rage at strata of his own being. However unimpressive the result may seem as verbal poetry, it does possess the crackling intensity and integrity of feeling which the name of Swift has come to stand for, and which makes a deeper 'poetry' than any aural polish or rational structure can supply without it. True, until irony is employed to resolve them, Swift's clashing attitudes seem incoherent; but the violence of their clash is realized by the poet and directly felt by the reader.

Temple's figure merges with the muse. Her rules are undoubtedly his—at least, as Swift conceives them. The closing lines of Swift's accusations against her are ultimately addressed to his patron. As father, as inspirer, as censor, Temple had inevitably fallen short of the excessive hopes which Swift had placed in him. But the young idealist dare not admit either that the original standards were impossible or that his chosen hero has sunk below them; so he scourges himself for failing to please Temple. This is what Swift means when he describes the rules as 'madness'; since hope, though false, is the only benefit of delusion, nobody will persist in a madness which destroys hope: the impossibly high-minded code preached by the muse (i.e., by Temple) permits one to win greatness only through such means as destroy the rewards of greatness.

This poem is almost magical in the degree to which it fits its place as Swift's farewell to a long misconception. Biographically and structurally, it embodies just the features one would seek in such a performance. The paradoxical reasoning behind it, the little drama in which the paradox is acted out, the feverish changes of tone, the foreshortened ending, the dissatisfaction and restlessness openly admitted, all join to make it a remarkably appropriate tailpiece to a series of false starts.

Chapter Five

SWIFT AND TEMPLE

Behind the poem on Temple's illness lay a situation which can be reconstructed with moderate accuracy. Ten years after his master's death, Swift wrote to Lady Giffard, 'I pretend not to have had the least share in Sir William Temple's confidence above his relatives or his commonest friends—' and added bitterly, 'I have but too good reason to think otherwise.'[1] The case is put differently, more than fifteen years still later, in a sarcastic message to Temple's nephew, with whom Swift had picked a quarrel:

> I own myself indebted to Sir William Temple, for recommending me to the late king, although without success, and for his choice of me to take care of his posthumous writings. But I hope you will not charge my living in his family as an obligation, for I was educated to little purpose, if I retired to his house, on any other motives than the benefit of his conversation and advice, and the opportunity of pursuing my studies. For, being born to no fortune, I was at his death as far to seek as ever, and perhaps you will allow that I was of some use to him.[2]

Swift's reasoning may seem dark to a modern reader. What he means to acquit himself of is not ingratitude for favours received, but self-seeking motives in cultivating Temple's patronage. As he saw it, the relationship was of mutual benefit. The immediate advantages to a young man of learning political wisdom, morality, and literary art from a master of those sciences, and of living elegantly at the same time were balanced by the secretarial duties which Swift must have fulfilled scrupulously.

[1] Ball I. 172. [2] *Ibid.* III. 301.

For 'gratitude' as resulting from special indebtedness, there was no place in the relationship; each party received his due and discharged his functions. And no one could, in fact, argue that Temple 'deserved' more than he 'got' from Swift, in labour or in reverence.

But this was after the event. In Temple's lifetime, it must have been obvious that the master so enjoyed the pupil's company as to tilt the balance of obligation away from Swift, and not toward him. The protégé could hardly have refrained from looking hopefully forward to (not perhaps depending upon, or expecting as his due) some particular kindness from his employer, a perhaps supererogatory but direct assistance toward a career, fitted to Swift's visible talents, and of an eminence proportioned to his ambition. If we think of Hobbes and Cavendish, or Locke and Shaftesbury, we shall have an idea of what could happen.

An incident which could hardly have weakened such hopes is also an example of what Swift meant when he wrote that 'growing into some confidence' with Temple after 1691, he 'was often trusted with matters of great importance'.[1] The king's faith in Temple had not evaporated when the diplomat refused to come out of retirement. Even while the international crisis spread, and the English were more and more deeply engulfed in the war of the League of Augsburg, William found occasions to be his old friend's guest, and (according to Swift) 'took his advice in affairs of greatest consequence'.[2]

During the reign of William and Mary an issue which had every urgency except novelty was the tug-of-war between court and parliament. After securing his throne and pacifying his three kingdoms, William had gone forward with the campaigns against Louis XIV. But the staggering defeat at Beachy Head and the surrender of Mons to Louis did not enhance his authority. To keep parliament with him, he allowed his prerogative to be hemmed in, though he considered no government so futile as that of a monarch without independent power.[3] The extreme Whigs,

[1] *Autob.*, f. 8^{v}. [2] *Ibid.*, ff. 8^{v}–9.

[3] G. N. Clark, *The Later Stuarts* (Oxford 1934), p. 143.

who were keenest against France, were least willing to enlarge the king's freedom of action.

Dependent for supplies upon grants of money, William had no way to avoid summoning parliament annually; and he laid down a tradition which has lasted ever since. What he did resist was the revival of Charles I's Triennial Act, which required the summoning of a new House of Commons at least once every three years. As Burnet remarks, Whiggish men felt afraid that in a house of unlimited life the members

> might be so practised upon by the court, that they might give all the money and all the liberties of England up, when they were to have a large share of the money, and were to be made the instruments of tyranny; as it was in king Charles the second's time.[1]

While a bill with this object had been unsuccessful in 1689, a second attempt passed both houses in 1693, when the king's prestige was reeling under a load of military disasters; for the victory of La Hogue seemed to be obliterated by the loss of Namur and the massacre at Steenkirk.[2]

First read in the House of Lords on 12 January, the 'triennial' bill hung fire for two months.[3] 'The king let the bill lie for some time on the table; so that men's eyes and expectations were much fixed on the issue of it.'[4] He felt so sharply worried about its possible effect that he had the Earl of Portland, his favourite, take the opinion of Temple. The latter, to make sure that his arguments in support of the bill were fairly set forth, had Swift present them at Kensington, early in 1693, when he was only twenty-five.[5] The young secretary carried a written account from Temple and added reasons of his own; he spoke briefly to the king, and at length to Portland. 'But in conclusion', says Burnet, the king 'refused to pass it; so the session ended in ill humour'.[6] On 14 March

[1] Burnet IV. 185. [2] Ogg II. 382–4.

[3] *J.H.L.*, XV. 181. The concurrence of the Commons was desired 22 Jan. (*J.H.C.*, x. 786), and the bill was read for the first time in the lower house on 28 Jan. (*J.H.C.*, x. 796).

[4] Burnet IV. 187.

[5] Not twenty-one or twenty-three, as Swift said (*Autob.*, f. 9^{v}). [6] IV. 187.

the bill was vetoed and parliament was prorogued.[1] Two months later, William arrived in Belgium to begin another miserable campaign; for this was the year of the battle at Landen—'even more bloody than Aughrim'—where the young Duke of Ormonde distinguished himself.[2]

Swift, forty-five years later, does not conceal his still-rankling annoyance:

> This was the first time that Mr Swift had ever any converse with courts, and he told his friends it was the first incident that helped to cure him of vanity.[3]

Yet he would have been mean-spirited indeed if the reliance upon him which Temple showed in this business did not raise expectations of a full step toward making him a career. The errand had been precisely the sort on which Temple had been accustomed to send his son. No offer was, however, forthcoming. Yet as the months passed, Swift saw more and more of his friends settled: Congreve the hope of English letters; cousin Thomas about to be ordained and to take up (in 1695) the rectorship of Puttenham, Surrey; Peter Browne already a fellow of Trinity College; Henry Tenison in the Middle Temple since 1692, and shortly to enter upon his Irish parliamentary service, which would commence in 1695.

Reaching this period in his autobiography, Swift says that he was 'inclined to take orders'.[4] To his uncle William he wrote at the time (November 1692), 'I am not to take orders till the king gives me a prebendary; and Sir William Temple, though he promises me the certainty of it, yet is less forward than I could wish, because I suppose, he believes I shall leave him, and upon some accounts, he thinks me a little necessary to him.'[5]

The complexity of the situation is barely intimated by Swift. There are several layers of conflict: first, whether to remain in the comfortable but temporary status at Moor Park, or choose a permanent way of life; second, if he should leave, whether to be-

[1] *J.H.L.*, xv. 289; the bill came up again in 1694 and was enacted.
[2] Ogg II. 385. [3] *Autob.*, f. 9^{v}. [4] *Ibid.*, f. 9. [5] Ball I. 10.

come a priest, or enter another profession; third, if he should take orders, whether to do so immediately, and risk seeming mercenary, or wait until he was in a position really to select the priesthood as preferable to other available openings. The last dilemma, while not Swift's alone, was characteristic of him. Of his respect for the priestly calling there can be no doubt; that his own intention was sincere is obvious from the straightforwardness with which he mentions it. He never deceived himself, however, as to the likelihood of his therewith improving his worldly substance. So much can be inferred from Swift's words to his cousin Thomas, then in a predicament like his own but further knotted by an engagement to be married. Thomas felt properly hesitant; he had no income, and he did not like marrying without one: yet marry he would. 'All I can say', Swift answered tartly, 'is I wish to God you were well provided for, though it were with a good living in the church.'[1] When Thomas communicated further qualms, Swift saw only one path for a man who, though he might prefer other trades to that of cleric, could be sure of a place in the church:

> I cannot . . . give a judgement near enough upon your other hopes, but if they be not certain, I think there is no avoiding the choice of what is. . . [Yet] if that curacy were not disposed of which I once mentioned you, I think I should say it was, for it fits your present prospects almost as ill as it did your merit then.[2]

He was realistic about it all. Though piety was the first ingredient of a priest, it could not support sublunary life. And if this was Swift's counsel to another, he surely reckoned with the obstacles himself.

The conscience beneath his conflict, however, appears in one extraordinary phrase—that he 'had a scruple of entring into the church meerly for support'.[3] Could a gate be straiter? In these refined scruples, Swift shows again his leaning toward what St Jerome described when he wrote that 'many, who screen from all men's sight their poverty, charity, and fasting, desire to excite

[1] Ball I. 365. [2] *Ibid.*, p. 367. [3] *Autob.*, f. 9.

admiration by their very disdain of it.'[1] Swift had to give up the Temple establishment because it led nowhere. Having no estate, he could not go without an employment before him. His strongest patron, Temple, would arrange nothing respectable and wished to keep him at Moor Park. The church, his natural terminus, would be profaned if he went to it seemingly for lack of an alternative.

Not that Swift's compunctions were unique: they seem parallel, for example, to those felt by Jane Austen's Edmund, in *Mansfield Park*, more than a century later—though the turn of mind there is less fastidious:

> I see no reason why a man should make a worse clergyman for knowing that he will have a competence early in life. [His lady friend demurs; so he goes on:] But the motives of a man who takes orders with the certainty of preferment, may be fairly suspected, you think? To be justified in your eyes, he must do it in the most complete uncertainty of any provision. [No, she bursts out, to do so would be madness. He then concludes:] Shall I ask you how the church is to be filled, if a man is neither to take orders with a living, nor without?[2]

Swift was a more eager casuist than Edmund, but he managed to kill his sphinx. He extracted from Temple the offer of a post easily in his gift, 'an employ of about 100^{ll} a year' in the office of the master of the rolls in Ireland (a sinecure which Temple held).

> Whereupon Mr Swift told him, that since he had now an opportunity of living without being driven into the church for a maintenance, he was resolved to go to Ireland and take holy orders.[3]

Free to exercise his franchise, Swift refused the clerkship, left Moor Park in the early part of May 1694, and joined his mother in Leicester. The closing scene must have been dramatic; a month later, he described it to his cousin Deane:

[1] *To Eustochium*, par. 27.
[2] Condensed from R. W. Chapman's edition (Oxford 1934), p. 109.
[3] *Autob.*, f. 9.

> He was extremely angry I left him; and yet would not oblige himself any further than upon my good behaviour, nor would promise any thing firmly to me at all, so that everybody judged I did best to leave him. I design to be ordained September next, and make what endeavours I can for something in the church.[1]

He was clearly without a concrete opportunity, for he went on to say that he would gladly become chaplain to the English traders' settlement in Lisbon if either Deane or Willoughby Swift, then merchants in Portugal (Deane had gone there from the Kilkenny School in August 1688), possessed 'interest to bring me in'.[2] Such a proposal, conceived at the height of a vast military campaign, a year after the loss of the Smyrna convoy, and the same month as the disaster of Camaret Bay, is a mark of how far the bitterest war could at this time seem from the destinies of private citizens. More pertinently, it also indicates that Swift never anticipated the delays which ordination itself might require.

Temple's side in this business should seem the effect of neither whimsy nor spite. If he had indeed any fatherly feelings for Swift, they would have worked in the wrong direction. Not only would he have wished to hold on to the young man's company, but the memory of his son's fate would have made protective measures appear kinder than efforts to give Swift independence. So long as John Temple had lived under his father's loving authority, he had been safe. He might carry messages from Temple to either Charles II or James II, but he was not allowed to meet the Prince of Orange at Torbay. When John Temple took a post of his own, though given him for his father's sake, the result was the most painful tragedy of Temple's life. Swift too might carry messages to court and lighten his master's solitude; but one could hardly expect Temple to play Daedalus a second time, and to Swift's Icarus.

On the level of pure selfishness, Temple could not have hoped to secure another secretary so talented as Swift. Here were an excellent listener, a witty speaker, a good book-keeper, an admiring disciple, and a humble subordinate, all ready to serve him at a

[1] Ball I. 12. [2] *Ibid.*

gesture. Swift could make fair copies of his essays, translate his French and Latin letters, explain his wishes to menials or visitors, keep his accounts, provide society for his wife and sister, manage the household when the family were away—all at a negligible expense and even with some appearance of benevolence on Temple's part.

In Temple's own past there were few experiences which might give him an insight into Swift's condition. Any diplomat spends most of his career waiting for others to make up their minds. But after the nightmare impasses at Nimeguen, the longest suspense which Swift might endure would sink below notice. Apart from his courtship of Dorothy Osborne, Temple had been the most obedient son possible—by his political philosophy, fatherhood and the very notion of authority were merely two different views of the same object. He could not have felt that his demands upon Swift's confidence were unfair.

Furthermore, it was not in Temple's nature to be a strong pleader, whether for himself or for others. It is even possible that his protégé caught from him the disdain which Swift was often to show for the normal methods of rowing one's own boat. It might indeed be no imprudence that Temple, heir to a considerable fortune, should brush past occasions for enriching himself and say, 'I have resolved never to ask [the king] any thing, otherwise than by serving him well',[1] or 'I never could go to service for nothing but wages'[2]; but it would seem either naïve or arrogant (and all the more admirable) that a man so ill provided for as Swift should suppose he owed it to his integrity to act a similar role. Meanwhile, if Temple were meaning to impose his code of honour upon Swift, he would certainly not meet the young man's demands.

Nor is there much reason to suppose that Temple regarded the priesthood as the ideal career for Swift or anyone else. With his cool piety, his resentment of the church's material strength, and his leanings toward a Dutch toleration, he would probably have hoped that Swift would interest himself in a more dashing or more public occupation.

[1] *Letters* II. 289; cf. I. 301–2. [2] *Memoirs* III. 170.

Chapter Six

KILROOT

i

Although one cannot describe Swift's becoming a priest as inevitable, it should appear quite natural. From the circumstances of his infancy, he grew into a lofty idealist. His intense moral anger, a frequent and noble heritage of men who have endured severe discipline in childhood, could have found no better vent than a pulpit. His appreciation of a father's employment must have made the paternal privileges of a clergyman seem deeply attractive. The tradition of his family was heavy with clerical ties (both grandfathers and two uncles Thomas, namesakes of the Goodrich hero). Cousin Thomas, his nearest thing to an older brother, and perhaps the most steadying element of his school and college days, was preparing for the church. Until the end of the eighteenth century a young man with Swift's education and attachments would have seemed fated to take up the vocation. One can only salute the integrity with which he deferred the obvious until it should possess the purity of a free decision. In his power of recognizing the tough, nasty facts of a case at the same time as he chose the high-minded, rather than 'realistic', resolution of it, Swift reveals his finest (and most poetic) trait.

By the canons of the church, he might not be ordained either before he was twenty-three or until he could certify to having 'a living in readiness'.[1] Although these conditions might sometimes be dispensed with, they would in the normal course have kept him a layman until the end of 1690. In February 1692 he said he was thinking 'of entering into the church'.[2] The Oxford M.A. that summer was probably a step on the way to ordination. In

[1] Landa, pp. 3–4. [2] Ball I. 5.

November 1692 he told his uncle William that Temple was having the king provide him with a prebend.[1] When, in June 1694, he said he intended to be ordained 'September next',[2] he was thinking no doubt of the embertides of September, one of the four periods set by the canons for the admission of candidates to orders.[3]

From Leicester, then, he went to Dublin, where he worked through the summer to move favourable powers in his own behalf. Several bishops were familiar with his uncles; and Narcissus Marsh, recently provost of Trinity College, was now Archbishop of Dublin. Nevertheless, Swift found that holy orders were closed to him, because the passage of so many years since his taking a university degree aroused suspicious curiosity about what he had been doing in the meantime. It was a canonical requirement that one should present testimonials of 'good life and behaviour' for a period of three years preceding ordination; and although the application of this rule had been notoriously lax, Swift had struck an era and a regime of tightening standards. Unless he could produce a certificate of good conduct, he was blocked.

To the delicate and humbling task of winning an endorsement from Temple he at last nerved himself, in a letter of October 1694, the only direct communication preserved between the two men. The conclusion of his appeal must stir the sympathies of anyone who has had to beg a benefit from an already resentful superior; Swift was not to use such language again until Gulliver left the land of the Houyhnhnms. Nevertheless, if the explanation we have given of their relationship is reliable, Swift neither forfeits his dignity here, nor sinks to self-abasement:

> May it please your honour,
>
> That I might not continue by any means the many troubles I have given you, I have all this while avoided one, which I fear proves necessary at last. I have taken all due methods to be ordained, and one time of ordination [i.e., the embertides of September] is already elapsed since my arrival without effecting it. Two or three bishops, acquaintances of our family, have signified to me and

[1] Ball I. 10. [2] *Ibid.*, p. 12. [3] Landa, p. 6.

them, that after so long a standing in the university, it is admired I have not entered upon something or other, above half the clergy in this town being my juniors, and that it being so many years since I left this kingdom, they could not admit me to the ministry without some certificate of my behaviour where I lived; and my Lord Archbishop of Dublin [i.e., Narcissus Marsh] was pleased to say a good deal of this kind to me yesterday, concluding against all I had to answer, that he expected I should have a certificate from your honour of my conduct in your family.

The sense I am in, how low I am fallen in your honour's thoughts, has denied me assurance enough to beg this favour, till I find it impossible to avoid; and I entreat your honour to understand, that no person is admitted to a living here, without some knowledge of his abilities for it, which it being reckoned impossible to judge in those who are not ordained, the usual method is to admit men first to some small reader's place till by preaching upon occasions, they can value themselves for better preferment. This (without great friends) is so general, that if I were four-score years old I must go the same way, and should at that age be told, every one must have a beginning. I entreat that your honour will consider this, and will please to send me some certificate of my behaviour during almost three years in your family; wherein I shall stand in need of all your goodness to excuse my many weaknesses and follies and oversights, much more to say any thing to my advantage. The particulars expected of me are what relate to morals and learning, and the reasons of quitting your honour's family, that is, whether the last was occasioned by any ill actions. They are all entirely left to your honour's mercy, though in the first I think I cannot reproach myself any farther than for infirmities.

This is all I dare beg at present from your honour, under circumstances of life not worth your regard. What is left me to wish, next to the health and felicity of your honour and family, is, that Heaven would one day allow me the opportunity to leave my acknowledgments at your foot for so many favours I have received, which, whatever effect they have had upon my fortune, shall never fail to have the greatest upon my mind, in approving myself, upon all occasions,

Your honour's most obedient and most dutiful servant,

J. Swift.

I beg my most humble duty and service be presented to my ladies, your honour's lady and sister. The ordination is appointed by the

Archbishop by the beginning of November, so that, if your honour will not grant this favour immediately, I fear it will come too late.[1]

Temple was above spite, and he sent the statement so quickly that Swift could be ordained deacon 28 October and priest 13 January 1694/5. Both ceremonies were performed in Dublin, at Christ Church Cathedral, by William Moreton, Bishop of Kildare (Moreton held the deanery of Christ Church *in commendam*).[2]

Swift had now resigned himself to profit in his own country rather than honour in England. But he had also to interest some large-handed, powerful person in his needs, for merit was no guarantee of a benefice. The name of the philanthropist is still unknown, but somebody recommended Swift to Lord Capel, chief of the three lords justices then ruling Ireland for the court.[3] This action was so effectual that only two weeks after his final ordination the new priest was presented (by the crown) to his first living, the prebend of Kilroot in the diocese of Down and Connor.[4] Of course, the speed was to be expected, with the promise of a benefice being a prerequisite for admission to orders.

This lord justice, Henry, Lord Capel of Tewkesbury, was the younger brother of that Earl of Essex who had been so treacherous a colleague of Temple's under Charles II. He had been a privy councillor with Temple, and his residence at Kew was almost next to Temple's at Sheen. Capel's father, the heroic Lord Capel of Hadham, had devoted a life of 'courage, virtue, and fidelity' (as Clarendon said) to the royalist cause; the Puritans beheaded him in 1649, soon after the king. The son, shortly to be sole governor of Ireland with the title of Lord Deputy,[5] was an immoderate 'Whig' (as the word was used at the turn of the cen-

[1] Ball I. 13–15. [2] Landa, pp. 7–8.

[3] Deane Swift (p. 106) identifies Swift's recommender as Temple; but he is practically excluded by the language, at this point, of Swift's autobiographical essay. Landa (pp. 9–10) suggests Ashe, who is indeed the most likely person. However, it is safest to leave the issue unresolved: e.g., Richard Tenison, Bishop of Meath, was the father of Swift's friend, had been chaplain to Capel's brother, and was one of Swift's predecessors at Laracor; he too might have recommended Swift to Capel.

[4] He was presented to the prebend of Kilroot by patent dated 28 Jan. 1695; he was instituted 5 March and installed 15 March (Cotton).

[5] 27 May 1695; he died a year later.

tury), steadily placing Protestant English welfare before Catholic Irish,[1] and pressing the Nonconformists' claims to legal toleration.[2] Dartmouth called him 'a very weak, formal, conceited man'; but Shrewsbury said he was 'liked and beloved by all parties'.[3] Expressly proud of his father's glorious reputation, Capel did not apparently find Swift's affiliations distasteful; and Capel's connection with Ireland had some depth, his brother having been lord lieutenant about twenty years earlier. It is clear of course that Swift outwardly had not yet assumed a political colour, and simply accepted the powers that be. However, if he had been labelled a fellow-traveller of the nonjurors, or a critic of the king's measures in Ireland, Capel would not have been selected as the man to prefer him.

ii

The Church of Ireland—which is of course the name not of the Roman Catholic Church but of the Anglican or Established Church in Ireland—was to be the scene of Swift's entire ecclesiastical career. Twenty years of manœuvring would bring him no bishopric, deanery, or prebend in England. Not that Swift wholly mistook his chance. The drive against him had begun before he was born. An English university man commonly had precedence over a rival from Ireland when benefices were assigned in the inferior kingdom; but a clergyman of Irish breeding and education—though of purely English descent—was in the natural course shut out not only from every good employment in the mother country but also from the major dignities of his native land. Yet a historical irony arises just here where none is wanting; for out of the three Trinity College students who were translated to the English episcopal bench in the eighteenth century, two were classmates of Swift—Thomas Wilson and Edward Chandler.

The Church of Ireland at this time was an ailing giant, asthmatic within and throttled from without. After the Reformation

[1] Burnet IV. 277. [2] Landa, p. 20. [3] Burnet IV. 278–9, n.

it was almost a foreign thing to the natives, for the proportion of Protestants among them was of the order of a fifth to a twentieth; and by 1695 most of the Protestants were dissenters from the Established Church. Having so few worshippers to employ them, the buildings fell away with disuse; the wealth drifted into the wrong hands; and the pastors failed in their sense of mission. Only 'a face of Christianity' was saved.[1]

A typical diocese was Ferns, practically identical with the county of Wexford, about fifty miles long and twenty miles wide. It contained a hundred and thirty-one parishes, of which William King said (when he became Archbishop of Dublin),

> 71 were in the hands of impropriate lay proprietors, 28 appropriated to the bishop and cathedral dignitaries, and only 32, usually the poorest, in the hands of the officiating clergy. Neither bishop, dean nor archdeacon was resident in the diocese. It was served by only thirteen beneficed clergymen, few of whom had an income of as much as £100 a year, and nine curates, each paid about £30 per annum.[2]

The livings, from the most meagre curacy to the primacy of all Ireland, were tending to become sinecures for ecclesiastical politicians and pamphleteers; and the clergy were pressed to use divine service, property rights, literary gifts, and seats in the House of Lords as devices for strengthening the government in power. By the time Swift took orders, a parson who owned no political identity might get a good name but hardly great riches.

To resist the defiance of Catholics and Presbyterians, and an English government's greed, the Church of Ireland had the support of Anglican landlords—the 'ascendancy'—who wished to keep the nation under their own control. But between them and their priests stood one bitter grudge: the payment of tithes. By paying less than the true value of the tithes, by converting land from tillage to pasture (for which the tithes were less), by paying an agreed-on but permanently set sum (rather than a proportion of the harvest, etc.), by taking long leases of episcopal lands at

[1] Davis IX. 58. [2] As summarized in Phillips III. 182.

low rents, or by simply refusing to pay tithes at all (and engaging the clergy in expensive, often disastrous litigation), the landlords tried to reduce their obligations to their ministers. Yet the principle by which the same men laid claim to their vested political ascendancy was that they were Anglicans and not Presbyterians or Roman Catholics. As the church weakened, under the hammer of its other destroyers, it had to compromise more and more ruinously in this relationship.

At the head of the Church of Ireland stood the Archbishop of Armagh, who was primate. Three other archbishops followed him in the hierarchy: Dublin, Cashel, and Tuam. Under each of these four were three to seven additional bishops, whose dioceses the archbishops had to oversee in addition to tending their own. The primate managed the diocese of Armagh, supervised the seven inferior prelates of his archbishopric, and was also head of affairs of the body of the church. Although the rest of the clergy might receive their appointments from a variety of sources, the bishops were always and deans usually chosen by the English government. Their incomes were seductive, their powers were broad (every bishop sat in the House of Lords), and the faithful wanted feeding. No administration could let the deanery of St Patrick's, valued at a thousand pounds a year, or the archbishopric of Armagh, abundant in patronage, slip into unco-operative hands.

Normally, a cathedral had a body of clergymen to carry on its business and services; they were the 'canons', and made up a 'chapter', the head of which was called 'dean'. Certain of the properties belonging to the cathedral were usually assigned to individual canons, and the right to use the income so arising was a 'prebend'; the holder of it, a 'prebendary'. To most prebends were attached parochial benefices in the diocese, which the prebendary served as vicar or rector and from which the bulk of his income was derived.

When Swift went to Kilroot, the primate was Michael Boyle, now closing a long life of eminence in the church. He was a decayed octogenarian, senilely absent-minded, very hard of hearing, and nearly blind[1]—an appropriate emblem of the Anglican establishment in Ireland. Edward Walkington, Bishop of Down and Connor, presided over the diocese to which Swift's first parish belonged. Like Boyle, he was a native of Ireland, educated at Trinity College. Capel had advised his promotion as a man who would get along with the dissenters concentrated in the area; and he was popular, learned, well connected. The other virtues which recommended him to the lord deputy were moderation, sobriety, a talent (regularly exercised) for preaching, and a habit of residing at the scene of his duties.[2]

iii

The parish which Swift served had since 1609 been a union of two vicarages and one rectory: Kilroot, Templecorran, and Ballynure. Together they formed the 'corps' of the prebend of Kilroot in the cathedral of Connor. The distinction between vicarage and rectory was not at all one of spiritual duties or authority. In theory the priest of any parish church had originally been a rector, supported by tithes which his parishioners set aside for him, and enjoying during his tenure the use of certain buildings and lands. In the Middle Ages and at the Reformation these 'rectorial' tithes or properties had often been handed over to somebody else—'impropriated'. But some resources had still to be held back for a 'vicar', who possessed spiritually the same rank as a rector but received different—usually more modest— 'temporalities'. Logically, there could be a vicar only where there was no rector.

Since the income of many livings was too little for the needs of even a parson's family, several parishes, adjoining or not, were frequently thrown together as a single 'cure'. The merger might be occasional and for the sake of one man, who was simply granted from time to time extra benefices. His holdings were then a 'plurality'; and if they were assigned *in commendam*, he enjoyed the receipts so long as no regular incumbent was named. Michael

[1] Ware I. 130. [2] *SPD. 1694–95*, pp. 480, 512.

Boyle, when Bishop of Cork, Cloyne, and Ross, had for a while taken the profits of six parishes to himself, 'under colour that he could not get clergymen to serve them'.[1] But his pluralism brought down a scolding from the government, and he filled the openings. Some benefices were attached to particular dignities *ex officio*, and whoever got one got the other: so the Bishop of Kildare, from 1681 to 1846, held *in commendam* the deanery of Christ Church Cathedral, Dublin. When several livings were permanently combined, and all their duties and temporalities were entrusted to the same minister, they became a 'union', such as that of Kilroot.

Swift was not entering a healthy and prosperous diocese. The prebendal stall of Kilroot was one of four (in the cathedral of Connor), created and endowed by James I (1609) during a campaign to strengthen the Church of Ireland. But the diocese of Connor did not flourish. Out of sixty-seven of its churches which were visited in 1622 only seven were found to be in good repair. As for county Antrim, where Kilroot lay, an inquisition of 1657 revealed that 'in the 65 parishes 30 churches were in ruins, 27 had no incumbents, 51 had no glebes, and the tithes of 32 were impropriate to laymen'. In 1693 another report on Down and Connor emphasized its lamentable condition—

> the clergy wrongfully dispossessed of their glebe lands, incumbents restrained from claiming their legal rights for fear of offending their patrons or parishioners, non-residence widely prevalent, churches falling into disrepair and ruin.[2]

So many complaints had been made that an ecclesiastical commission was appointed to look into the diocese. The then bishop (1693), Thomas Hackett, 'was facetiously known as the Bishop of Hammersmith [near London] because of his prolonged residence there'; he found himself finally deprived. In the wake of the commission's work there were additional

> suspensions, excommunications, and deprivations for such varied

[1] Ware I. 569. [2] Landa, pp. 10–11.

offences as drunkenness, fornication, adultery, neglect of cures, pluralism, diversion of funds, excessive procuration and visitation fees, non-residence, illegal use of the bishop's seal, and simony.[1]

The stables were still being cleansed when Swift arrived from Dublin. During March and April 1695 he was installed in his prebend at Lisburn, went through the required forms for induction at Templecorran and Ballynure, and at the end of April read divine service and preached at Lisburn.[2] His parishes were in the north-east of Ireland, on the shore of Belfast Lough. Even today it is a bleak and exposed neighbourhood, though with fine views of the hills behind the farmlands and of the edge of county Down across the bay. Templecorran and Kilroot together formed an uneven rectangle, with one short side of sea-front. Inland and due west lay Ballynure, cut off from them by St Nicholas's parish, which included the important fishing port and market town of Carrickfergus. There was no church at Kilroot, only a non-functioning ruin. Swift did not appear there to read divine service at the time of his induction, and he probably never preached there.[3] At Templecorran and Ballynure there were churches, less than eight miles apart—the one at Ballynure seems to have been in poor repair but usable—and his Kilroot parishioners may have worshipped at nearby Templecorran.[4]

Every parish was supposed to have some land—or 'glebe'—and a house (manse or glebe house) for the priest's own use. It was a common thing, especially in unstable Ulster, for the house to be uninhabitable and the glebe impropriated. There is no sign that Swift found a manse in any of his parishes, though there may have been a glebe in one.[5] He may have lived either in the village of Templecorran or in Carrickfergus. From the town he could have ridden to each of his churches in less than an hour, unless the weather and the roads were bad.

Neither had Swift (on a hundred pounds a year) an abundance of income to enjoy,[6] nor was there a glut of parishioners to overwork him. An accurate description of his territory, written on the

[1] Landa, p. 13. [2] *Ibid.*, p. 15. [3] *Ibid.*, p. 22. [4] *Ibid.*, p. 23.
[5] *Ibid.*, p. 22. [6] *Ibid.*, p. 16.

spot (1683), by Richard Dobbs, one of his parishioners-to-be, is still preserved:

> The parish of Kilroot is but small, the whole tithes not worth forty pounds per annum, and the great tithes belong to the Earl of Donegal, the small tithes to the prebendary [i.e., Swift's predecessor], one Milne, a Scotchman; the inhabitants (except my family and some half a dozen that live under me) all Presbyterians and Scotch, not one natural Irish in the parish, nor papist, and may afford 100 men. Next adjoining to this parish, adjacent to the sea, is . . . the parish of Templecorran; the small tithes belong to the prebendary aforesaid, the great to the bishop, and may be worth fifty pounds per annum . . . the inhabitants all Scotch, not one Irishman or papist, all Presbyterians except the parson and clark, who I think is his son.[1]

For an Anglican clergyman in Ireland, one of the severest trials was that the government, which could not afford to alienate the powerful community of Nonconformists, actually gave encouragement to them. 'King William not only renewed the *regium donum* to the Ulster Presbyterians; he increased it.' Capel tried to strengthen their legal toleration. The Act of Uniformity was not enforced.[2]

Not only was Ulster in general heavily Presbyterian, but Swift's diocese, especially Antrim, was still more densely so than the rest of the province. 'The Nonconformists are much the most numerous portion of the Protestants in Ulster', one bishop complained:

> Some parishes have not ten, some not six, that come to [the Established Church], while the Presbyterian meetings are crowded with thousands covering all the fields. This is ordinary in the county of Antrim especially, which is the most populous of Scots of any in Ulster.[3]

Even within Antrim, no parishes were more seriously infected than Swift's; and he himself said his sermons were 'calculated for a church without a company or a roof'.[4] Shortly before his ap-

[1] McSkimin, p. 378. [2] Landa, p. 20. [3] *Ibid.*, pp. 20–1. [4] Ball I. 29.

pointment, the dean of Connor had said that many cures in this part of the diocese were neglected, 'particularly the cure of Ballynure and Killrott belonging to Mr Miln [is] not served by himself or any curate'; as a consequence, 'several considerable persons in the parrish of Ballynure particularly Mr Dobbs & his lady & Mrs Stewart & several others . . . were forced to frequent the Presbyterian meetings for want of a fitt minister to attend that cure'. The first Presbyterian minister in Ireland had been presented to Templecorran and Kilroot. Swift's immediate predecessor had been a Commonwealth minister until, at the Restoration, he decided to conform.[1] Belfast, only a few miles from Kilroot, was the centre of the strength and wealth of Presbyterianism.

As a final sign of the weakness of Swift's outpost, there is the startling fact that his own bishop, Edward Walkington, believed the prebend was not rightly Swift's, for he had been (erroneously) persuaded that it still belonged to the previous incumbent. William Milne had emigrated to Ireland from Scotland in 1657. He was ordained by the presbytery of Antrim and given a parish next to Kilroot. In 1660 he abandoned Presbyterianism, and in 1662 Jeremy Taylor reordained him; a year later, he was presented to Kilroot.[2] During the general investigation of the diocese by the ecclesiastical commission of 1693, Milne was charged with non-residence, intemperance, and incontinence. He was first suspended but later deprived, although a maintenance of twenty pounds a year was set aside for him out of the income of the prebend.[3]

Early in 1697, Walkington said that Milne had never been deprived of his prebend but merely suspended. Writing to Anthony Dopping, then Bishop of Meath, Walkington mistakenly argued,

> [Milne] was censured by your lordship here at Lisburn for some misdemeanours, and his penalty was a suspension from his office and benefice during the kings pleasure, this censure was by the poor man himself and by most of the hearers mistaken for deprivation, and the mistake was so current, and universall that one Mr.

[1] Landa, p. 19. [2] *Ibid.*, p. 12, n. [3] *Ibid.*, p. 14.

> Jonathan Swift putt in for the poor man's living, and obtain'd the kings patent for it, during which time the poor man has been maintain'd by the charitable contribution of the clergy or otherwise he must have starv'd.[1]

Further research must have shown that Milne had no case; and he was certainly not reinstated. Swift probably never heard of the bishop's doubts, being in England at the time; nevertheless, the proceedings of the commission were notorious; and one of the witnesses against Milne had been John Winder, rector of Carnmoney, who became Swift's friend and eventually his successor at Kilroot. It was impossible for Swift to avoid knowing the details of Milne's scandalous conduct. Even if he had not just come from the civilization of Moor Park, even if he were not infused with the highest ethical ideals, even if he did not possess a both hereditary and inculcated repugnance for Puritanism, the circumstances of his entry into the church must have shocked him. The geographical isolation of his parishes, the meanness of their church buildings and temporalities, the paucity of worshippers, the threatening crowds of the hostile sect, the profound corruption of his own prebendal antecedents—to be undisturbed by such a congeries of evil symptoms would seem a mark not of wisdom but of vice.

iv

Yet he found some people who were worth knowing. In Carrickfergus and Belfast princely homes were maintained by the Earl of Donegal, heir of the Chichesters. The rectory of Kilroot was of course impropriate to the Earl. Swift put himself on speaking terms with the Countess,[2] and was—sooner or later—introduced to her niece, Lady Jenny Forbes.[3] Within Kilroot parish the great house was Castle Dobbs, belonging to Richard Dobbs, who was one of Swift's churchwardens at Templecorran and who had

[1] Landa, p. 12.

[2] Ball I. 18. The lines praising her, in *Apollo's Edict*, I believe to be not Swift's but Mary Barber's: see *Poems* I. 355–6.

[3] Ball II. 248–9.

often been mayor of Carrickfergus.[1] He was now about sixty or more, loved to improve his house and his lands, and felt obvious pride in his family's long connection with the place. Since 1664 he had been high sheriff of county Antrim. Swift paid visits to Dobbs, borrowed Glanvill's *Scepsis Scientifica* from him, and lent him a volume of Temple's *Miscellanea*. The Glanvill he found, as one might have guessed, 'a fustian piece of abominable curious virtuoso stuff'.[2]

Carrickfergus was still the focal centre of the Lough, only starting to be eclipsed by Belfast. Carrickfergus Castle, thrusting out to sea on a rocky promontory, was among the best-preserved ancient fortresses in Ireland. During the late Middle Ages it had been 'the only firm holding of the English in Ulster'. Around it grew a flourishing maritime trade. On the pier under its walls, after the castle surrendered to Schomberg, William III had landed in 1690, five years before Swift's arrival. On the edge of the town stood its most imposing residence, the Chichesters' many-windowed, many-bayed Joymount, built by Sir Arthur at the beginning of the century. The handsome church of St Nicholas (as yet unsteepled) dated from Norman times; although the original structure fell into ruin, it was repaired, at Chichester's expense, while Joymount was being finished—'a mean beggarly restoration', says a recent rector. The north aisle still ends with the elaborate Jacobean monument, alabaster and marble, bearing effigies of Sir Arthur and his family.[3]

In 1696 the mayor of Carrickfergus, elected for a second time, was Henry Clements, one of Swift's churchwardens at Ballynure.[4] His family, like those of Dobbs and Donegal, had done what they could to resist James II during the Troubles; both he and his brother Edward were attainted by the Dublin parliament of 1689. Clements witnessed Swift's preaching and reading divine service at Ballynure in April 1695. Swift liked him and accepted an invitation to his mayor's feast.[5]

[1] McSkimin, pp. 417–19; Landa, p. 15, n. 2. [2] Ball I. 28.

[3] See E. M. Jope, *A Guide to Carrickfergus Castle* (Belfast 1957), p. 3; J. C. Rutherford, *St Nicholas' Church, Carrickfergus*, 1957, p. [9].

[4] Landa, p. 15, n. 2; McSkimin, pp. 418–20. [5] Ball I. 29; Landa, p. 15, n. 2.

Most of the parishes next to Swift's were the corps of George Warter Story, who had succeeded Ward as dean of Connor. When Schomberg's army came over in 1689, Story came with them as a regimental chaplain. He served throughout the Williamite campaigns, and wrote a history which became 'by far the most important authority for the war on the Williamite side'. At the same time as his deanship (December 1694) he had received the rectory of St Nicholas.[1]

Of all the acquaintances which Swift formed at this time, the longest-lived was with John Winder, whose sea-front vicarage of Carnmoney lay between Ballynure and St Nicholas's parish. According to one report, he too had been an army chaplain, and was the son of a colonel.[2] The husband of one of his great granddaughters sketched Winder as having 'a moderate estate' in county Antrim and as forming 'several respectable connexions'.[3] Yet what Swift says to him suggests a man not well provisioned with money or great friends. Although he was probably married at this time, his first child was born after Swift left Kilroot. Winder's two sons became parsons; his elder daughter, a parson's wife; but his younger daughter married one of the most eligible gentlemen in the county, with whom she had an only child eventually to be famous as a brilliant diplomat and created Earl Macartney.[4]

Swift had enough respect for Winder to tell him, '[I] never entertained one single ill thought of you in my life.'[5] The vicar of Carnmoney was a considerate friend, abnormally sensitive, who admired Swift so much that he made copies of his sermons. However, sincere intimacy with an earnest young clergyman, admittance to what elegance the society of Belfast and Carrickfergus could afford, and the freedom of an independent style of life, all came short of the heights which Swift had breathed in Moor Park; he says himself that he grew 'weary in a few months'.[6] In the spring of 1696, a way of release opened: Temple asked him to rejoin the family.[7] Swift did not hesitate long.

[1] *DNB*. [2] Cotton v. 246. [3] Mason, p. 235, n.
[4] Ball IV. 282, n. 3; *DNB* (Macartney). [5] Ball I. 26. [6] *Autob.*, f. 9v.
[7] Ball I. 18.

Though he resided no more than a year at Kilroot,[1] he made up his mind to go away weeks or perhaps months before he actually left. One cause for the delay was the comfort of Winder's presence: 'Had I been assured of your neighbourhood, I should not have been so unsatisfied with the region I was planted in.'[2] A much stronger deterrent was Jane Waring.

V

The family home of the Warings was the inland town named after them, about thirty miles southwest of Carrickfergus. Jane's father, Roger, had died in 1692, when he was not yet fifty.[3] An accomplished pluralist, he had, from 1682 to 1690, been Archdeacon of Dromore, residing in Waringstown until the Troubles.[4] Then he must have left Ireland about the same time as Swift and for the same reasons, since he was another person attainted in Dublin, 1689. The act of attainder had fallen mainly upon those who went to England so as to escape from the government of the dethroned king. It took in about twenty-five hundred people, of whom almost a hundred were clergymen. William Waring, the head of the family, moved to the Isle of Man in March 1689. Though he returned alone, a few months later, his wife and children remained behind until peace was established.[5] Roger may have stayed abroad too long, for a new archdeacon was collated in August 1690.[6]

When Swift met Jane Waring, she had poor health and was probably living in Belfast with her widowed mother.[7] He gave her a poetical nickname, 'Varina', by latinizing the *W* of 'Waring' and altering the *g* to a feminine *a*; she became the first of the three frail, fatherless, first-born young women to whom he successively attached himself. So large and prominent a family as the

[1] Landa, p. 24. [2] Ball I. 30. [3] Burtschaell gives his age in 1658 as fifteen.

[4] Edward D. Atkinson, *An Ulster Parish* (Dublin 1898), pp. 31–3.

[5] *Ibid.*, pp. 34, 37, 51.

[6] H. B. Swanzy, *Succession Lists of Dromore* (Belfast 1933), p. 43.

[7] His letters were apparently addressed to her in Belfast; see Nichols, 1808, XVIII. 243, n.

Warings[1] Swift could hardly fail to meet, especially as his uncle Adam (whose property lay on the south coast of county Down, in Carlingford Bay) knew them,[2] and Swift had been at Trinity College with two of Jane's cousins.[3] At the same time, in his travels and visits through the area, he would have seen something of Henry Jenney, Roger Waring's successor; for the Jenneys yielded only to the Warings as personages in the local society. But Swift could ride a horse from Kilroot to the city of Belfast in a few hours, and he probably did so often.

Jane herself was the eldest of eight children, but not yet twenty-one years old when Swift moved to his new situation.[4] Her half-orphaned state and her illnesses (reminding him of Hetty Johnson at Moor Park) must have made it easy for him to sympathize with her and to wish to supply the guidance which he had missed at her age. The comparatively wide gap between them, in years (he was a third again as old as she) and in education, would have encouraged him to assign Hetty's filial role to the girl. Like his mother's flirtatious cousin, Elizabeth Jones, she was a parson's child. Like his sister, whose name she bore, she was the eldest in her family. There were plenty of elements to make Swift feel at home. But this time, if he began (as in 1691) 'without any other design than that of entertaining myself',[5] the affair soon found a deeper level. No doubt Swift was impelled in that direction not only by his solitude but by the effect of his cousin Thomas's marriage.

By the end of the year, Swift had enough assurance to be corresponding with Varina during a visit which he made to Dublin.[6] Although the earliest letter preserved between them is dated 29 April 1696, the marriage engagement which he proposes in it has obviously been for some time an unfailing source of heady conversation to the pair. Varina apparently considered his proposal ill-timed. She could not see herself enjoying life either in the vicinity of Kilroot or on Swift's income. 'Is it possible', he wrote,

[1] Atkinson, pp. 24–54. [2] Ball I. 31, n. 2. [3] *Ibid.* I. 16, n. 1.
[4] She was born 8 Oct. 1674 (Swanzy, p. 43). [5] Ball I. 5.
[6] Nichols x. 14, n.

> you can[1] be yet insensible to the prospect of a rapture and delight so innocent and so exalted? Trust me, Varina, Heaven has given us nothing else worth the loss of a thought.

His conditions are mild. She may live where she pleases until the wedding day; and the ceremony will take place only when she is satisfied with his income. 'I will push my advancement with all the eagerness and courage imaginable, and do not doubt to succeed.'

Although the temperature of the message is properly exalted, the argument is didactic and even avuncular. Apart from talk about his love, he repeatedly begs Varina to mind her health and to give up her whimsies and affectations: 'It is true you have known sickness longer than you have me, and therefore perhaps you are more loath to part with it as an older acquaintance.'

His urgency was due to a shift in his plans. Ireland was a disappointment. He held himself ready to remain there if she would engage herself to him, and not otherwise. If she preferred to remain sickly and single, and he left the kingdom before she was his, he would 'endure the utmost indignities of fortune rather than ever return again, though the King would send me back his Deputy'. For Temple had felt Swift's loss and was not only inviting him to return but promising not to leave him where he found him:

> I am once more offered the advantage to have the same acquaintance with greatness that I formerly enjoyed, and with better prospect of interest.

For all Swift's fountains of eloquence, Varina remained unwilling. That her prudence was well founded is almost certain. Swift accuses her of being mercenary and makes acid reflections on the character of all women; yet his concrete terms do not quite reach the unqualified promise of marriage. If one pokes among the rhetoric, one finds his admission that his friends 'still continue reproaching me for the want of gallantry, and neglecting a close

[1] Ball misprints 'cannot' (I. 19); other texts read 'can'.

siege'. Evidently, the hectic tone of these appeals made a serenade which Varina did not often hear from him, and which arose in part from Swift's very sense of their hollowness. She was a good listener ('your pity opened the first way to my misfortune'); but if she had behaved herself with less caution at this point, Swift would probably have expressed himself with more. Although he uses the style which one associates with utter recklessness, he manages to make a very hard demand—that she give him her decision immediately, because he is going to England in two and a half weeks. Yet he knows she desires more time, for he complains of 'your unreasonable scruples to keep me here'. That he looks for a negative seems clear, since in the midst of his rhapsody he says, 'In one fortnight I must take eternal farewell of Varina.' Swift was being true to the character he had given himself four years earlier: 'I confess I have known one or two men of sense enough, who, inclined to frolics, have married and ruined themselves out of a maggot [i.e., an infatuation]; but a thousand household thoughts, which always drive matrimony out of my mind whenever it chances to come there, will, I am sure, fright me from that.'[1]

While their correspondence was nevertheless to continue,[2] the tone was to alter. His stipulations would grow more exact; her demurrals would soften. Soon it would no longer be a question of manners or of physical health. Varina's family and her character would be found wanting. Unless she radically rearranged her way of life and cut down her material needs, he would find himself unable to keep up his own side of the understanding. Varina would infer, correctly, that she had a rival.

[1] Ball I. 6, 18–19.

[2] Nichols (x. 14, n.) mentions unpublished letters of 20 Dec. 1695, from Dublin; and 29 Jun. 1696 and 28 Aug. 1697, from Moor Park (besides the two in Ball).

Chapter Seven

MOOR PARK AGAIN

i

Swift did return to Moor Park in 1696. Without giving up his prebend, he accepted Temple's invitation. During his absence the household had suffered. Thomas Swift had stepped into the office of secretary, perhaps at his cousin's recommendation.[1] In January 1693/4, however, Thomas was presented to the rectory of Puttenham, about five miles west of Moor Park, toward Guildford. While Temple may have helped him to obtain this living,[2] the duties must have limited the attention which he could give to his patron. Here was one occasion for the recall of Jonathan.

Another was the death of Lady Temple, buried in Westminster Abbey, February 1694/5, soon after the funeral of her friend, Queen Mary. Temple's brother John commented to a relative, 'You have heard, I believe, of the greate losse, that wee have lately had here, by the death of my Sister Temple, which hath been a greate trouble to us all in this family, and with a greate deale of reason, for a better woman I never knew, and no body could be kinder, then she had alwayes been, both to mee and my children.'[3] So Sir William's immediate circle shrank to the dimensions of his sister, his French daughter-in-law and her mother, his two grand-daughters, Mrs Dingley, Mrs Johnson,

[1] In a sermon published 1710, Thomas Swift labelled himself 'formerly chaplain to Sir William Temple'; in its dedication, he called Temple 'my own wise patron'; he witnessed Temple's will 1695; and he wrote a letter for Temple to a bookseller, Feb. 1694/5 (Ball I. 387–8; Woodbridge, p. 231).

[2] See William Wotton, *Observations on A Tale of a Tub*, 1705, p. 67.

[3] Dated from East Sheen, 9 Mar. 1694/5, to Thomas Flower.

and young Hetty.[1] Yet the summer before this was probably the time when he impressed a visitor as leading an ideal life:

> far enough from the town to be protected from visits, the air wholesome, the soil good, the view limited but pretty, a little stream which runs near making the only sound to be heard; the house small, convenient, and appropriately furnished; the garden in proportion to the house and cultivated by the master himself. He is free from business, and to all appearances free from ambition; he has a few servants, and some sensible people for company. . . I saw Monsieur Temple healthy and gay; and though he is gouty and getting on in years, he tired me in walking, and except for the rain which interrupted us would, I believe, have forced me to ask for quarter. . . This good old man thought I should not be sufficiently repaid for my trouble if I saw only his little house; and though I assured him that I was more interested in men than in buildings, and that I was content with the honour of having seen him, he insisted that before returning to London I should go to [Petworth], the country house of the Duke of Somerset. He gave me horses and servants to take me there, and fearing that the Duke might be gone to London, he asked my Lady Temple to write to the Duchess.[2]

The picture of her asking the Duchess of Somerset to receive a young Swiss traveller is the last direct view we have of Dorothy Osborne. What her passing meant to the man who had courted her for six years, through war, smallpox, and the disapproval of both fathers, is foreshadowed in his sister's record: 'He was often heard to say how happy his life had been if it had ended at fifty.'[3]

About the middle of May 1696 (just after James II's 'invasion' collapsed) Swift departed from his parishes.[4] He probably moved from Belfast to Dublin, to Holyhead, to Leicester, and there paused to visit his mother. Then came London, while the government's worst financial crisis was being complicated by the arrest of Sir John Fenwick; and at last Moor Park. Here, at the end of

[1] Woodbridge, pp. 217–18, 233. [2] *Ibid.*, p. 232.

[3] Temple, *Early Essays*, p. 21 (the remark was written before the death of Lady Temple).

[4] On Wednesday, 29 Apr. 1696, he said he planned to leave Kilroot for Dublin on Monday fortnight (18 May), there to take leave of the lord deputy and go quickly to England; but if Capel's illness was as serious as he had heard, he might sail directly from Belfast or Carrickfergus; Capel died 30 May (Ball I. 18).

June, one of Swift's first gestures was to write Varina a letter, in diction perhaps less molten than before.[1]

Although he waited another year and a half before resigning Kilroot, Swift does not seem to have felt disappointed by the reception Temple gave him. He had been granted a licence of absence from his cure, extendible if he so desired.[2] However, according to Swift's sister, Temple 'was so fond of him . . . that he made him give up his living in [Ireland], to stay with him at Moor Park, and promised to get him one in England'.[3] Her impression exaggerates the warmth of Temple's feelings, for he urged Swift to write for a 'further licence'. Yet we know that Swift decided to resign the prebend while he was still in Ireland. He even promised Winder that he would do what he could to get him appointed as Swift's successor. Few people besides Winder seem to have encouraged such imprudence; and even Winder was reported to have advised against it.[4] Nevertheless, Swift carried out the scheme; and his friend was installed exactly three years after himself.[5]

One can hardly miss the smell of bridges burning. Not only is there the violence of Swift's threat to Varina—'I will endure the utmost indignities of fortune rather than ever return again'—but on the very eve of his resignation, Swift's hopes in England were dashed. Temple had recommended him to the Earl of Sunderland, whom the king brought out of seclusion, at the time of the peace negotiations, to serve as lord chamberlain. But the earl gave up his office soon after the treaty was signed at Ryswick.[6] Instead of hesitating at this turn, Swift plunged ahead: 'Ten days before my resignation [of Kilroot], my Lord Sunderland fell and I with him.'[7] One seldom shoves a treasure aside with such eager reluctance if it does not hold a strong allurement. Swift was probably showing that he lived, as he had hoped Varina would do, above the 'paltry maxims' of that prudence which is 'calculated for the rabble of humanity'.[8]

[1] I am assuming that Swift followed his usual course and that Nichols is right about the correspondence with Varina (x. 14, n.).

[2] Landa, p. 24. [3] Ball I. 30. [4] *Ibid.* I. 24. [5] Cotton III. 266.

[6] Ogg II. 437–41. [7] Ball I. 24. [8] *Ibid.* I. 20.

ii

Meanwhile, in the new order at Moor Park, Swift functioned less as a clerk than as a companion and literary aide. After 1695, Temple wrote practically nothing for publication. However, his poems,[1] a number of essays, a volume of memoirs, and what appeared as three volumes of letters, had all to be prepared for the press. The first two volumes of the letters had been mainly collected by one of Temple's secretaries; and Swift did little with these but transcribe them in chronological order and translate those in French or Latin. A few in Spanish were probably translated by Lady Giffard, if we may judge from the flourish of praise which Swift bestows upon that labour.[2] The additional letters in these volumes (besides those collected by the earlier secretary) and all the letters in the third volume were chosen as well as recopied by Swift, under Temple's direction: 'I had begun to fit them for the press during the author's life', Swift said later; 'but never could prevail for leave to publish them: Tho' he was pleased to be at the pains of reviewing, and to give me his directions for digesting them into order.'[3] Similarly, Temple's 'third' volume of *Memoirs* had to be 'copied from the originals by Sir William Temple's direction, and corrected all along by his orders'.[4] Exactly this sort of work had been Swift's province from his first days at Moor Park.[5]

The measure of his advance over those days is given by the tone of a letter which he wrote early in 1698. Sir William and his sister had gone to London, taking with them Mrs Dingley, Mrs Johnson, and her daughter Esther—a kind of companion and waiting woman, it seems, to Lady Giffard. Ralph Mose was Temple's steward; Swift and he had charge of the establishment during the family's absence. The letter was almost certainly ad-

[1] The poems, though not published, were privately printed; and a copy, perhaps unique, is in the British Museum.

[2] Davis I. 258. [3] *Ibid.* I. 259.

[4] Ball I. 172; the 'first' volume of Temple's *Memoirs* was not published or preserved. Cf. Swift's remark on the third volume of Temple's *Letters*: 'They were corrected by himself; and fairly transcribed in his life time' (Davis I. 266).

[5] Ball I. 171–2.

dressed to the seventeen-year-old girl; for in it the recipient is coupled with Lady Giffard's pet bird of paradise, as 'fellow-servant' to her ladyship, and Swift jokes about an association with 'my lady's chamber floor'. In one sentence he suggests the ease with which he now lives in Moor Park, the warm-but-teasing relationship with Hetty, and his famous habit of saying the kindest things by their opposites:

> I desire your absence heartily, for now I live in great state, and the cook comes in to know what I please to have for dinner: I ask very gravely what is in the house, and accordingly give orders for a dish of pigeons, or, &c.[1]

When everybody was home, there must have been pleasant, if hierarchical, social evenings together. Frequently, Temple would give the young people a little money for stakes, and they would all play cards.[2] Swift also used to visit London, though we do not know how often; he later described himself as being at this time a 'gentleman much in the world'.[3] Temple sometimes sent him on errands to court, possibly in order to remind the king of Swift's name.[4]

The uncertainty of his position went on, of course, and he did not like being a dependent; yet though he tried 'other courses' (unspecified) for preferment after Sunderland's withdrawal, they were fruitless.[5] Temple did recommend him to the king, but with how much force we do not know.[6] The baronet took himself seriously; there was not much in his past that he could think about without the danger of painful contrasts; and Swift had sometimes to put up with more reserve or gloom than he was ready to make allowances for. Years later, when a powerful friend acted diffident, Swift said,

> One thing I warned him of, Never to appear cold to me, for I would not be treated like a school-boy; that I had felt too much of that in my life already (meaning from sir William Temple)... I think what I said to [him] was right. Don't you remember how I used to be in

[1] Ball I. 21-2. [2] *Journal* II. 561. [3] *Tale*, p. 4. [4] Longe, p. 216.
[5] Ball I. 24. [6] *Ibid.* III. 301.

pain when Sir William Temple would look cold and out of humour for three or four days, and I used to suspect a hundred reasons?[1]

However familiar he might feel with Moor Park, it was not Swift's home. His sister, who had been there with him, and was eventually to return and work for Lady Giffard, now lived in Dublin.[2] His cousin Thomas, with a parish and a wife to look after, perhaps found himself too busy to haunt the young genius. Anyhow, Swift, for all the confidences which he had reposed in him, had already begun to sound contemptuous of Thomas in 1693.[3] Like many apparently close friends who have been connected by less sympathy than proximity, the two parsons lost rapport with advancing age. They possessed so many experiences in common that any clash of temperament must have made a bold impression. Swift obviously acted the dominant part; and if he had wished to strengthen the tie, he could have done so: it was Thomas who saved his letters, not Swift who saved his cousin's.

If Swift felt ambitious, the strict morality but thin emotional indulgences of his childhood had trained him to put a low rating upon his natural abilities or charm. He did not look for disinterested affection, though he could evoke it. To signs of contempt he was unreasonably open. Frequently, he gave offence to begin with, for fear of receiving it to end with. Instead of finding practicable standards of conduct in himself, he therefore made heroes of men like Temple and Sancroft. The comparative lack of friction between Sir William and his protégé is a credit to the older man's urbanity.

Nothing about Temple impressed Swift so much as the high road which he had left. Refusing twice to become secretary of state was an act of as much virtue as genius. There is no sign that Temple underplayed the role of Cato Uticensis. After Swift came to know intimately the men who ruled England, he might smile at the 'splutter Sir William Temple [made] about being secretary of state'.[4] While he still lived at Moor Park, however, Swift

[1] *Journal*, 3–4 Apr. 1711. [2] Ball I. 8. [3] *Ibid.*, pp. 367–8.
[4] *Journal*, 3 Nov. 1711.

had no reservations about his patron's magnificence. Throughout Swift's life, he never referred to Temple except by his full name; the most private allusions are always respectful; the public allusions are always admiring: 'this great and good person' (1700), 'a certain great man . . . universally reverenced for every good quality that could possibly enter into the composition of the most accomplish'd person' (1709).[1]

iii

Temple's glory and integrity seemed not superior to his literary gifts: 'I never read his writings', Swift said in 1692, 'but I prefer him to all others at present in England.' 'This author', he said in 1700, 'has advanced our English tongue, to as great a perfection as it can well bear.'[2] Both Temple and his sister helped to direct the aspiring writer's first exercises. They had him undertake a translation of Virgil.[3] He wrote his ode to the Athenian Society only after 'Sir William Temple speaking to me so much in their praise, made me zealous for their cause.'[4]

The strenuous course of reading which Swift undertook at this time may have owed something to Temple's advice and was probably meant as a propaedeutic to literary composition. When he prepared sketches of English history, he used Temple's *Introduction* and started from Temple's sources. After Temple gave up the idea of writing a complete history of England, he spoke of turning the job over to younger men, in words which could easily have referred to Swift.[5] Of a list of books read by Swift in 1697 and 1698,[6] history—political and ecclesiastical—accounts for a third of the titles. The classics, from Homer to Petronius, come to less than a quarter. Literature of travel, some books concerning Christian doctrine, French belles-lettres (e.g., Voiture, Fontenelle), and works on esoteric aspects of religion are (ranged from the more to the less important) other distinct groupings. Lucre-

[1] Davis I. 259, 6. [2] Ball I. 365; Davis I. 258. [3] Ball I. 365.
[4] *Ibid.*, p. 363.
[5] See my 'Swift's History of England', *JEGP.*, LI (Apr. 1952), 177–85.
[6] See *Tale*, pp. lvi–lvii.

tius he read three times; Virgil, twice; Lucius Florus—a compilation based upon Livy—three times.

Copying out, during more than a decade, the works and letters of his patron set Swift a model of the highest value, Temple's prose style; for Lamb underestimates that in calling it 'plain natural chit-chat'. It is marked at its best by the use of short sentence elements with little affectation of periodic structure. The phrases are idiomatic, the vocabulary colloquial, the imagery striking and homely. In place of the slow cadences of Jacobean and Caroline rhetoric, Temple has a varied, unstressed rhythm. There are good examples in even his early essays:

> Amongst all those passions which ride men's souls none so jade and tire them out as envy and jealousy; their journey is longer than any of the rest, they bate seldomer, and commonly ride double.[1]

The unobtrusive parallelism gives coherence; the quiet metaphor gives life; the tone, learned from Montaigne, of independent observation and personal reflection, gives character. Temple had a gift for anecdote, character-drawing, narrative history, and lucid (if superficial) exposition. Accuracy of information hardly mattered, since his data were rather illustrative than demonstrative; he used facts to embody moral generalizations, not to record what happened. He possessed little genius for large organization in the manner of Hooker; like most essayists of the Restoration, he conceived his works in paragraphs raying out from a central theme and unified by attitude or style. Structure in the sense of an articulated skeleton, the kind of outline-logic taught at the universities and employed to support a sermon or a formal oration, he hardly attempted. Recreation, not proof, was his aim.

Taking over the essential qualities of Temple's style, Swift transfigured it through his violence, his wit, and his irony. However, of the brilliant style which makes *A Tale of a Tub* the greatest prose satire in English, there is small promise in Swift's early

[1] *Early Essays*, p. 166.

poems. The proper source to examine for such foreshadowings is not his verse but the first specimens of the genre in which Swift shows his most shining literary virtues—letters. Although now seldom handled as aesthetic objects, there is no doubt that the six volumes of his general correspondence and the two volumes of the letters to Esther Johnson contain a higher achievement than all but the best-known of his essays and poems. In this art, Swift may have an equal; he has no superior.

In his good letters, Swift plays with the correspondent as a witty author plays with a reader.[1] The famous irony appears here when Swift's poems are still grim with sobriety and sticky with one-sided idealism. He tries a great range of comic devices, especially with intimates on whose affection he can rely: practical jokes, flattery disguised as insult, word play, farcical exaggeration. But when he wishes to sound serious, he can communicate bitter self-containment, gratitude, warm friendship, sarcastic contempt, deep admiration, all through turns of phrase rather than superlative epithets. The heart of Swift's literary effectiveness is not his vocabulary but his syntax.

The earliest letter preserved, written when he was twenty-four, to his cousin's husband, is a remarkable accomplishment as a respectful but sternly dignified epistle. His gift for phrase-making is already ripe—'my mind was like a conjured spirit', 'the people is a lying sort of beast'. His habit of humble, Bunyanesque metaphor appears throughout: 'But whenever I begin to take sober resolutions, or, as now, to think of entering into the church, I never found it would be hard to put off this kind of folly at the porch.' The purity of language and expression, the distinctly articulated sentence structure, the tough but elegant management of periodic units, the clarity of meaning, the intensity of feeling, the boldness of self-analysis, which permeate the letter, make it easy for one to understand why the recipient, to whom it was in part a rebuke, decided to save it:

[1] There is a fine analysis of this aspect of the *Journal to Stella* in Dr Mackie L. B. Jarrell's unpublished Ph.D. dissertation, 'Swift's "Peculiar Vein of Humor" ', University of Texas, 1954.

And as to that of my great prospects of making my fortune, on which as your kindness only looks on the best side, so my own cold temper, and unconfined humour, is much greater hindrance than any fear of that which is the subject of your letter, I shall speak plainly to you, that the very ordinary observations I made with going half a mile beyond the university, have taught me experience enough not to think of marriage till I settle my fortune in the world, which I am sure will not be in some years; and even then I am myself so hard to please that I suppose I shall put it off to the other world.[1]

A letter to cousin Thomas, three months later, demonstrates Swift's infinite capacity for turning his ordinary tasks into a drama:

It makes me mad to hear you talk of making a copy of verses next morning, which though indeed they are not so correct as your others are, [is] what I could not do under two or three days, nor does it enter into my head to make anything of a sudden but what I find to be exceedingly silly stuff by great chance. I esteem the time of studying poetry to be two hours in a morning, and that only when the humour sits, which I esteem for the flower of the whole day, and truly I make bold to employ them that way, and yet I seldom write above two stanzas in a week—I mean such as are to any Pindaric ode—and yet I have known myself in so good a humour as to make two in a day, but it may be no more in a week after, and when all is done I alter them a hundred times, and yet I do not believe myself to be a laborious dry writer, because if the fit comes not immediately I never heed it, but think of something else.

The same letter shows his talent for exposing his own frailties without sacrificing our respect, because the style of the exposure is so masterly that we must envy the writer:

I have a sort of vanity or foiblesse, I do not know what to call it, and which I would fain know if you partake of: it is—not to be circumstantial—that I am overfond of my own writings; I would not have the world think so, for a million, but it is so, and I find when I write what pleases me I am Cowley to myself and can read it a hundred times over. I know it is a desperate weakness, and has nothing to

[1] Ball I. 4–5; Ball's text reads 'myself I am'.

> defend it but its secrecy, and I know farther, that I am wholly in the wrong, but have the same pretence, the baboon had to praise her children, and indeed I think the love in both is much alike, and their being our own offspring is what makes me such a blockhead.[1]

Even in addressing Varina, when he sinks nearest the bathos of the pindaric odes, he cannot suppress his nervous genius: 'I am once more offered the advantage to have the same acquaintance with greatness that I formerly enjoyed,' 'It is true you have known sickness longer than you have me, and therefore perhaps you are more loath to part with it as an older acquaintance.'[2] But it is not until we reach the message to Esther Johnson that true humour appears: sympathetic identification of oneself with the subject ridiculed; affectionate raillery; harmless, careless wit, more to be valued for the good nature than the bright mind behind it—'Here are three letters for you, and Molly will not send one of them', he lies; 'she says you ordered her to the contrary': but then he relents, confessing, 'Here is a great bundle and a letter for you; both came together from London.'[3] Perhaps this air of direct speech, unscreened by ink and paper, but simple, open, and fresh, is the most solid foundation of Swift's epistolary art.

iv

In comparing the styles of Temple and Swift, the question of influence is, as always, perilous, since their common traits often seem more innate than acquired; and even when a trait does appear to have been taught or learned, it is often the effect either of general fashion or of common masters. During the Restoration, for example, nobody required an introduction to the names of Montaigne and Sir Thomas Browne. Yet if Swift was not brought to them by Temple, he was certainly encouraged to read them. They are palpable influences upon Temple's early essays of the 1650's and on Swift's writing a generation afterward.

That Swift derived his literary style immediately from Temple

[1] Ball I. 362–4; Ball's text reads 'partake of it: it'. [2] *Ibid.*, pp. 18–19.
[3] *Ibid.*, pp. 21–2.

one can take for granted, since besides transcribing and editing hundreds of pages of his patron's writings, he also translated scores of the French and Latin letters into English, all under Temple's correction. (William Wotton thought he could identify Temple as the author of *A Tale of a Tub* by the vocabulary.[1]) In both men's prose one finds the same colloquial elegance, the same command of idiom, the avoidance of technical terms, of pretentious jargon, or the appearance of pedantry; they share the taste for homely similes,[2] though Swift's seldom run so long as Temple's; and they like to use lists. But Dryden also has these traits; and while he had welcomed technical terms into the *Annus Mirabilis*, he explicitly disavows them in the dedication of his *Aeneid*, where he claims to be writing like Virgil, 'to men and ladies of the first quality, who have been better bred than to be too nicely knowing in the terms'—a remark which might have come from Temple. (Hobbes and Rymer made similar attacks upon 'terms and jargon'[3]; and when Swift came to write on language, he too would show less interest in enrichment than in purgation.[4])

In his letters, Temple employs a graceful style, direct but charming, much like Addison's; but Swift has far more variety of tone and change of level. While Temple often brightens his manner with the risqué gallantries which Swift avoids, he never uses the coarse expressions, the word play, or the complicated ironic flatteries with which his protégé (who learned some of them from Voiture) is identified; and of course he lacks the crisp, nervous, aphoristic talent that gives distinction to many of Swift's routine messages. Temple avoids giving details even where he obviously should (and could) supply them[5]; Swift glories in his instances.

Temple's periods are much longer (though not weightier) than Swift's; but the degree of difference is less than at first appears: in a persuasive analysis, Macaulay, distinguishing the truly in-

[1] *Tale*, p. 314.

[2] Cf., in Temple's *Observations upon the U.P.*, p. 257: 'But as any rough hand can break a bone. . .'

[3] Spingarn II. 64, 68, 170. [4] Davis IV. 10–16.

[5] E.g., *Observations upon the U.P.*, p. 250.

volved syntax of Hooker or Clarendon from that of Temple, says that a careful judge

> will find that [Temple's apparently long sentences] are not swollen by parenthetical matter, that their structure is scarcely ever intricate; that they are formed merely by accumulation, and that . . . they might, without any alteration in the order of the words, be broken up into very short periods.[1]

Temple has only the seed of Swift's genius for phrase-making, aphorism, and startling analogies; Swift's conciseness, energy, variety, and violence are foreign to Temple's style. Yet when he does happen to strike out a 'thought', the result can be remarkably like Swift: 'We bring into the world with us a poor needy uncertain life, short at the longest, and unquiet at the best.'[2]

Rarely does Temple indulge in either bitter or teasing sentiments; but when he does, he comes nearest the vigour we associate with Swift:

> I shall not engage in answering the complements of your letter, tho' I should have much more justice on my side; but I am very ill furnished with that sort of ware, and the truth is, there is required so much skill in the right tempering, as well as the distribution of them, that I have always thought a man runs much hazard of losing more than he gains by them; which has made me ever averse, as well as incapable of the trade.[3]

This lacks Swift's nervous syntax, his degree of insinuation, his conciseness, and his irony; but it has his command of idiom, his simplicity of phrase and language, his talent for making structure follow feeling, and—most important—his directness, which lets one feel an emotion as if it were carried by the tone of a voice.

On the contrary, it is in Swift's rare elegiac cadences that his style most closely agrees with Temple's, the prolonged, receding rhythms in which both of them take a melancholy view of historical ironies: e.g.,

[1] *Works*, ed. Lady Trevelyan, 1873, VI. 280. [2] *Miscellanea* I. 175–6.
[3] *Letters* I. 73–4.

> [Temple:] And thus an adventure has ended in smoak, which had for almost three years made so much noise in the world, restored and preserved so long the general peace, and left his majesty the arbitrage of all affairs among our neighbours, by the Emperor and Spain's resolutions, as well as Sueden and Holland's, to follow his measures for the common safety and peace of Christendom.[1]
> [Swift:] And now it is done, it looks like a dream, to those who will consider the nobleness of his birth, the great merits of his ancestors and his own, his long unspotted loyalty; his affability, generosity, and sweetness of nature.[2]

Such Virgilian pathos is of course far more characteristic of Temple than of Swift. It is, indeed, the essential strains or impulses that most deeply divide the two. Where Temple chastens his natural formality to give it the ease of speech, Swift must guide the vigour of his colloquial instincts and impose the clarity of form upon them. Temple works to keep his language from sounding too fastidious; Swift's danger is leaning towards coarseness. Temple's periods tend to rhetorical fullness, even where an abrupt movement would be more effective; Swift's rhythms, more broken and more spontaneous, have the air of nature but seldom grow awkward. It is in *A Tale of a Tub*, therefore, where he is under least restraint, that Swift stands farthest from his master.

[1] *Letters* II. 307. Cf. the Ciceronian echo in Temple's curtain on the Battle of Hastings: 'This was the man, these the forces, and such the circumstances that contributed to so famous an enterprise, by which the fate of England was determined...' (*Introduction to the History of England*, pp. 119–20).

[2] Davis VIII. 132–3.

Part III

Chapter One

A TALE OF A TUB (I)

i

The composition of *A Tale of a Tub* produces little stir in Swift's biography because he has left no reference to the work made during its progress and almost none after its completion, apart from the *Apology* and a letter to the publisher.[1] As the book now stands, much of its apparatus belongs to a later time than the first finishing of it. The notes, the *Apology*, the dedication to Lord Somers, the 'Bookseller [i.e., publisher] to the Reader' were not part of the original plan. We are left with the allegory of the three brothers, spread over five 'sections' (II, IV, VI, VIII, XI); five digressions interrupting the 'tale'; a dedicatory epistle, preface, introduction, and conclusion. Two of the five digressions have an evident order. That on madness is properly in the climactic position, and, since it expounds a theory of vapours, follows the 'Aeolism' episode in the tale. The last, untitled digression ('Section X') is certainly intended as a conclusion to all five. The other three have no more excuse for their locations than what Swift provides for the third ('Section VII'):

> I have chosen for it as proper a place as I could readily find. If the judicious reader can assign a fitter, I do here empower him to remove it into any other corner he pleases.

Although the scheme is odd enough—deliberately so—it does have precedents, such as L'Estrange's version of Quevedo's *Visions* and Donne's *Ignatius His Conclave*, both of which are ex-

[1] Ball I. 183–5.

amples (known to Swift) of discursive, segmented satire with a centrifugal design.

The earliest part of the *Tale* to be conceived was probably the religious allegory. Of this the root ideas—a magical legacy and three brothers who fall out—are common in folk lore and literature.[1] Swift's version is similar to the old story of three rings left by a rich merchant to his three sons: though all the rings look alike, only one is genuine, and the owner of it is heir to the whole paternal estate. Conventionally, the father is God; the children are the Jewish, Christian, and Mohammedan faiths; and the implied meaning is that we should, regardless of our church, strive through charity to deserve God's blessing. Boccaccio took this plot for his third novella in the *Decameron*, and Lessing has embodied it in *Nathan the Wise*. After the Reformation it is sometimes applied to the threefold division of Christianity, with the sons representing the Lutheran, Calvinist, and Roman Catholic communions; the father's will (i.e., the New Testament) grows important; the rings fade out; the meaning becomes not eirenic but anti-Catholic. There are close parallels to Swift's treatment in an early seventeenth-century German play (based upon a Renaissance Latin source)[2] and in a notorious sermon preached (1686) by John Sharp, later Archbishop of York.[3] Swift replaces the estate by three seamless coats (the Christian faith); he gives the will a fundamental role; names the sons Martin, Jack, and Peter; and turns the ridicule against both Geneva and Rome: the plea for charity is now an aggressive, satirical defence of the Church of England. Since all the elements of his plot were in the air, we need not exercise our minds as to his 'sources'.

There may be some truth in the tradition that Swift produced the allegory while he was at Trinity College, and that he showed sketches of it to friends there or in Kilroot.[4] Temple, of course,

[1] Cf. J. A. Macculloch, *The Childhood of Fiction*, 1905, pp. 350–80.

[2] Martin Rinckhardt, *Der Reichslebischer Christlicher Ritter*, 1613. See C. M. Webster in *MLN.*, XLVIII (1933), 251–3; also C. J. Horne and H. Powell, 'A German Analogue for *A Tale of a Tub*', *MLR.*, LV (1960), 488–96.

[3] *Tale*, pp. xxxi-xxxvi.

[4] *Ibid.*, pp. xxxiv-xxxvi. Lyon says it 'appears from some sketches . . . in his own hand' that Swift (*c.* 1685–8) wrote an account of the kingdom of absurdities

frowned on satire. If Swift had such works under way when he first came to Moor Park, he probably tabled them. Returning to Ireland in 1694, he might have felt emancipated enough to let his instincts have their way. Nevertheless, no allusion which can be dated points to a period earlier than 1696; and the *Tale* shows traces of many books which he read in 1697 and 1698. In 1709 Swift said, 'The greatest part of that book was finished above thirteen years since, 1696, which is eight years before it was published.'[1] Since he had a habit of remembering dates as earlier than the truth, this statement probably puts the farthest limit on the writing of the text which we know. Delivered from the cures of three parishes, untroubled by Varina's proximity, restored to the leisure and the bluestocking ambience of Moor Park, and moved by Temple's authorial example, he probably began to compose the *Tale* during the latter half of 1696.

The five digressions (sections III, V, VII, IX, X) hardly refer to the course of the intervening plot, and seem to have been struck off later, during 1697–8. They contain attacks upon pedantic scholarship, 'modernism' in literary style and taste, political and military crime, mechanistic natural philosophy, occultism, Roman Catholicism, and, above all, Puritanism. The 'Introduction' and 'Conclusion', very much to the same purposes, carry signs of the 1697–8 period of composition. The 'Preface' anticipates most of the themes in the succeeding pages; it offers a mocking but not misleading declaration of aims, and ends in a pseudo-dissertation on the nature of satire. Like the 'Epistle Dedicatory', just preceding, it sounds as though it had been done right after, or at the same time as, the body of the book. The 'Epistle Dedicatory', which contains much free-flying bombardment of contemporary authors and scholars, is subscribed December 1697.

(p. 15). Lyon also believed that several people saw a draft of the *Tale* while Swift was at T.C.D. (p. 25).

[1] *Tale*, p. 4.

ii

The character of Martin probably belongs to the earliest part of *A Tale of a Tub*. Certainly it is the weakest ingredient. If one seeks a biographical explanation, one may say that in a book dominated by the principles which Swift shared with Temple, the figure representing Swift's positive religious values could not be strong, because Christian devotion never meant so much to Temple as it did to Swift. True, they both conceived of Christianity as a simple, easy, rational faith, single, coherent, and harmonious, independent of studied erudition[1]; but the reverence which drew Swift into the clergy was alien to Temple. One may also say, thinking historically, that after experiencing the desolation of Kilroot, Swift could hardly recapture the mood of his ode to Sancroft. Or, thinking of Swift's character, we may say that especially in a comic setting he had trouble paying straightforward tribute to what he cherished most.

But, in its literary aspect, the treatment of Martin is weak because it clashes with the programme of the book as a whole. This programme is for the author to imply a virtue which he desires to recommend, but to state it either not at all or else ironically—by pretending to depreciate it. In seventeenth-century England it would scarcely have been feasible for a writer to communicate his love for the Established Church by the medium of mock-insults. Swift would have accomplished his aim best by leaving Martin out. However, the central allegory which he chose almost precluded that possibility.

For one who admires the *Tale of a Tub*, therefore, the safest way to demonstrate its merits is to admit the flaw and then to consider what Swift accomplishes in spite of it. However, in order to succeed in this task, one must start from the objects which he implicitly proposes for our respect and emulation. That few of his favourable critics have done so, may be due either to their misunderstanding of the nature of his satire or to their unwillingness to face the conventionality of his recommendations.

[1] Temple, *Miscellanea* III. 260–70.

Unfortunately, those who occupy themselves wholly with techniques and targets can find little genuine structure in *A Tale of a Tub*. The patterns which they offer are usually so abstract and so remote from the concrete detail of the book as to seem, for practical purposes, irrelevant. If we root ourselves firmly in the principles which Swift advocates, however, we shall have to confess that these are neither original nor dazzling. Literary critics who dislike the conclusions of the supreme moralists, from St Luke to Freud, will find *A Tale of a Tub* diminished by this perspective. But there is no other way to bring order into the chaos of commentary upon what is, after all, an affirmation of quite accessible wisdom. Those who believe that rationality carries one away from virtue, or that agony and mindless mysticism are the invariable tokens of true religious faith, may call *A Tale of a Tub* a great satire; but unless they agree that it satirizes them, they cannot understand it.

A good clue to Swift's scheme is his remark in an *Examiner* paper written many years after the *Tale*: 'In describing the virtues and vices of mankind, it is convenient, upon every article, to have some eminent person in our eye, from whence we copy our description.'[1] For the virtues implicitly recommended by *A Tale of a Tub*, the eminent person is of course most often Sir William Temple; for the vices, Richard Bentley and William Wotton lead the train, but other antagonists of Sir William's virtues march close behind. This is in no way to suggest that one cannot comprehend and enjoy the book without a knowledge of Temple; certainly Swift never made such a demand upon his reader. Swift's view of Temple was itself a construction, and he respected him as embodying ideals which were largely implanted before the two met. With this in mind, we may state the problem as not to discover how Temple appears in *A Tale of a Tub* but, using the figure of Temple as a reference, to see what sort of person Swift is urging us to imitate. My only postulate is that behind the book stands not a list of philosophical propositions but the idea of a good man.

[1] Davis III. 10–11.

This idea belongs to the tradition usually called Christian humanism and descending to Swift from the great line of Spenser, Sidney, and Milton. However, the hero has been tamed into the shape of a gentleman; for nobody so appalled as Swift was by the effects of Puritan self-confidence could advise men to use epic standards as the test of merit. When Temple examined 'heroic virtue' in his finest essay, it was the Roman talents that he exalted —justice, government, prudence, and advances in the practical arts—not self-sacrificing magnanimity or sublime patriotism demonstrated on the battlefield; it was his grandfather who had fought beside Sir Philip Sidney, but it was Henry Sidney who became Sir William's adored friend.

Swift sets before us the Christian gentleman, a landed proprietor educated in humanist culture, conscious of his duties as a subject and a master. This model conforms cheerfully to the Established Church; he willingly supports the government of England as redesigned in 1688–9, and he is a responsible head of a family. As a father and as a landlord, he lives by the rules of Christian morality and labours to improve the condition of those who depend upon him. He uses polished manners, rereads the Greek and Latin classics, keeps his hereditary property in order, and maintains his elevated place in society. While everybody cannot hope to enjoy such a position, Swift argues, only fools would prefer another.

The satire is therefore directed against the fools and their antecedents: those who oppose 'the direct rules of the gospel, the current of antiquity, the religion of the magistrate, and the laws of the land'.[1] Swift takes up the alternatives to his model in religion, in culture, in politics, and in manners. When he described the genesis of the book, he said,

> The author was then young, his invention at the height, and his reading fresh in his head. By the assistance of some thinking, and much conversation, he had endeavour'd to strip himself of as many real prejudices as he could; I say real ones, because under the notion of prejudices, he knew to what dangerous heights some men have

[1] Davis IV. 27.

> proceeded. Thus prepared, he thought the numerous and gross corruptions in religion and learning might furnish matter for a satyr, that would be useful and diverting: He resolved to proceed in a manner, that should be altogether new, the world having been already too long nauseated with endless repetitions upon every subject. The abuses in religion he proposed to set forth in the allegory of the coats, and the three brothers, which was to make up the body of the discourse. Those in learning he chose to introduce by way of digressions.[1]

The danger in this account is that it encourages one to split the book into parts and to search for coherence in what qualities the objects of his satire possess together. But since Swift is ridiculing the alternatives to the good life, his targets are wildly various; and the search would only take us into a jungle.

The convenient frame is the limitation of Swift's era. If we consider the possibilities available to religious men, for instance, in 1696, we may say that those who rejected the Church of England could be either Roman Catholics or Dissenters; and if Dissenters, they were most likely to be Presbyterian. They might also belong to other Protestant sects: Independents (or Congregationalists), Baptists, Anabaptists, Quakers, and so forth; or they might doubt the divinity of Christ and be Socinians or deists. Nobody admitted to atheism ('free-thinking'), and hardly anybody would publicly accept the name of deist; in ordinary usage the type of great mystic, Boehme, was classified as a maniac. Though most of these groups felt small respect for one another, the Calvinist sects and the Roman Catholic Church were normally conceived as the most extreme opposites along the same axis. While the Roman Catholics made the bulk of the people in Ireland, they were as powerless there as in England, where they constituted a docile minority. Among the sects which acted as dangerous, expanding rivals of the Established Church, the Presbyterians (who were usually the ones intended by 'nonconformists' or 'dissenters') were easily the strongest.

In politics the situation seemed rather less knotty. Absolutism,

[1] *Tale*, p. 4.

as illustrated by Louis XIV, could have no open supporters in England (no matter how many statesman accepted French bribes), least of all when the two nations were at war; the Jacobites, for self-evident reasons, had to veil their longing for the 'abdicated' king. But the Commonwealth was a fresh memory, especially to Swift, whose Antrim had been smothered in Cromwellians. In Swift's experience, therefore, a man who disliked the constitution of 1688–9 would look much more menacing if he criticized it by republican principles than by regrets over the death of divine right. Since open advocacy of a republican constitution was not possible, such tendencies took the form of 'new-Whiggish' political manœuvres, descended from the controversy over the Exclusion Bill. An older body opposed to the court was the 'country party', or the grouping of landed gentry fearful of any demand that might increase the taxes upon their estates.

In literature and learning, one division was philosophical. Here, Swift assumed that the central position belonged to the accepted moralists, from Plutarch to Montaigne, who warned men against the frailty of their nature and praised the stern but humble pursuit of duty. Swift was able to celebrate the same virtues in Socrates as in Sir Thomas More, in Cato as in 'King Charles the Martyr'. To this plain sort of moral 'philosophy' was opposed either the old scholasticism or the new systems of Descartes and Hobbes; and in a lunatic fringe were to be found a procession of quack sciences (alchemy, astrology), hopeless researches (the longitude, squaring the circle, the philosopher's stone), occult studies (numerology, the cabbala, rosicrucianism, the work of Paracelsus). Both scholastic metaphysics and the modern (but outmoded) systems of Hobbes and Descartes appeared, to Swift, useless speculations beside the irrefutable validity of moral wisdom. The ethics of Plato (i.e., the early dialogues), Epicurus, and Zeno deserved respect in so far as they anticipated Christian doctrine; but neo-platonism, extreme stoicism, epicurean physics, all belonged to another department and had more significance as illustrating folly than as teaching virtue. Scholasticism of course possessed few defenders by this date. Long before Bacon, it had been the fashionable butt of humanist sneers.[1] But the geometrical 'method' of Descartes and the parallel, mechanistic scheme of Hobbes (whose critique of scholasticism Swift accepted) had admirers. Nevertheless, their reduction of the world and of mankind to soulless machines, their loud boasts of great accomplishments by easy devices, their dismissal of earlier philosophy as futile, their promising panaceas while supplying little to help man's condition—such appearances made it necessary for Swift to reject their work. As for the virtuosi and amateur experimenters—the Royal Society and the Dublin Philosophical Society—not only did they fall into the same class; but if Swift had any knowledge of his university teachers' extracurricular studies, the very pedants who expounded Aristotle's physics and logic must have seemed the first converts to the new (though now fading) obsession.

In polite letters the things of worth were again plain to the dullest eye: Homer, Virgil, Horace, and the usual diet of classics; Molière, Boileau, Jonson, Cowley, Milton, Temple, etc., among the moderns. Swift felt no inclination to limit his literary taste to ancient works; he enjoyed and recommended a healthy assortment of English, French, Spanish, and Italian authors. He must have agreed thoroughly with Temple's protest against 'that which is called the authority of the ancients'; for Temple wrote,

> I suppose authority may be reasonably allowed to the opinions of ancient men in the present age; but I know not why it should be so to those of men in general that lived in ages long since past; nor why one age of the world should be wiser than another; or if it be, why it should not be rather the latter than the former; as having the same advantage of the general experience of the world, that an old man has of the more particular experiments of life.[2]

Similarly, Temple, probably under St-Evremond's influence, wrote a panegyric on English dramatic humour which was

[1] Neither *A Tale of a Tub* nor *The Battle of the Books* was an attack on Bacon or on Baconian tradition.

[2] *Miscellanea* I. 68.

echoed by Congreve: 'There is no vein of that sort either antient or modern', said Temple, 'which excels or equals the humor of our plays.'[1] It is true that this judgment, though accepted by Rymer and Dennis, was later qualified by Swift in favour of 'the Spaniards and Italians'[2]; but the recognition of modern superiority remains unchanged. For Swift, the true enemies of the proponents of good taste were—under whatever comprehensive label—pedantic critics, sensational journalists, and self-advertising poetasters: e.g., Bentley, L'Estrange, Blackmore, Wesley. When he grows sarcastic against 'moderns', it is such hacks and mercenaries that he means, and not modern authors generally. That these contemptibles had sometimes the insolence to find fault with the classics, or to argue that merely being modern gave them advantages over the ancients, in no way touched the merits of a Cervantes or a Congreve.

We should remark Swift's great unconventionality in one respect, the weighting of his ridicule. Of three standard subjects for satire—women, the law, and medicine—he gave hints, but no more. With physicians and courts of justice, his experience, whether personal or second-hand, was modest; he had as yet no aspirations tied up in them, no disappointments sad enough to curse them for. Out of his inbred modesty, he denied himself the usual style of anti-feminine campaign; for he had not yet created his own expression of that theme. Anyhow, as he said, he was resolved

> to proceed in a manner, that should be altogether new, the world having been already too long nauseated with endless repetitions upon every subject[3]

—and so avoided the topics most commonly affected. There is one further motif which in a more particular way singles itself out by its absence; this is the parvenu. Except in an episode of 'Section II', where the three brothers, freshly come up from their late father's country home, try to copy city fashions, there is hardly a

[1] *Of Poetry*, p. 337. See Spingarn I. lviii-lxiii, III. 311. [2] Davis XII. 33.
[3] *Tale*, p. 4.

stab at the newly rich who pretend to be aristocrats. Plenty of middle-class traits are tumbled about: the narrow education; the hypocrisy; above all, the dissenting creeds. Yet the social climber of Molière and Congreve gets barely a nod.[1] It may be another case of recognizing and therefore rejecting a coin too current to have character; or it may have been a target so close that he might cut himself with the knife he threw at others. He was, many years later, to say (misleadingly),

> All my endeavours, from a boy, to distinguish myself, were only for want of a great title and fortune, that I might be used like a lord by those who have an opinion of my parts—whether right or wrong, it is no great matter, and so the reputation of wit or great learning does the office of a blue ribbon, or of a coach and six horses.[2]

To appreciate how false this calculated misrepresentation is, one must add up the number of times Swift let his talents and integrity spoil his career. But his saying it first, indicates how alert he was to the chance of others' saying it.

Having briefly surveyed the positives and negatives of *A Tale of a Tub*, we may turn to its occasion. Though there is no direct evidence on this problem, most scholars assume that the heaviest impulse behind the composition of the satire was Swift's year at Kilroot. The most bitter and extensive ridicule in *A Tale of a Tub* is that devoted to the Dissenters; and neither Moor Park nor London could have provided Swift with the frightening hordes of them which he met in Ulster. The long removal from Temple's presence may have enabled Swift to recognize his congenital leanings toward comic irony and to exercise them in essays which he did not preserve. Returning to Moor Park and the sight of literary eminence, as well as visiting London and receiving the stimulus of conversations there, Swift may have been impelled to make a fresh assault upon Parnassus.

Besides such currents, the only occasion discoverable which has any concreteness is Temple's fight with Wotton and Bentley. William Wotton had courteously taken issue, in print, with

[1] The nod occurs in the clothes satire of section II.

[2] Ball IV. 78.

Temple's essay on *Ancient and Modern Learning*; Richard Bentley had added, to a second edition of Wotton's book, an ungloved attack on Temple for praising the *Epistles of Phalaris*; and the Hon. Charles Boyle, later Earl of Orrery, had lent his name to an elaborate riposte, ridiculing Bentley more than Wotton. According to Swift's prejudiced account, Wotton had

> in a way not to be pardon'd, drawn his pen against a certain great man then alive [i.e., Temple], and universally reverenced for every good quality that could possibly enter into the composition of the most accomplish'd person; it was observed, how he was pleased and affected to have that noble writer call'd his adversary, and it was a point of satyr well directed, for I have been told, Sir W.T. was sufficiently mortify'd at the term. All the men of wit and politeness were immediately up in arms, through indignation, which prevailed over their contempt, by the consequences they apprehended from such an example . . . till my Lord Orrery had a little laid the spirit, and settled the ferment. But his lordship being principally engaged with another antagonist [i.e., Bentley], it was thought necessary in order to quiet the minds of men, that this opposer should receive a reprimand . . . and the author [i.e., Swift] was farther at the pains to insert one or two remarks on him in [*A Tale of a Tub*].[1]

If the satire on Dissenters was immediately inspired by Kilroot, the satire on 'corruptions in learning' might be similarly due to the *Phalaris* affair; for Bentley and Wotton take more punishment than any other persons referred to in *A Tale of a Tub*.

But the literary appeal of the book resides in its armoury of satirical techniques. The power, vigour, and joy which Swift communicates flow from the abundance of his resources. He moves so fast from one device to another, employs each with such skill, combines them so suddenly, and exhibits such manifest pleasure in his own motions, that the reader can only share his delight. The fundamental method of the satire and the irony is for Swift to make believe that he possesses the faults which he means to attack, and that he detests the qualities which he means to praise. By exaggerating and exemplifying the 'corruptions' as he

[1] *Tale*, pp. 11–12.

recommends them, he of course makes them absurd. Most of the people whom he satirizes are writers of one sort or another; so Swift can, as it were, act out their vices for us through parodies of their work. When he cannot directly bestow a fault upon 'himself', he praises it. The result is to bewilder anyone who tries to find a consistency in the character of the 'author'. As he switches masks from Presbyterian to Roman Catholic, from schoolman to Cartesian, from pedant to poetaster, from republican to absolutist, he in effect repudiates such coherence. If one should succeed in isolating some threads of uniformity, they would have to be either genuine traits of Swift himself or else qualities so vague as to be detached from the workings of this book. Either way, they become irrelevant to Swift's literary art. At the source of his incandescence there is not a consistent *persona* but an ironical pose, which wins its literary effect only to the degree that it is seen through.

Swift's more subtle and original method of ridicule is to treat each object as if it were its opposite. Swift can do this because both are false alternatives to his honest recommendations. Robert Boyle, measuring the elasticity of air, may feel contempt for a mad astrologer; but to a man convinced that moral philosophy is the only kind worth studying, the virtuoso seems as foolish as the quack. Similarly, the Puritan may loathe the papist as an idolater of anti-Christ; yet the Anglican not only spurns them both as distractions from true religion, but he also charges them with being in league.[1] Swift will therefore 'praise' the scientist for being a brilliant quack, or 'recommend' Calvin as the best guide to Rome. The modern reader has difficulty telling the opposites from the parallels, and without an annotated edition he is sure to go astray. However, Swift's contemporaries, familiar with other satires against Puritan enthusiasm, met little trouble of this sort.[2] Even today, anyone acquainted only with the plays of Jon-

[1] W. P. Holden, *Anti-Puritan Satire* (New Haven 1954), p. 61.

[2] See Clarence M. Webster, 'Swift's *Tale of a Tub* compared with Earlier Satires of the Puritans', *PMLA.*, XLVII (1932), 171–8; and 'Swift and Some Earlier Satirists of Puritan Enthusiasm', *PMLA.*, XLVIII (1933), 1141–53; also Holden, *passim.*

son or with Butler's *Hudibras* should find the clusters of associated traits which are damned in *A Tale of a Tub* at least slightly familiar. Temple seems to make such links automatically:

> I have always look'd upon alchymy in natural philosophy, to be like enthusiasm in divinity, and to have troubled the world much to the same purpose. And I should as soon fall into the study of the Rosycrucian philosophy, and expect to meet a *nymph* or a *sylph*, for a wife or a mistress, as with the elixir for my health, or philosophers stone for my fortune.[1]

Malvolio already has the combination of arrogance, hypocrisy, lechery, credulity, superstition, avarice, and commercial interests which Swift includes among the attributes of the Puritans.[2]

The most elusive but powerful of Swift's methods is his reversing the normal connotations of the 'polarized' kind of imagery which he had employed in his early poems. Emile Pons has shown how near the metaphors of *A Tale of a Tub* are to those of the odes.[3] The difference is that while in the odes they were intended to be sincere and to support the poet's argument, in the satire they are intended to be ironical and to undermine the 'author'. Illusion and truth, appearance and reality, vapour and solid, light and darkness, hero and crowd, upward flight and sudden fall, these are applied just where they do not belong. The vapour which means spirit becomes the vapour which means flatulence; the light which illuminates becomes the phosphorescence of rotting wood in the dark. The intangible is treated as tangible. This is Hobbes's sceptical method of reducing ideals to delusions; and Swift, whose flavour is remarkably close to Hobbes's, may have learned it from him. However, as Empson says, 'the language plays into [Swift's] hands' because 'the spiritual words are all derived from physical metaphors'.[4]

But this level of his technique also reflects the deepest moral

[1] *Some Thoughts upon Reviewing the Essay of Antient and Modern Learning*, in *Miscellanea* III. 255.

[2] Cf. the cluster of people in Eachard's *Free and Impartial Inquiry*, 1673.

[3] *Swift, Les Années de jeunesse et le "Conte du tonneau"* (Strasbourg 1925), pp. 246–7, 325–6, and *passim*; cf. Davis I. xvi.

[4] *Some Varieties of Pastoral*, 1935, p. 60.

implication of Swift's comic irony, a principle which he shares with St Augustine: that *inter urinas et faeces nascimur*,[1] that the seat of love is the foulest place in our body, that our most exalted, most spiritual aspirations are bound to our soiled flesh. As Montaigne says, 'Man is the onely creature, whose wants offends his owne fellowes, and he alone that in naturall actions must withdraw and sequester himselfe from those of his owne kinde. . . Whereas in other creatures, there is nothing but we love, and pleaseth our senses: so that even from their excrements and ordure, we draw not only dainties to eat, but our richest ornaments and perfumes.'[2] Swift's repeatedly forcing this truth on our attention suggests that it frightened him more than it does most (but not all) men; yet Swift was perfectly capable of keeping himself clean and falling in love. Temple, who was also fascinated by the imagery of air and vapours,[3] worried less about cleanliness and enjoyed a more conventional family life; but he never faced this paradox. Swift's warning is not to confuse the intangible with the good, or the anus with evil. For purposes of invective it may be proper to use such associations (and Swift rarely failed to do so); but in religion and morality it is disastrous to believe either that refining a sin makes it a blessing, or that the humble origin of a noble impulse makes it vicious. If one falls into the mud through staring at the heavens, the way to keep on one's path is not to darken the sky.

As the framework for these patterns, Swift often adopts the rhetorical schemes taught him at the university: the oration, the sermon, the formal praise or dispraise, the demonstration or disproof. In academic rhetoric, praise and dispraise were treated as equivalent: one ran through identical heads, consistently approving or condemning the facts marshalled under each: as St

[1] For all his gross errors of fact, attribution, and interpretation, Professor Norman O. Brown has, on this limited subject, something important to say, in his *Life against Death*, 1959, pp. 186–8.

[2] Florio's translation, ed. 1908, II. 222–3; see also K. Williams, p. 150.

[3] Temple's preoccupation with air and vapours, his referring of human character to the state of the 'finer spirits of the brain' or to the 'fumes of indigestion', and similar chains of imagery are illustrated in his *Miscellanea* I. 45–6 and *Observations upon the U.P.*, pp. 125–7, 186–7.

George Ashe said, 'All things are capable of abuse from the same topics by which they may be commended.'[1] This is one reason for Swift's power: he was accustomed to follow the same plan for opposite ends; to be ironical, he had only to change expected positives into negatives. By a reverse form of the same device, one may treat a noble character as a subject for either a direct attack or meiosis; in the dedication to Somers, Swift gives this treatment to his lordship. In rhetorical tradition, the device is an ancient one, going back to Isocrates' eulogy of Busiris, the wicked king of Egypt.

Syllogistic demonstration had an analogous effect: it was taught purely as method, detached from the truth or falsity of the result. One recalls that in the final exercises for the B.A. degree at Trinity College, each candidate had to write twenty-four syllogisms on the wrong side of each question but only twelve on the right. To be ironical, Swift therefore goes through the gestures of logic, but gives such absurd reasons and reaches such absurd conclusions that the proposition he offers to prove becomes incredible.[2] Contrariwise, he will pretend to explode a proposition which in reality is one of his rules of life; but again, though employing all the machinery of logic, he operates it on glaring fallacies, and strengthens the case which was ostensibly to be destroyed. Thus he can make great play with the school distinction between accidental and essential properties, especially in examining the central problem of the satire—the nature of man. In the logic handbooks, for instance, it was regularly explained that man was *vestitus* by accident but reasonable by essential nature. Swift merely treats dress as essential and reveals the degree to which we are (though we ought not to be) our clothes[3]; or he treats unreason (i.e., madness), rather than reason, as essential to humanity, and unmasks the vulgar conception of what a great man is.[4]

Another framework is the type of fable or anecdote which be-

[1] See Appendix D.

[2] Cf. John M. Bullitt, *Jonathan Swift and the Anatomy of Satire*, 1953, pp. 116–22.

[3] Section II. [4] Section IX.

gins to appear in the poem to Congreve. Swift has little gift for narrative plot; and he changes this defect into a satirical device by substituting bathos for climax at the turning-point of an episode. Instead of a dramatic struggle followed by triumph or tragedy, we get an impasse or an anticlimax; any action is hurriedly summarized, but the enveloping commentary, and the speeches, are extended. Swift's power lies in the extraction of many meanings from the juxtaposition of contrasting figures, usually in a static but tense tug-of-war; so his fables succeed best either when they are short or when they comprise a series of such evocative but quick juxtapositions filled out by speeches (usually one to a side), mock-moralizing, and commentary. In *A Tale of a Tub* the fable of the three brothers, though spread over four sections (II, IV, VI, XI), will be found to contain little sequential narrative but many discrete sub-fables, static speeches (i.e., not controversy progressing dialectically), and authorial exegesis. In these occupations, Swift's ear for talk is a formidable talent, and supplies an excitement which makes up for the lack of dramatic suspense. The little anecdote in the preface to *A Tale of a Tub* is a good specimen; it is of course a parable concerning the rivalry of writers for public attention:

> A mountebank in Leicester-Fields, had drawn a huge assembly about him. Among the rest, a fat unweildy fellow, half stifled in the press, would be every fit crying out, Lord! what a filthy crowd is here; Pray, good people, give way a little, Bless me! what a devil has rak'd this rabble together: Z——ds, what squeezing is this! Honest friend, remove your elbow. At last, a weaver that stood next him could hold no longer: A plague confound you (said he) for an over-grown sloven; and who (in the devil's name) I wonder, helps to make up the crowd half so much as your self? Don't you consider (with a pox) that you take up more room with that carkass than any five here? Is not the place as free for us as for you? Bring your own guts to a reasonable compass (and be d—n'd) and then I'll engage we shall have room enough for us all.[1]

[1] *Tale*, p. 46.

iii

The attitude behind the *Tale*, then, is intensely moral. The book is a criticism of men, not of theologies or tastes. Swift means to contrast two types of behaviour; the symptoms by which he identifies the wrong type are chosen from aspects of life familiar to him but not already exhausted as material for comedy. He is therefore persuaded that any one of these streaks will serve to diagnose the same underlying disease, and each therefore stands for the others. 'Modernism', properly defined, shows links with atheism; an epicurean philosopher will make a bad literary critic; for all originate in one failing: the dismissal of orthodox goods (Anglicanism, humane letters, reason) and their replacement by eccentric satisfactions (pedantry, superstition, enthusiasm). This error is too gross to arise from self-interest; Swift therefore attributes it to ignorance or madness.

What makes the *Tale* bewildering is of course that Swift does not put his real merchandise before the reader. It must be refined from the ironies which he marshals instead. Since he is attacking tendencies and not products, he can use a single example in several contexts, protecting it when it has benign implications, destroying it when it has others. Through his centrifugal symbolism, each motif can be transformed into any of the rest. They are not even limited by chronology, for human nature is stable beneath the changes of civilization: our essential character, as Temple said, 'seems to be the same in all times and places'.[1] So Jack blends with Peter, Tigellius with Bentley, critic with fanatic. But Homer as an epic poet is differentiated from Homer as a reputed seer, the statesman as patriot from the statesman as egotist, erudition as wisdom from erudition as pedantry.

It is correct to read every part of the *Tale* as an adaptation of one attitude: that wilful rejection of the Established Church, limited monarchy, classical literary standards, and rational judgment is an act of pride, and leads to corruptions in government, religion, and learning. The book would then be a collec-

[1] *An Essay upon the Original and Nature of Government*, opening sentence (*Miscellanea* I. 45).

tion of essays treating, from this point of view, several of the endless varieties of corruption. Ironically, the author pretends to admire his exhibits. He is so sure of his own creed that he assumes intelligent readers share it and will not fail to penetrate his plain sense.

Under the stunning complications of its surface, the *Tale* has an intellectual symmetry. Everywhere in it, Swift is preaching the same lesson. His countrymen's lives should possess the virtue and cultivation of Graeco-Roman antiquity, improved by Christian ethics and a cheering hope of salvation. To put themselves in this condition, they had only to accept the doctrines of the Church of England and the political constitution of 1688, to let their understanding instruct them in decisions outside the province of revelation, and to form their taste from the monuments of unageing intellect. Instead of doing so, they swarmed after crazy sectarians, threw the reins to their passions, and either ignored the classics or anatomized them to dust. Where order belonged, they established chaos.

Chapter Two

A TALE OF A TUB (II)

i

To see how the full apparatus of the satire actually works, we may look at three of its sections, beginning with a rather straightforward one, *A Digression concerning Criticks*. Before taking even this up in detail, however, we should remark that the whole intricate pattern of preliminaries and 'sections' in *A Tale of a Tub* amounts to a general parody of the elaborate arrangements often bestowed in the seventeenth century upon books whose content did not deserve them; it embodies the spirit of La Bruyère's epigram, 'Si l'on ôte de beaucoup d'ouvrages de morale l'avertissement au lecteur, l'épître dédicatoire, la préface, la table, les approbations, il reste à peine assez de pages pour mériter le nom de livre.'[1] Through the superficial formality of his pattern, Swift encourages the reader to look for a cleverly knit argument, advancing with the rhythm of reason to a set of propositions evolved from it if not proved by it. Nothing of the sort is forthcoming. The *Digression in the Modern Kind* might easily be moved to the position of 'Section x'; the *Conclusion* delivers no conclusions; 'Section xi' contains an apparently impertinent study of ears; the text is irregularly broken by files of asterisks where we expect crucial transitions. An object of this game is to show up the excessive elaboration of framework in much polite literature of the age. But such structural parody glances more specially at Dryden's *Virgil*, with its texts of the great poems set adrift among commendatory verses, separate dedications, notes, observations, a life of Virgil, a preface to the *Pastorals*, an essay on the *Georgics*, and a postscript. Similarly, the business of presenting

[1] *De l'Esprit*, no. 6.

the expository parts of *A Tale of a Tub* as 'digressions' probably points at Fontenelle's '*Digression*' *sur les Anciens et les Modernes*, in his *Poésies Pastorales* (1688).

However, the general ideas which are themselves defended in the digression on critics can be traced to Temple's *Some Thoughts upon Reviewing the Essay of Antient and Modern Learning* and to *Dr. Bentley's Dissertation Examin'd* (published over the name of Charles Boyle—and therefore called 'Boyle's' *Examination*, though largely prepared by Francis Atterbury).[1] The objects attacked are identified mainly with Richard Bentley, William Wotton, and their writings; yet Wotton here is a thoroughly subsidiary figure, receiving most of his punishment elsewhere within the *Tale*. As the fundamental method of his satire, Swift uses a parody of the polemical and erudite manner adopted by Bentley in the *Dissertation upon the Epistles of Phalaris*.[2] Finally, the internal structure of the digression is that of a formal speech, part demonstration, part eulogy.

Several of Swift's minor devices appear here. One is to mention his true values briefly near either the outset or the end of a satire, and to dismiss them with a sneer. Thus he defines two admirable senses of *critic*—an impartial judge of literature and a textual editor—but says they are both 'utterly extinct'.[3] What he does in the remainder of the 'digression' is to pretend he admires the kind of pedantry which he attributes to Bentley and Wotton. For this project, the main device is the animal metaphor which had found only casual expression in the poems. Now Swift makes capital of a phrase used in the Boyle-Bentley exchange, and pretends that the ass, in antiquity, was employed as a symbol of the 'true' critic.[4] Since he explores the rather unsubtle implications of this theme through a parody of Bentley's own philological proofs, his success is irresistible.

The exhilarating texture of the section depends more on Swift's wild, punning conceits than on any other ingredient; as a

[1] See Temple, *Miscellanea* III. 256–60; Boyle's *Examination*, pp. 224–7.

[2] See Miriam K. Starkman, *Swift's Satire on Learning in A Tale of a Tub* (Princeton 1950), pp. 101–4.

[3] *Tale*, p. 93.

[4] Boyle's *Examination*, p. 220; Starkman, pp. 103–4.

device of comic irony, these have an almost generous flavour: the reader feels that the author is grateful to his objects for giving him such happy occasions to exercise his intellectual muscles. Here, for example, is a figure in which Swift compares critics with deadly substances which never change their natures; the punning close depends on the fact that hashish and a gallows rope are both derived from the hemp plant:

> For it hath been observed both among antients and moderns, that a true critick hath one quality in common with a whore and an alderman, never to change his title or his nature; that a grey critick has been certainly a green one, the perfections and acquirements of his age being only the improved talents of his youth; like hemp, which some naturalists inform us, is bad for *suffocations*, tho' taken but in the seed.[1]

Another example, almost adolescent in its rawness, is the explanation of why critics are like ancient mirrors; here the joke hinges on the moral connotations of 'brass' and on the use of 'mercury' (which was of course the backing of glass mirrors), in Swift's day, to signify wit:

> Now, whoever considers, that the *mirrors* of the antients were made of *brass*, and *sine mercurio*, may presently apply the two principal qualifications of a *true modern critick*, and consequently, must needs conclude, that these have always been, and must be for ever the same. For, *brass* is an emblem of duration, and when it is skilfully burnished, will cast *reflections* [i.e., aspersions] from its own *superficies*, without any assistance of *mercury* from behind.[2]

Swift's tone suggests the cocksure arrogance of one who has taken over wholesale the opinions of others. The quarrel is expressly with 'pedantry'. Temple said he had 'no mind to enter the list, with such a mean, dull, unmannerly pedant'.[3] What may trouble the modern reader is the confusion, all around, between manners and morals. In his attack upon pedantry as exemplified by some university dons,[4] Swift was following the consensus of

[1] *Tale*, p. 101. [2] *Ibid.*, p. 103. [3] *Ibid.*, p. xlviii.

[4] It would be wrong to describe the Temple-Boyle-Swift campaign as either an

thoughtful men, from Montaigne to Locke. When vulgarized among polite gentlemen in the late seventeenth century, the attitude assumed the form of a 'fashionable flight from learning'. It was, said John Norris in 1678, 'a piece of *errant pedantry*, and defect of good breeding to start any question of learning in company'; while, said Norris, the fellows of the Royal Society might improve in learning, 'in point of *civility* they decline'. As Boyle put it, 'The first and surest mark of a *pedant* is, to write without observing the receiv'd rules of civility and common decency: and without distinguishing the characters of those he writes to, or against: For pedantry in the pen is what clownishness is in conversation; it is *written illbreeding*.' Pedantry thus becomes a matter of manners; and for this invidious distinction anyone not a gentleman by birth is implicitly at a disadvantage; Bentley's fault is to be an upstart. Swift was later to fling contempt upon such notions, but in 1696 he agreed with Temple, who had assigned much of the blame for the decline of true learning to

> the scorn of pedantry, which the shallow, the superficial, and the sufficient among scholars, first drew upon themselves, and very justly, by pretending to more than they had, or to more esteem, than what they [could] deserve; by broaching it in all places, at all times, upon all occasions; and by living so much among themselves, or in their closets and cells, as to make them unfit for all other business, and ridiculous in all other conversations.[1]

Bentley's *hubris* was admittedly colossal. He was the greatest classical scholar in England before the nineteenth century; but his erudition hardly excuses his offensive condescension. Yet though he gave ample provocation, and though the answers of both Swift and Atterbury ('Boyle') are so clever that their lack of

---

attack upon or defence of the universities as such: Bentley, like Temple, was an ornament of Cambridge, and 'Boyle' regarded himself as the loyal son of Christ Church, Oxford (*Examination*, sigg. A4ᵛ–5).

[1] Temple, *Miscellanea* II. 71; W. E. Houghton, 'The English Virtuoso in the Seventeenth Century', *JHI.*, III (1942), 216–17; T. Scott XI. 49–57; Boyle's *Examination*, p. 93, and cf. p. 222. Wotton himself made remarks sympathetic with Temple's position (*Reflections*, pp. 415–16), and Boyle praised Wotton's book for 'a vein of learning running through it, where there is no ostentation of it' (p. 25).

scholarship is irrelevant, the attacks have a hollowness which finally weakens their achievement, because the clergymen and the scholars really belong in the same party. For all his arrogance, moreover, Bentley stood solidly behind his *Dissertation*; he did not pretend to be writing anything except a piece of scholarship, but classical philology was half his life; not only are his facts sound: his deepest feelings are bound up in the work; it is his own exposition of his original ideas. *A Tale of a Tub* was anonymous; *Dr. Bentley's Dissertation Examin'd* was pseudonymous; but everybody knew who was the author of both the *Dissertation upon Phalaris* and the *Reflections upon Ancient and Modern Learning*.

What Swift resented was not in fact the kind of learning—corrupt or pure—which his victims possessed. Wotton had, he said, 'in a way not to be pardon'd', drawn his pen against Temple; 'all the men of wit and politeness' were up in arms.[1] Yet the writers of Boyle's *Examination* say Wotton 'is modest and decent, speaks generally with respect of those he differs from'.[2] Wotton actually fought, as a modern scholar says, 'in reasonable and accepted terms, and distinguished himself by the thoroughness and justness of his analysis. Although Swift engaged in a good deal of personal diatribe against him, Wotton's ideas were perfectly orthodox.'[3] Temple, furthermore, never seems to have asked Swift to write against either Bentley or Wotton.[4] After all, a riposte had been published which Temple had approved; and Swift's parody of Bentley comes perilously near to being as well a parody of Boyle. One suspects that Swift's hopes were treading on his sense of reality, and that he felt eager to render a service which no one had called for, because while the talents of the participants were inferior to his own, their prestige was much higher. Who, after all, was an obscure Irish parson to put himself in the place of the distinguished baronet and the heir of a great earl? Was not Swift showing that he was a better ally for Temple than the Christ Church wits? that a Wotton in Swift's clothing could outlord the Hon. Charles Boyle?

[1] *Tale*, pp. 11–12. [2] *Ibid.*, p. 11, n. 2. [3] Starkman, pp. 15–16.
[4] *Tale*, p. xlviii.

At the heart of the digression on critics one finds little that Swift really stood for. The arrogance which he denounced appears more in him than Wotton (who is a peripheral figure in this digression but a focus of the ridicule elsewhere). Swift fundamentally respected learning of the sort which Bentley exemplifies. Neither victim could be described as a hack pamphleteer or a poetaster. Swift's attack on Wotton (a parson his own age) was not for pedantry but for daring to criticize Temple, however courteously; and Swift may be said to have borrowed his emotion. The wit, for all its fanciful exuberance, is narrow in connotation and lacks the rich cross-references to religion and to the human body that will be found in other sections; it touches no moral depths. The comic thrusts are skinny word-play, lacking 'humour'. The 'true critic' is indeed apotheosized so that the link with Bentley becomes a shadow; the whole essay is a dazzling performance; yet these admirable transmogrifications and pyrotechnics are not what we mean by *Swift*.

ii

The remarkable violence of Swift's irony is not only due to his 'polarized' imagery and to his playing foul against fair with the human body, but also to what might be called his nettle-grasping instinct. He often writes as though he were disproving the insinuation that he feels uneasy about his subject. It is as if he wished to appear so sure of his own piety, his continence, his modesty, his rectitude, that common prudential maxims should not apply to him. In the holiest places he could affect to sound coarse—not out of irreverence but as a demonstration that his faith was too serene for any such expressions to impugn it. What he fails to anticipate is that other worshippers may hear the coarseness without appreciating the piety.

This leaning belongs to the hypocrite-in-reverse character which is often assigned to Swift. Through it, he separates himself from those who substitute the show for the reality in religion. By caricaturing the postures of Tartufe, he does not ridicule the church but the hypocrisy. To an uninformed outsider, unfortunately, the two sorts of ridicule look alike. Similarly, in literary forms, the mock-heroic Swift does not attack the epic but the pretensions of men who hope to achieve greatness by putting on the trappings of Achilles. To some outsiders, however, the parody seems an affront not to pretensions but to poetry. Yet the genius who assumes that his religion or his literary taste is unquestioned does not stoop to concern himself with their blunders. Hence the troubles of Molière and Swift with their contemporaries.

'Section XI' of *A Tale of a Tub* has some good illustrations of Swift's nettle-grasping. It is part of the satire upon Jack, the one of the three brothers in Swift's religious allegory who stands for Calvinism. In spite of the explosive effect of the satire, Swift, in his charges against the Puritans, is 'far less fierce and unrelenting' than many of his predecessors. His ultimate conception of Jack is, after all, 'more of a zealous fool, with no sense or reason in him' than of a cunning, dangerous Tartufe. Furthermore, much of Swift's material was not very fresh: he said 'little that was new about the Puritan alone. Many of his most amusing thrusts were a century old when he wrote them.'[1] Even motifs which seem 'characteristic' of Swift had been exploited by a train of writers including not only obvious names like Burton, Jonson, and Butler but also Sir Thomas Browne, Meric Casaubon, Henry More, and John Eachard. Accusations that Puritans mistook flatulence for inspiration, that their zeal was a cover for sexual excitement, that they suffered from a martyr complex, that women were peculiarly susceptible to enthusiasm—were staples of such literature.[2]

Swift's audacity in manipulating these motifs is what makes them his own. In a satire on predestination, for instance, he has Jack first bang his nose against a post and then claim that 'Providence thought fit' to arrange this collision, and again that 'Providence either forgot, or did not think it convenient to twitch me

[1] Webster, in *PMLA.*, XLVII. 177–8.

[2] Webster, *ibid.*, XLVIII. 1141–53; see also William P. Holden, *Anti-Puritan Satire* (New Haven 1954), pp. 40–3 and *passim*. One burlesque of Puritan sermons was entitled *A Tale in a Tub* (John Taylor, 1642; see Holden, pp. 73–5).

by the elbow, and give me notice to avoid it.' One wonders how Swift could have been puzzled to find Wotton describing such phrases, delivered by an ordained clergyman, as 'a direct prophanation of the majesty of God'. Later, Swift himself confessed the rashness of his involving the deity so directly in a piece of broad ridicule, when he altered 'Providence' to 'Nature' and 'Fortune'.[1]

Not only does Swift use words which in an absolute sense appear shocking, but his similes have cross-references to other bold implications of his argument. Although, therefore, 'Section XI' possesses less fluency and a less regular organization than the digression on critics, its imagery has more depth and the whole essay more power. In Jack, Swift treats the doctrines, practices, and evolution of the Calvinists, employing far-fetched tropes which would nevertheless be easily penetrated by an audience familiar with the theme. The most bizarre of these tropes is a history of ears which breaks into the already rough-hewn tale of Jack.[2] This operates analogously to the 'ass' in the digression on critics.

As Swift develops the 'ear' figure, he suggests two fundamental connotations of Puritan zeal: political rebellion and sexual excitement. Ear-clipping was a penalty for certain crimes; and the Puritans, by cutting their hair short, gave themselves round heads and prominent ears. Swift can therefore suggest, through the rise and fall of ears, the Civil War and the Restoration. But he also draws a parallel between ears above and genitals below; by such displacement he suggests that in their avowed desire for spiritual light, the Puritans were really looking for erotic pleasure. A weaker but distinct innuendo is that the dissenting minister's overwrought, sensational preaching—addressed to the 'ears' of the congregation—was a substitute for true piety rationally expounded. Finally, there is a reference to philosophy; for Swift emphasizes the eagerness of the ignorant Puritan worship-

[1] *Tale*, p. 193 and n. 1; p. 324.

[2] Cf. the faces pictured on the title page of *Heads of All Fashions*, reproduced in Holden, p. 62.

pers to hear the minister's wild speculation; their idle, dangerous curiosity, undermining established wisdom, is the kind of hunger which maintains the systems of the scholastics and the Cartesians alike.

> 'Tis true, indeed, that while this *island* of ours, was under the *dominion of grace*, many endeavours were made to improve the growth of *ears* once more among us. The proportion of largeness, was not only lookt upon as an ornament of the *outward* man, but as a type of grace in the *inward*. Besides, it is held by naturalists, that if there be a protruberancy of parts in the *superiour* region of the body, as in the *ears* and *nose*, there must be a parity also in the *inferior*: And therefore in that truly pious age, the *males* in every assembly, according as they were gifted, appeared very forward in exposing their *ears* to view, and the regions about them.[1]

One of the happiest extensions of 'cross-referential' overtones is the treatment of avowed opposites as equivalents. Much as the Calvinists might fear the Established Church, it was Rome that loomed for them as the anti-Christ. Swift therefore has a fine passage describing Jack as if he were Peter:

> Their lodgings were at the two most distant parts of the town, from each other; and whenever their occasions, or humors called them abroad, they would make choice of the oddest unlikely times, and most uncouth rounds they could invent; that they might be sure to avoid one another: Yet after all this, it was their perpetual fortune to meet. The reason of which, is easy enough to apprehend: For, the phrenzy and the spleen of both, having the same foundation, we may look upon them as two pair of compasses, equally extended, and the fixed foot of each, remaining in the same center; which, tho' moving contrary ways at first, will be sure to encounter somewhere or other in the circumference.[2]

In the abruptness with which he introduces such overtones, the speed with which he circulates among them, and the nakedness with which he exhibits them, Swift seems to be protesting too much that these things hold no terrors for him—that *he* is not worried or tempted by political unrest, by lust, by emotional

[1] *Tale*, p. 201. [2] *Ibid.*, pp. 198–9.

oratory, by Hobbes and Descartes. Both as a moralist and as a literary artist, Swift miscalculates; for however worthy his ideals may be, and however sinful his opponents, he never reckons with the fright which he may give to the reader. By their very success, his methods of communicating a violence of feeling distract one from Swift's values and his targets both: one looks instead at the author, and marvels at his audacity.

Here (in part) is Swift's satire on Jack's obsession with Scripture as the sole recourse in every function of life:

> He had a way of working it into any shape he pleased; so that it served him for a night-cap when he went to bed, and for an umbrello in rainy weather. He would lap a piece of it about a sore toe, or when he had fits, burn two inches under his nose; or if any thing lay heavy on his stomach, scrape off, and swallow as much of the powder as would lie on a silver penny, they were all infallible remedies. With analogy to these refinements, his common talk and conversation ran wholly in the phrase of his Will [i.e., Scripture], and he circumscribed the utmost of his eloquence within that compass, not daring to let slip a syllable without authority from thence. Once at a strange house, he was suddenly taken short, upon an urgent juncture, whereon it may not be allowed too particularly to dilate; and being not able to call to mind, with that suddenness, the occasion required, an authentick phrase for demanding the way to the backside; he chose rather as the more prudent course, to incur the penalty in such cases usually annexed. Neither was it possible for the united rhetorick of mankind to prevail with him to make himself clean again: Because having consulted the Will upon this emergency, he met with a passage near the bottom (whether foisted in by the transcriber, is not known) which seemed to forbid it.[1]

To digest such a satire without suspecting possible sneers at one's own beliefs, one would have had to be not only Protestant but Anglican, and not only Anglican but a high-churchman, and not only a high-churchman but a very special distruster of other Protestant sects. In 1688, comprehension—or the inclusion of the Presbyterians in the Anglican communion—had been 'a high-church policy'; Sancroft himself (unlike Francis Turner) had

[1] *Ibid.*, pp. 190–1.

been 'a warm friend of members of the foreign Reformed churches in England and a cordial advocate of comprehension at home'. On Swift's treatment of the Roman Catholics a parallel, if weaker, comment can be made; for although the period (largely war time) from 1685 to 1714 was one of open hostility between the Gallican and Anglican churches, a rapprochement of the two had been canvassed, before the revocation of the Edict of Nantes, by men like Bossuet and Wake; and when Wake became Archbishop of Canterbury (1716), he was to revive the project; even during the war years, nonjuring Jacobites like Charles Leslie and Henry Dodwell sought to heal this schism. Similarly, while Swift seems to have set great store by the authority of the primitive church, the reputation of the pre-Nicene fathers was sinking quickly between 1680 and 1730.[1]

In theology as in philology, Swift's note of confidence should not imply that all right-thinking folk stood behind him, but that he was wholeheartedly borrowing the standards of a small, powerful group. As a contrast, we may quote a statement made by Sir William Temple's old tutor, Cudworth, in 1674: 'Certainly in our English Church, just as in Noah's Ark were all sorts of animals (if I may so express it), are all kinds of Protestants: Calvinists, Remonstrants [i.e., Arminians], and I believe even Socinians, all dwelling here, united with no apparent discord in one and the same communion.'[2] In the face of such varied evidence, Swift's apology for the *Tale* can only be described as question-begging—viz.,

> Why should any clergyman of our church be angry to see the follies of fanaticism and superstition exposed, tho' in the most ridiculous manner? since that is perhaps the most probable way to cure them, or at least to hinder them from farther spreading. Besides, tho' it was not intended for their perusal; it raillies nothing but what they preach against. It contains nothing to provoke them by the least scurillity upon their persons or their functions. It celebrates the Church of England as the most perfect of all others in discipline and

[1] Norman Sykes, *From Sheldon to Secker* (Cambridge 1959), pp. 82–7, 114–32, 142; George Every, *The High Church Party 1688–1718*, 1956, pp. 70–3.

[2] Rosalie L. Colie, *Light and Enlightenment* (Cambridge 1957), p. 40.

doctrine, it advances no opinion they reject, nor condemns any they receive.[1]

Unless, in fact, one either agreed with the details of Swift's principles, or else felt disrespect for all churches, one could hardly read such a passage as that on Jack's addiction to Scripture, and not flinch. Furthermore, by deliberately narrowing the limits of a sympathetic audience within the community of Christians, Swift effectively enlarged it outside; and people of moderate piety might easily question the religion of a priest who seemed to encourage scepticism. Thus he laid himself open to charges which he could not refute without weakening the very self-confidence which lay behind his provocations.

[1] *Tale*, p. 5.

Chapter Three

A TALE OF A TUB (III)

i

But the full force of Swift's abilities is only felt when he widens the angle of his satire to include everybody. The logic is that if Puritans, pedants, mechanical philosophers, and the rest are so numerous, they must represent corruptions which are incipient in all, and which Swift associates with irrationality. Normally, these are considered not essential properties but diseases, and in that sense accidents. Our most essential property is, by contrast, said to be reason, or the opposite of madness. Swift stands the traditional contrast on its head, making madness the essential property and reason the corruption.[1] To prove the paradox, he shows how much better we can account for human history and behaviour as the outcomes of madness than as the effect of reason; and his demonstration is the material of *A Digression concerning the Original, the Use and Improvement of Madness in a Commonwealth.*

This digression embodies an irony familiar to Swift's generation and recognized throughout the eighteenth century: that the corruption of reason can be cured by reason alone. Our restless itch for knowledge, when it trains the reason upon proper objects, brings wisdom; but when it thrusts the reason upon objects outside reason's province, brings delusion. As Temple said,

> The same faculty of reason, which gives mankind the great advantage and prerogative over the rest of the creation, seems to make the greatest default of humane nature; and subjects it to more troubles, miseries, or at least disquiets of life, than any of its fellow creatures.[2]

[1] Martin Price, *Swift's Rhetorical Art* (New Haven 1953), p. 93.
[2] *Miscellanea* II. 75.

Yet we can be reclaimed from delusion by nothing but reason, 'called in, to allay those disorders which it self had raised'.[1] In attributing both political and philosophical upheavals to insatiable, idle curiosity, operating by way of the corruption of the understanding, Swift is not original, either. Although the bond between irrationality and evil—knaves and fools—is one of his leitmotivs, it is an article which he shares with the longest line of Western moralists. 'This restless humor, so general and natural to mankind', writes Temple,

> is a weed that grows in all soils, and under all climates, but seems to thrive most, and grow fastest, in the best; 'tis raised easier by the more sprightly wits and livelier imaginations, than by grosser and duller conceptions. . . From this original fountain issue those streams of faction, that with some course of time and accidents, overflow the wisest constitutions of governments and laws, and many times treat the best princes and truest patriots, like the worst tyrants and most seditious disturbers of their country.[2]

Thus the revolutions of governments and of intellectual systems are traced to the same source. Eighty years after Swift's satire, Gibbon, when excoriating the neo-Platonists, still nursed this tradition: in his version, the link is made between religious, philosophical, and civil disorders:

> By mistaking the true object of philosophy, their labours contributed much less to improve than to corrupt the human understanding. The knowledge that is suited to our situation and powers, the whole compass of moral, natural, and mathematical science, was neglected by the new Platonists, whilst they exhausted their strength in the verbal disputes of metaphysics, attempted to explore the secrets of the invisible worlds. . . As they agreed with the Christians in a few mysterious points of faith, they attacked the remainder of their theological system with all the fury of civil war.[3]

Still later, we find Hazlitt, whose moral constitution shared several ingredients with Swift's, independently asserting the tra-

[1] *Miscellanea* II. 87.

[2] *Miscellanea* III. 10–11 (*Of Popular Discontents*); cf. *Tale*, p. 169.

[3] *Decline and Fall*, ed. Bury, 1900, I. 392–3.

dition in its widest, most 'Swiftian' form, and tying the irrational to ultimate evil:

> There is a love of power in the mind independent of the love of good, and this love of power, when it comes to be opposed to the spirit of good, and is leagued with the spirit of evil to commit it with greediness, is wickedness... This character implies the fiend at the bottom of it; and is mixed up pretty plentifully (according to my philosophy) in the untoward composition of human nature. It is this craving after what is prohibited, and the force of contrast adding its zest to the violations of reason and propriety, that accounts for the excesses of pride, of cruelty, and lust.[1]

In Hazlitt's formulation, the principle becomes so general that it seems neither a special insight nor part of a current, but simply an attitude which occurs to many moralists when they reflect upon the vagaries of human behaviour. But in Swift the attitude has unique depth and strength because its roots are religious and emotional, starting from that centre where his innermost ideals met his innermost feelings. Although Swift's illustrations come from a great range of social types, the prime specimen always before his eyes is the fanatic: the digression on madness takes the psychology of religious zeal to be the paradigm of all folly.

Since, however, the object defended in the digression is reason, one must consider that before examining the targets attacked. Those faculties which nowadays are separated into intelligence, moral insight, and intuition were, in Swift's time, still included under a single head: the same power that enables us to tell true from false, he assumed, also distinguishes right from wrong; and in the shape of 'discursive reason', or ratiocination, it produces the kind of logical analysis of which Euclid is the model.

The material on which the reason or understanding works is given to it by the senses, and the record of their reports is the memory. However, there is also a power which can take the remembered sensations and divide and recombine them in new patterns independent of experience: this is the imagination or fancy; and it falls peculiarly under the influence of our feelings or

[1] *Selected Essays*, ed. Geoffrey Keynes, 1930, p. 274.

passions; for those people whose emotions are least controllable have the most powerful fancies and the weakest understanding. The lure of the imagination is the pleasure which it can give, illusory perhaps, but more attractive than the honest reports of the senses or the impartial analysis of reason. As Temple said (with echoes of Hobbes),

> All the pleasures of sense, that any man can enjoy . . . grow fainter with age, and duller with use; must be revived with intermissions, and wait upon the returns of appetite, which are no more at the call of the rich, than the poor. . . But the pleasures of the imagination, as they heighten and refine the very pleasures of sense, so they are of larger extent, and longer duration.[1]

Although, therefore, the senses are indispensable, they should only serve, not dominate, the reason; and although the imagination is not essentially bad, it must never displace either the senses as the windows or the reason as the governor of the soul. But the understanding itself has boundaries too; and these seemed to Swift most apparent in the realm of discursive (rather than moral or intuitive) reason; for when that is given free play, it can become dangerous speculation. Modern readers have trouble following the twists of the digression on madness because Swift was more anxious about the menace of speculation than the menace of conformity, whether in religion, philosophy, politics, or learning. He shared Locke's wish,

> to prevail with the busy mind of man to be more cautious in meddling with things exceeding its comprehension, to stop when it is at the utmost extent of its tether, and to sit down in a quiet ignorance of those things which, upon examination, are found to be beyond the reach of our capacities.[2]

Or as Swift would say in 1712, 'True learning, like all true merit, is easily satisfied; while the false and counterfeit is perpetually craving, and never thinks it has enough.'[3]

[1] *Observations upon the U.P.*, sigg. A6^{v}–7.
[2] *Essay concerning Human Understanding*, I. i. 4. [3] Davis IV. 20.

It is in problems of faith above all that the issue grew urgent; and here it was expressed as a conflict between credulity and incredulity.[1] The arguments by which Anglican divines attacked the papist doctrine of transubstantiation, for instance, had to be such as would not boomerang against their own doctrine of the trinity. To protect their own creed, they used a distinction between what was 'above' and what was 'contrary to' reason. While transubstantiation was said to be contrary to reason, the trinity was said to be above reason. Some quotations from South and Tillotson will make the case clear:

> The case between transubstantiation and the Trinity is very different; the former being contradicted by the judgment of that faculty [i.e., the senses], of which it is properly the object; the latter being not at all contradicted but only not comprehended by the faculty [i.e., the reason], to which the judgment and cognizance of it does belong.
>
> He that can once be brought to contradict or deny his senses, is at an end of certainty; for what can a man be certain of if he be not certain of what he sees? In some circumstances our senses may deceive us, but no faculty deceives us so little and so seldom: And when our senses do deceive us, even that errour is not to be corrected without the help of our senses.
>
> Credulity is certainly a fault as well as infidelity: and he who said, *blessed are they that have not seen and yet have believed*, hath no where said, *blessed are they that have seen and yet have not believed*, much less, *blessed are they that believe directly contrary to what they see.*[2]

With these commonplace distinctions before us, we may state the Anglican position generally as that the better one reasoned, the more Christian one became, that revelation and the understanding, being in perfect harmony, must strengthen one another. Unreason and sin become thus almost equivalent. Through such arguments, moreover, one disposes not only of Puritan 'enthusiasm' and papist superstition, but also of mechanical systems like those of Epicurus, Descartes, and Hobbes.

[1] Cf. Andrew Marvell, *Mr. Smirke* and *Defence of John Howe, passim.*

[2] Robert South, *Sermons*, 1824, II, 494–5 and *passim*; John Tillotson, *A Discourse against Transubstantiation*, 1684, pp. 38, 42.

By leaving no place for 'spirit' in the Christian sense, by dividing faith from reason, and by making the laws of nature (human or physical) independent of immediate Providence, the 'systems' denied exactly what the Anglican position affirmed. Hence it is that with the digression on madness Swift 'satirizes, in the greatest detail, the contemporary neo-Epicurean and Hobbesian philosophies'.[1]

ii

Though the implications of the digression on madness are complex indeed, its design is straightforward; for Swift's stratagem of camouflaging his real movements under an appearance of systematic argument appears in each expository 'section' of the *Tale*. The digression on madness has two divisions: the theory of madness and the application of the theory. In the first, he begins with two propositions: that the greatest deeds are due to madness and that madness is caused by vapour on the brain. As evidence, he uses three categories: acts of military conquest (Henry IV and Louis XIV of France), acts of philosophic innovation (Epicurus and Descartes), and acts of religious innovation (the nonconformist sects). By analysis of these classes, Swift proves that new kingdoms, new philosophies, and new religions are all established by madmen. He provides only asterisks where there should be an explanation of how individual differences make the same madness lead to military activity in some, philosophical in others, and religious in others. The entire first section ends with two famous paragraphs on the function and value of madness.

The second division begins with two propositions: that madness is brought on by an excess of vapours; and that this excess, properly disposed, would be of service to the community. Swift takes his examples from Bedlam Hospital and shows how each kind of lunatic, correctly adapted, could fulfil some ecclesiastic, civil, or military responsibility. A violent maniac becomes a colonel; a babbler, a lawyer; an anxious compulsive, a city merchant; a megalomaniac and pathological liar, a courtier; a

[1] Starkman, p. xix.

coprophiliac, a physician; and 'a taylor run mad with pride', a bishop. In a final paragraph he extends the plan to include other persons puffed up with vapours, such as fops, musicians, authors, and statesmen.

This scheme has an air of logical discourse and the shape of a formal speech. It is a defence of reason in the Erasmian design of a praise of folly, and its development is a parody of logic. Swift makes one expect normal procedures: a principle followed by illustrations; a series of postulates and corollaries building up to a proved conclusion. He then frustrates this expectation by using cases which contradict his ostensible principle, or arguments which defy his premise. If the reader knows the real, unexpressed proposition which is being advanced, he will see that the proofs and examples do, ironically, support it. But they do so in no articulated form. The composition which results amounts to a recasting of the *Moriae Encomium* two centuries after the original.[1]

To Erasmus as well may be traced, ultimately, Swift's inverted *decorum personae*, his acting the dunce (here and elsewhere) because he is exposing fools. But only in the work of Marvell had Swift's talent for applying that principle been adumbrated. Pretending that his *Rehearsal Transpros'd* must take a clownish form because its victim, the Bishop of Oxford, is a clown, Marvell has to excuse himself when he slips into serious argument, for that is a violation, as it were, of the crazy decorum; otherwise, however, Marvell consistently makes his own pose a caricature of the one he attributes to the bishop.[2] Swift has no serious argument to apologize for; but he picks up Marvell's comical *decorum* and embodies it in the most brilliant shape it has yet received.

The second of the two central paragraphs of the digression can be anatomized to show his full, elaborate method in detail. Here,[3] Swift says that knowledge of surfaces (credulity) is better than knowledge of interiors (curiosity). To prove this, he says what

[1] Cf. Pons, pp. 385–8; Ronald Paulson, *Theme and Structure in Swift's Tale of a Tub* (New Haven 1960), pp. 79–80.

[2] John S. Coolidge, 'Martin Marprelate, Marvell, and *Decorum Personae* as a Satirical Theme', *PMLA.*, LXXIV (1959), 526–32.

[3] *Tale*, pp. 173–4.

would seem to argue against it: that man's reason pries into the depths while his senses are satisfied with appearances. To prove this in turn, he says what again seems a contradiction: that reason is correct (though therefore to be *not* followed but rejected) in deciding that most bodies, when investigated, prove worthless within though attractive without. The conclusion is that since outsides are thus 'superior' to insides, we ought to make the most of our appearance and ignore our essence.

The real proposition here is that man's moral essence or reason —his inside—is infinitely more important than his physical accidents—the outside. Reason and judgment are therefore analytical or introspective, while the senses, passions, and imagination (when divorced from the understanding) may be tricked by appearances. It is better to be sadly wise and know oneself, Swift really says, than to be complacently self-deceived.

Such axioms are neither argued nor ironically implied in a coherent order; they are repeatedly illustrated by innuendo, through absurd assertions and fantastic instances. In this paragraph, for example, Swift says with a straight face that surface counts for more than substance, but means ironically that it is worth nothing by comparison. He says with contempt that reason is mistakenly occupied with internals, but he means seriously that reason is correct in its business. He says that natural law requires us to put our 'best furniture forward' but means that unnatural vanity is behind man's obsession with show. Supposedly to illustrate how much appearances are preferable to reality, he comments, 'Last week I saw a woman *flay'd*, and you will hardly believe, how much it altered her person for the worse.' Between the bland understatement of the reaction, and the loathesomeness of the event, lies a gap the parallel to which separates the foolishness of the narrator in being surprised, from the inevitability of the operation's causing disfigurement. The least consequence of flaying is its effect on the victim's beauty. The agony is what matters. Only grotesque immorality would see things so far out of proportion: pride is so blind that hellish pain holds less terror for it than bad looks. Ostensibly, the anecdote shows the value of a good complexion; really, Swift is saying that irrational vanity will consider ugliness the most deplorable result of being skinned alive.

The succession of these assertions and instances has a pseudo-logic in accordance with the outward argument. But actually it is irrational, except to this extent: that only certain motifs are repeated, that each of them connotes others, and that they are juxtaposed so as to heighten their effectiveness through contrast and paradox. The complete digression admits of interpretation by this method; and its force is that only madness can account for the zeal of those men who, rather than live at peace with orthodoxy, reason, and good taste, insist on upsetting themselves and others with dangerous, or at best unprofitable, newfangleness.

By madness Swift implies two features: an extravagant addiction to one's own opinions and an excess of vapour on the brain. Stubborn insistence upon personal convictions—however unlikely or iconoclastic—had another name besides madness: pride. To be puffed up with clouds of self-importance meant to be filled with the sin of vanity. Swift is once more ironical when he says madness causes great and beneficent innovations; for he means that zeal against orthodoxy is the growth of egoism. What to a lunatic looks like progress, to a sane man looks like pride; and this was Temple's judgment of natural philosophy.

If such 'madness' be opposed to reason, we face the medieval definition of a person as 'the individual substance of a rational nature': the common element, what we *share* with others, is by this definition reason; the separate element, whereby we *differ* from others, is will. Hence, the more wilful, proud, sceptical we are, the more irrational and individual we are; on the contrary, the more reasonable, the more like others. Madness, sin, and perverse individuality are thus essentially opposed to sanity and conventionality. As Hooker said, 'The most certain token of evident goodness is, if the general persuasion of all men do so account it.'[1]

[1] *Laws of Ecclesiastical Polity* I. viii. 3; cf. Michael Oakeshott's introduction to his edition of Hobbes's *Leviathan* (Oxford 1946), p. lv and n., also p. 28 of the text.

So it is that Swift contrasts curiosity and credulity. Curiosity may be bad when it idly and insatiably pokes into the foundations of settled, unsearchable beliefs; for it then becomes the pride or incredulity which caused Adam's fall. But curiosity is good and reasonable when it encourages self-criticism within the orthodox framework, when it enhances modesty or destroys falsehood. Credulity, however, is bad in so far as it idly follows a wicked or irrational authority, as it accepts immoral assurances as to the grace of an individual, as it strengthens complacency and corruptions.

In this digression, Swift reaches the height of his literary achievement. He has given elaborately formal, evocative expression to a rich, powerful moral insight. It was to be almost another thirty years before he would repeat, and even surpass, the achievement; and that was to be only once, in Gulliver's voyage to the Houyhnhnms.

Chapter Four

THE BATTLE OF THE BOOKS

The Battle of the Books is one of Swift's most detached and enjoyable productions. It is a shame that the work must be closely identified with its occasion, because Swift employs the presumed arguments as an excuse for independent comedy. To make the *Battle of the Books* into a chapter in the history of ideas can be as misleading as to make *Le Malade Imaginaire* an illustration of seventeenth-century medical practice. Furthermore, the ancients-moderns *querelle* was not—as has been asserted—a conflict between emerging science and reactionary humanism, but an essential part of the humanistic tradition itself.[1] Even moral issues are almost irrelevant here; Swift's humour is ultimately as remote from 'ideas' as a brilliant piece of comic prose can be. Yet the achievement arises from a cross-play of allusions; and until these are recognized, the charm of the 'history' cannot be appreciated. Unless one knows that Dryden translated Virgil, one misses the wit of his giving Virgil 'rusty iron' armour in exchange for gold. If one does know it, however, the episode becomes less an argument that the modern is inferior to the ancient than a little farce out of *commedia dell'arte*. The biographical, moral, literary, and intellectual aspects of the *Battle of the Books* constitute its accidents, not its essence.

If we nevertheless examine the work as a moral satire, its positive basis will be seen to be the teachings of Temple in his essay *Of Poetry*. The *Battle* is a defence of taste as an expression of character; and Swift implies ultimately that a good book is one which a 'good' man approves. By this principle one may use literature as

[1] Hans Baron, 'The *Querelle* of the Ancients and the Moderns', *J.H.I.*, xx (Jan. 1959), 3–22.

a measure of social health. In a good society, bad writers cannot flourish because they will find no readers.

The enemies of good taste are those who offend on both sides: the poetasters, hack journalists, pedants, who manufacture trash; and the corrupt judges who read and recommend it. That Swift gives this class the name of 'moderns' is less an attempt at definition than a tribute to Sir William Temple; for Swift traces their descent from antiquity. Similarly, the leaders of the moderns happen to be identified as William Wotton and Richard Bentley not because these are the worst writers or worst critics of the age but because they had disagreed with Temple.

The situation which led Swift to write his book goes back to the time of his second departure from Moor Park. Wotton, in his methodical *Reflections upon Ancient and Modern Learning* (1694), had taken up Temple's essay *Of Ancient and Modern Learning* (1690) and defended modern arts and sciences against Temple's intimation that no significant advance had been made on the accomplishments of the ancients. Temple had bestowed unusual praise on the letters of Phalaris and the fables of Aesop, which he accepted (though admitting the doubts of scholars) as the earliest works of their kind, and authentic compositions of the historical Phalaris and Aesop. Unfortunately, the dean of Christ Church, Oxford, decided, partly as a gesture in Temple's direction, to make *Phalaris* the text of an editorial exercise which he used to assign to bright undergraduates. The student chosen was the Hon. Charles Boyle, but the main work of preparing the edition (1695) was carried out by older men in the college. Through a wicked coincidence, one of the manuscripts required belonged to the King's Library ('St. James's Library'), of which Richard Bentley had just been made Keeper: and instead of facilitating the necessary collations, Bentley saw fit to hinder them. Here, therefore, were the tinder and wood for an academic blaze.

The match was soon applied: for Wotton, in the second edition of his *Reflections* (1697), made room for a *Dissertation* by Bentley, bluntly impugning both Temple's judgment and Boyle's edition (in which that judgment was paraphrased), and demonstrating that the fables and epistles could not be authentic. By now Swift had returned from Kilroot, and was at Moor Park, writing *A Tale of a Tub*. Soon a rebuttal of Bentley appeared, in the form of an *Examination* attributed to Boyle but again prepared by his seniors (March 1698); and this stimulated Swift either to create or to revise some of his own 'digressions' and other expository chapters, for material from it is incorporated not only into the *Digression on Critics* but as well into the many quick thrusts at Wotton and Bentley which are scattered throughout the *Tale*.[1]

It seems to have been, however, the memory of the recent war with Louis XIV that determined the plan of the new satire, for the Treaty of Ryswick was only settled in the autumn of 1697. The closing campaigns of the War of the League of Augsburg had produced a stalemate. The attempted invasion of England had been a fiasco (April 1696). Neither side could claim a triumph in the treaty: conquests made by either were to be returned to the other within six months.[2] Swift gave his story the appearance of a sensational pamphlet reporting a fresh battle; but he gave the battle an ending as inconclusive as the terms of the peace. Implicitly, he thus made the narrator a journalist, or one of the moderns, although the tone of the account obviously favours the ancients. If Swift seems to imply that England is the defender of the ancients and France of the moderns, he has convention on his side; for Temple had derived the immediate controversy over the relative merits of the two literary parties from Perrault and Fontenelle; and one of the chief documents in the controversy was a poem by Perrault flattering Louis XIV by asserting that *le siècle de Louis le Grand* was not inferior to classical antiquity.

Swift may also have drawn analogies between the recent war and the war of the Trojans and Latins in the *Aeneid*. In the plates of Dryden's translation Aeneas was given the face of William III; in Virgil's epic, Aeneas, an idealized Augustus, is the bringer of

[1] A. C. Guthkelch's edition of the *Battle of the Books*, in the King's Classics (1908), follows the controversy in detail, giving lengthy extracts from relevant works. For some additions to the list of books which Swift may have read while he was writing the *Battle of the Books*, see Appendix G.

[2] Ogg II. 439.

civilization; and Swift's London was commonly conceived of as a new Rome (*Nova Augusta*). Since the *Battle of the Books* takes its design mainly from the *Aeneid* (Dryden's version appeared in July 1697), and since Temple is the hero, Swift could be suggesting a parallel, through King William, between Augustus-Aeneas and Sir William. In Swift's own career, Temple appears indeed to have been the great civilizer, covering provincial brick with cosmopolitan marble.

Certainly the story is founded upon Virgil, though with many allusions to Homer. It consists of a historical introduction which is interrupted by the fable of the spider and the bee; then the mobilization of the opposing sides, interrupted by the episode of Momus and Criticism; and at last a fragmentary account of several battles, closed by the long episode of Bentley and Wotton meeting Temple and Boyle. The historical introduction, with the newly arrived Moderns challenging the property rights of the old inhabitants, the Ancients, seems parallel to the difficulties between Aeneas and Latinus (*Aeneid* VII); and the catalogue of the forces goes back to both Homer and Virgil (*Iliad* II. 484–877, *Aeneid* VII. 641–817). The meetings of Momus with Criticism, and of Criticism with Wotton, are derived from the Allecto-Juno-Amata-Turnus sequence in the *Aeneid* (VII. 286–465). Among the battles, the encounter of Virgil with Dryden is a parody of Glaucus and Diomedes (*Iliad* VI. 119–236); Blackmore and Lucan recall Hector and Ajax (*Iliad* VII. 244–302); Creech and Horace recall Turnus and Aeneas (*Aeneid* X. 636–88); Aphra Behn is Camilla (*Aeneid* XI); and Pindar attacking Cowley suggests Diomedes attacking Aeneas (*Iliad* V. 302–4). In the final episode, the portrait of Bentley and his chastisement by Scaliger follow closely the Thersites-Odysseus exchange in Homer (*Iliad* II. 211–69); Bentley and Wotton are modelled on Nisus and Euryalus (*Aeneid* IX. 314–449); and the attack on Temple is a parody of Arruns' attack on Camilla (*Aeneid* XI. 759–867).

Additional allusions seem stitched into these. For example, Jupiter enthroned, with a chain of 'second causes' attached to his toe, suggests not only the famous gold chain of the *Iliad* (VIII. 19) but Lucian's *Icaromenippus*[1] and Bacon's idea of second causes as 'nature's chain', of which the highest link is 'tied to the foot of Jupiter's chair'.[2] Of such allusions, the most interesting is an elaborate parody of *King Arthur*, Blackmore's doggerel epic on William III; for the whole of Swift's Momus-Criticism episode seems to caricature the parallel episode in that poem.[3] Blackmore's manner invited parody, and others were already mimicking him[4]; but Swift's effort may reflect certain personal alignments. Blackmore was sympathetic with Dissent; he followed the new Whigs; he associated himself with the commercial and financial interests of the City of London. Swift was a devout Anglican who did not trust the Dissenters; an old Whig, with views which enlightened 'Tories' would soon accept; and an admirer of the landed gentry. To Swift, perhaps, Blackmore's principles seemed as detestable as his prosody.

Certainly the mock-epic situation, in which these parodies and echoes are submerged, belongs to the seventeenth century. In one of Boccalini's *Advertisements from Parnassus*, Apollo has to marshal his belletristic followers for the defence of Parnassus against the powers of Ignorance.[5] In de Callière's *Histoire Poétique* the ancients and moderns fight about the twin peaks of Parnassus.[6] In the fifth canto of Boileau's *Le Lutrin* (which is itself a document in the ancients-moderns controversy), Chicane plays the role of Allecto (Swift's Criticism); and the two parties under-

[1] Paragraphs 25–6.

[2] *Advancement of Learning*, Bk. I, *ad init.* (World's Classics ed., p. 11). This application of the image is commonplace: cf. Hobbes, *Leviathan*, pt. II, chap. 21, *ad init.* (Cambridge English Classics, ed. A. R. Waller, p. 148). See also A. O. Lovejoy, *The Great Chain of Being*, 1936, *passim.*

[3] See Blackmore's *King Arthur*, 1697, pp. 61–77 (Bk. III, ll. 1–451). For a detailed comparison, see *MLN.*, LXX (Feb. 1955), 95–7. (Blackmore combined Scylla in the *Odyssey* with Juno and Allecto in the *Aeneid.*)

[4] See Albert Rosenberg, *Sir Richard Blackmore* (Lincoln, Nebraska, 1953), pp. 36, 39–70; Richard C. Boys, 'Sir Richard Blackmore and the Wits', *University of Michigan Contributions in Modern Philology*, no. 13, Ann Arbor 1949.

[5] Advertisement LXXXVI. See Traiano Boccalini, *Advertisements from Parnassus* [trans. by N.N.], II (1704), 83–9. (The first English translation of Boccalini's *Advertisements* appeared in 1656.)

[6] For an acute comparison, see Craik I. 91–2.

go a mock-heroic battle in a bookstore, with the fighters throwing famous authors at one another:

Là, près d'un Guarini Terence tombe à terre.
Là, Xenophon dans l'air heurte contre un la Serre.

As the Renaissance retrieval of ancient science had become the antiquarian philology of Augustan scholarship, so humanism had stiffened into neo-classical hierarchies, themselves no less sterile than the scholastic dogmas against which the tradition had been once directed; and it was natural that some geniuses—first in Italy, then in France, and later in England—should test the dimness of the decline by the vitality of the dawn. Of course the new learning of Vossius and Bentley was no continuation of Erasmus and Montaigne. It grew out of a divorce between the materials of scholarship and the ends of wisdom. And this divorce is what Swift was attacking. The mock-epic serves his need for protest because it reminds the reader of the original grounds of our esteem for the ancients, at the same time as it suggests the mean purposes into which the classical heritage has been betrayed. In the single structure we recognize the *Aeneid* of Virgil, the *Aeneid* of Petrarch, and the *Aeneid* of Bentley. Thus the hiatuses in Swift's battle scenes are meant to burlesque the scholarly arguments which Bentley founded upon 'void spaces' in manuscripts.[1] The mock heroic poet is not ridiculing Homer or Virgil. He is attributing a heroic pretension to those moderns whom he wishes to satirize; then, standing them beside the monuments of Greece and Rome, he shows us how absurd is the gap between pretension and achievement.

Swift is, in this sense, appealing to the old scholarship against the new, and his appeal reaches its climax in the fable of the spider and the bee. Here he was perhaps modelling his work upon that of Sir Roger L'Estrange; for in L'Estrange's popular versions of Aesop one finds the same coarse language, the same lively dialogue, colourful letterpress, and elaborate moralizing,

[1] See Boyle's *Examination*, p. 221.

as in Swift's creation.[1] Swift may even have expected the reader to notice and feel amused by the parallel. In general, however, Swift's employment of Aesop as a character alludes to the second part of 'Boyle's' polemic: *Dr. Bentley's Dissertation upon the Fables of Æsop Examin'd*; in this part, furthermore, occurs a discussion of the animated 'picture' of Aesop's *Fables* described by Philostratus in his *Imagines*.[2] In 1698 there was also a Christ Church edition of Aesop, in which the fable of the dog in the manger was so interpreted as to reflect upon Bentley and his manuscripts of Phalaris.

The fable of the spider and the bee makes the link between *A Tale of a Tub* and the *Battle of the Books*.[3] The relation to the *Digression on Critics* is obvious, but deeper bonds exist. At his first appearance the spider was already 'swollen up to the first magnitude'; when he saw the bee's effect upon his fortress, he 'swelled till he was ready to burst'; before undertaking the verbal duel, he 'swelled himself into the size and posture of a disputant'; and he began arguing 'with a resolution to be heartily scurrilous and angry, to urge on his *own* reasons, without the least regard to the answers or objections of his opposite'. As the bee points out, the contents of the spider's swelling 'over-weening pride' are 'dirt and poison'.[4] Bacon is probably the source of these hints, and he indicates how they refer to the *Digression on Madness*; for Bacon says it is not the 'quantity of knowledge' alone that can 'make the mind of man to swell':

> It is manifest that there is no danger at all in the proportion or quantity of knowledge, how large soever, lest it should make it swell or outcompass itself; no, but it is merely the quality of knowledge, which be it in quantity more or less, if it be taken with the true corrective thereof, hath in it some nature of venom or malignity, and some effects of the venom, which is ventosity or swelling. This corrective spice, the mixture whereof maketh knowledge so sovereign,

[1] E.g., no. 258, the swallow and the spider (*Fables, of Æsop*, 1692, pp. 224–5). Around 1698 there was a burst of anthologies of satirical poems in imitation of the fables, with titles like *Æsop at Bathe*, *Æsop at Epsom*, etc.

[2] Boyle's *Examination*, p. 274.

[3] A similar comment is made by John Bullitt, in *Jonathan Swift and the Anatomy of Satire* (Cambridge, Mass. 1953), p. 117.

[4] *Tale*, pp. 228, 230–1.

> is charity, which the apostle immediately addeth to the former clause; for so he saith, 'knowledge bloweth up, but charity buildeth up.'[1]

So here, as in the *Digression on Madness*, flatulence becomes a symbol of pride, and thus pedantry is a kind of flatulence.

It is also Bacon who compares an introspective, reclusive, narrow-read pedant to a spider: the scholastics, Bacon says,

> shut up in the cells of monasteries and colleges; and knowing little history, either of nature or time; did out of no great quantity of matter, and infinite agitation of wit, spin out unto us those laborious webs of learning which are extant in their books. For the wit and mind of man, if it work upon matter, which is the contemplation of the creatures of God, worketh according to the stuff and is limited thereby; but if it work upon itself, as the spider worketh his web, then it is endless, and brings forth indeed cobwebs of learning, admirable for the fineness of thread and work, but of no substance or profit.[2]

For Swift, of course, the model of a contentious pedant, obsessed with the novelty of his futile minutiae, was Bentley: part of the division of Boyle's *Examination* devoted to Aesop was a burlesque dialogue between Bentley and another scholar, in which the former spiderishly refutes a charge of plagiarism: 'I tread in no man's footsteps.'[3]

Although some scholars have argued that Swift's spider has more definite connotations than arid pedantry divorced from experience of the world, and though they have tried to tie it specifically to the new natural philosophers, their argument seems improbable.[4] The image was a commonplace and might be applied with any overtones which suited an occasion. Locke, for example, arguing with Stillingfleet, denied that his own doctrines

[1] *Advancement of Learning*, Bk. I, *ad init.* Cf. Martin Price, *Swift's Rhetorical Art* (New Haven 1953), pp. 4–5. On Swift's relation to Bacon, see R. F. Jones, 'The Background of the *Battle of the Books*', *Washington University Studies* VII (St Louis, 1920), 159 and *passim*; *Ancients and Moderns* (St Louis, 1936), p. 55 and *passim*.

[2] *Advancement of Learning*, Bk. I, *in med.* (World's Classics ed., p. 30).

[3] P. 250.

[4] E.g., Ernest Tuveson, 'Swift and the World Makers', *J.H.I.*, XI (1950), 54–74.

were borrowed from Descartes; they were, he says, 'spun barely out of my own thoughts, reflecting, as well as I could, on my own mind, and the ideas I had there, and were not, that I know, derived from any other original'.[1] Stillingfleet made the image invidious: 'Although those who *write out of their own thoughts* do it with as much ease and pleasure as a spider spins his web; yet the world soon grows weary of controversy.'[2] Hereupon, Locke flung it back at him in the same spirit: 'Should I . . . think I had some right to return the general complaint of length and intricacy without force; yet you have secured yourself from the suspicion of any such trash on your side, by making cobwebs the easy product of those who write out of their own thoughts, which it might be a crime in me to impute to your lordship.'[3] Yet both men, in this combat, were opposed to Descartes; Locke stood for the Baconian tradition; and Stillingfleet kept the methods of scholastic logic which Bacon's invention had been designed to asperse.

The final element of Swift's fable remains: the bee. This was supplied by Bacon in the *Novum Organum*; here is the famous passage contrasting empiricists, in natural philosophy, with dogmatists:

> The empirics, like the ant, amass only and use: the [dogmatists], like spiders, spin webs out of themselves: but the course of the bee lies midway; she gathers materials from the flowers of the garden and the field; and then by her own power turns and digests them. Nor is the true labour of philosophy unlike hers: it does not depend entirely or even chiefly on the strength of the mind, nor does it store up in the memory the materials provided by natural history and mechanical experiments unaltered, but changes and digests them by the intellect.[4]

This distinction, which was to impress Coleridge deeply, also struck Temple, who admired Bacon as among the greatest

[1] *Works*, 5th ed., 1751, I. 369.
[2] *The Bishop of Worcester's Answer to Mr. Locke's Second Letter*, 1698, p. 4.
[3] *Works* I. 438.
[4] Transl. G. W. Kitchin (Oxford, 1855), aphorism no. 95, p. 78.

modern thinkers; and in his essay *Of Poetry*, Temple adopted the bee simile with the literary connotations already belonging to it; only narrowing its meaning to signify the far-ranging, elaborate art of ancient genius.[1] Swift, knowing his master's essay, may have read Bacon with the added stimulus of Temple's recommendation. He manifestly employed both the broad and the narrow connotations of the images, ramified them by cross-reference to the *Digression on Madness*, and dramatized the outcome in his fable.

One source of the appeal of Swift's allegory is its underlying 'naturalness'; for the bee in fact goes with honey and wax, the spider popularly connotes dust and menace. Swift is also drawing upon such diverse clichés as *aranearum telas texere* (for hollow polemics) and 'Where the bee sucks honey, the spider sucks poison.'[2] Others had already come near the application made by him and Temple. Florio, for example, had complained that literary critics 'doo not seeke honie with the bee, but suck poyson with the spider'[3]; and we find a similar figure in Beaumont and Fletcher:

Sweet poetry's
A flower, where men, like bees and spiders, may
Bear poison, or else sweets and wax away.
Be venom-drawing spiders they that will;
I'll be the bee, and suck the honey still.[4]

The fable therefore provides an early example of one of Swift's most characteristic and effective devices: to pick up some commonplace distinctions, embody them in 'naturally' appropriate creatures, and dramatize the resulting juxtaposition in a comic scene with dialogue. He tells no story but brings home the ironies

[1] *Miscellanea* II (1696), p. 323.

[2] Cf. Herbert Davis, *The Satire of Jonathan Swift* (New York 1947), pp. 21–2; Morris Palmer Tilley, *A Dictionary of the Proverbs in England in the Sixteenth and Seventeenth Centuries*, proverb no. B 208.

[3] *Florios Second Frutes*, 1591, 'To the Reader'.

[4] *Four Plays . . . in One*, in the *Works* of Beaumont and Fletcher, ed. A. Glover and A. R. Waller (Cambridge 1905–12), x. 312. Professor Ronald Paulson traces the bee-poet analogy to Plato's *Ion* (*Theme and Structure in Swift's Tale of a Tub* [New Haven 1960], p. 91, n.).

implicit in the clichés. To this genre belong the fat man and the weaver in the 'Preface' to *A Tale of a Tub*.

Though Swift employs no suspenseful plot, he provides a succession of unpredictable flowerings not unlike his sentence structure in effect. Without periodicity, Swift's clauses turn on articulations which are the more evocative because one could not foresee them; e.g., concerning the spider in his web: 'In this mansion he had for some time dwelt in peace and plenty, without danger to his *person* by *swallows* from above, or to his *palace* by *brooms* from below'[1]—one is prepared to end this sentence at each comma, but one is pleased by what appears when one goes on, and the very touch of rhetorical parallelism is itself ironic. So, in the fable, the reader feels ready to stop gratefully after the preliminary dialogue, assuming there will be a brief, summary close. But two apparently climactic speeches follow, expatiating with unpredictable inventiveness on adumbrated themes. Again we presume a conclusion. Yet the truly climactic 'moral' by Aesop still follows, and only then does the scene end. The prose style, meanwhile, is Swift's best. Concrete, homely speech; fresh figures, with no varnish of 'rhetoric'; quick, colloquial rhythms; syntax so idiomatic, expressive, so plainly hinged and turned, that it seems the language of proverbs.

Among Swift's satires this episode is further remarkable in its lack of negative emphasis. The tone seems that of confident affirmation. Swift states his principles openly, as he rarely does in comic writing:

> As for *us*, the Antients, we are content with the *bee*, to pretend to nothing of our own, beyond our *wings* and our *voice*: that is to say, our *flights* and our *language*; for the rest, whatever we have got, has been by infinite labor, and search, and ranging thro' every corner of nature: The difference is, that instead of *dirt* and *poison*, we have rather chose to fill our hives with *honey* and *wax*, thus furnishing mankind with the two noblest of things, which are *sweetness* and *light*.[2]

Flights, language; sweetness, light; that is, elegance of expression

[1] *Tale*, p. 229. [2] *Ibid.*, pp. 234–5.

and clarity of sense—Lucian's χάριτες καὶ σαφήνεια—these are the real definition of 'ancient' virtues in Poetry; they exist, for Swift, in Rabelais as in Lucian, in Cervantes as in Horace; and they are embodied in his fable.

Chapter Five

THE MECHANICAL OPERATION OF THE SPIRIT

i

The structure of *The Mechanical Operation of the Spirit* is simple. It has four parts: some preliminaries; a 'Section I', on Dissenting congregations; a 'Section II', of which the first part is on Dissenting preachers; and a closing part of 'Section II' (not separately labelled), on the history of 'enthusiasm'. The preliminaries include a 'Bookseller's Advertisement', probably by Swift, stating that the work is incomplete and of doubtful authorship; and an epistolary opening, in which the discourse is addressed to a virtuoso in Australia.[1]

In 'Section I' Swift says he proposes to treat of Dissenting zeal in a new way, viz., as enthusiasm artificially excited at first but become natural through habit: this is a doctrine concerning hypocrisy which Swift was to make peculiarly his own, that what may have begun as an affectation can through long use become an elementary part (bad or good) of one's nature. He then proceeds to give a coarse caricature of the alleged manner and vices of Dissenters attending a conventicle, a caricature embodying most of the ancient, hack charges accumulated by their enemies. In not very comic irony, Swift simply describes these supposed hallmarks of Nonconformity as if they were premeditated techniques for inducing, in the minister and his hearers, fits which release their most uninhibited fantasies. Swift may be referring tangentially to the Roman Catholics' use of visible symbols and meditational exercises; for the title of the 'Discourse' probably

[1] The 'Bookseller's Advertisement' has hints that Swift himself felt the satire was

comes from a couplet in *Hudibras* sneering at such papist practices as

> *The tools of working out salvation*
> *By meer mechanick operation.*[1]

In 'Section II', after a long and dazzling introductory paragraph, Swift expounds, by mock-physiology, the relation between the 'real' internal constitution of the brain (an Epicurean 'crowd of little animals') and the workings of the mind. This is to explain how Nonconformist preachers think. Next, Swift analyses the speech of the ministers, as he had earlier analysed the behaviour of their congregations. Employing traditional lines of attack, he describes, in caricature again, their enunciation and their language; and he pretends that all these traits are deliberate means of arousing 'enthusiasm' (i.e., delusions of being divinely inspired) in the worshippers. Finally, he traces the allegedly nasal whine of their voices to a decayed nose ruined by the effects of venereal disease.

What follows amounts to a further section, though not so entitled.[2] This is a brief, punning mock-history of enthusiasm, from ancient times to the present. Here, by a rough pseudo-allegory, Swift not only pretends that pagans, Roman Catholics, and Dissenters are indistinguishable in this respect, but he also pretends to discover that the common element, and thus the essential cause, of all the phenomena is concealed (not stifled) lust. His irony, here, is in the style—I do not suggest influence—of Hobbes's amazing parallels, at the end of *Leviathan*, between

---

too violent; and Swift later describes the portion deleted from 'Section II' as 'neither safe nor convenient to print' (p. 276); cf. similar hints added in the fifth edition: pp. 17–18 and the italic note, pp. 261–2. There are hints of a different sort in the address to 'T. H. Esquire', at the 'Academy of the Beaux Esprits in New Holland': the initials may be an anagram of 'the squire'; the *Academy* is probably a thrust at the Royal Society; the epistolary style suggests the elaborate correspondence maintained by the philosophical societies; New Holland apparently is to connote the self-important provinciality of the philosophical societies—cf. the Iroquois and the Topinambo literati two pages later (p. 263); *beaux esprits* may possibly allude to hedonistic free-thinkers (see George Boas, *The Happy Beast* [Baltimore 1933], pp. 64–70).

[1] III. i. 1497–8, noted in *Tale*, p. 261, n. 1.

[2] *Tale*, pp. 282–9.

the papacy and the kingdom of fairies: 'The fairies marry not', Hobbes says, for instance; 'but there be amongst them incubi, that have copulation with flesh and bloud. The priests also marry not.'[1] Swift draws a closing parallel, appropriately but surprisingly, between a modern lover's manners in courtship and a Dissenting minister's manners in preaching; and this leads to the famous aphorism, 'Too intense a contemplation is not the business of flesh and blood; it must by the necessary course of things, in a little time, let go its hold, and fall into *matter*.'[2]

Swift's subject is thus Protestant Nonconformity in England—or, we might say, a further consideration of Jack, from *A Tale of a Tub*. Yet the author ironically gives himself the character not only of a Dissenter but also of a 'modern' and a virtuoso. Swift's purpose in adding such references was probably to account for the mechanistic terms of his analysis; for he employs something like the language and methods of Hobbes, the interpretation of human nature as wholly governed by the laws of matter and motion. Hobbes's mechanistic psychology was traditionally understood to encourage atheism, and all faiths abhorred him, the Puritans as much as the Anglicans. Swift is therefore implying that while Hobbes is wrong, his theories do fit the 'unnatural' behaviour of the sects. Conversely, since Hobbes detested the Puritans, Swift is ridiculing him by implying that they are his most eager imitators.[3] If the *Mechanical Operation* is primarily an attack upon Dissent, it is, in a more limited way, also a satire upon pseudo-scientists (Descartes and Hobbes, not Bacon or Locke) and pedantic scholars.

Among the *Tale*, the *Battle*, and the *Mechanical Operation*, the connection is not obscure. For instance, the pretended 'spirit' (of the hypocrites whom Swift is attacking) operates like the

[1] *Leviathan* IV. xlvii (ed. A. R. Waller, p. 518). [2] *Tale*, pp. 288–9.

[3] Much of Swift's language, in the *Mechanical Operation*, seems drawn from Hobbes: e.g., pp. 274–5, 'things invisible', 'invisible power', 'fear' and 'desire' as causes of religion; cf. *Leviathan* I. xi-xii (ed. A. R. Waller, Cambridge, 1904), pp. 68–71. See also David P. French, 'Swift and Hobbes—A Neglected Parallel', *Boston University Studies in English* III (Winter 1957), 243–55.

Spider's genius, 'entirely from within'.[1] Butler, in *Hudibras*, had described the Presbyterians as

> *Those spider-saints, that hang by threads*
> *Spun out o' th' entrails of their heads.*[2]

The ass which stood for a pedantic critic in the *Digression on Critics* and for a modern in the *Battle of the Books*,[3] becomes a Puritan preacher in the *Mechanical Operation*. The displacement of senses and reason by imagination and fancy, as in the *Digression on Madness*, reappears in the *Mechanical Operation* with the associated vapours of the Aeolists.[4] Jack's soliloquy upon predestination and the unreliability of the senses reappears in a direct attack by the author upon Dissenting preachers.[5] But the deepest self-echo is the assertion that enthusiasm, like the madness of the *Digression on Madness*, not only can be found in men of every time and place, but also 'has been able to produce revolutions of the greatest figure in history'[6]; for of course Swift accounted for Puritan fanaticism as merely the most poisonous form of that irrationality which springs eternally in *animal rationale* and which it must be our constant moral purpose to control. The flatulence which seems spirit to self-tricked hypocrites is mediately the vapours of all foolishness and ultimately the swelling of pride.

ii

Although the *Mechanical Operation of the Spirit* stands beside the *Tale* and the *Battle* through always being published with them, it stands far beneath them as a literary achievement.[7] One might treat the *Battle* as a generalization of the *Digression on Critics*; and one might treat the *Mechanical Operation* as a generalization of

[1] *Tale*, p. 271. [2] III. i. 1461–2. [3] *Tale*, p. 233. [4] P. 273.

[5] Cf. pp. 192–4 and 275–6. Professor Pons has traced such connections in his *Swift*, pp. 383–6 and *passim*.

[6] P. 266.

[7] Professor James Clifford's arguments as to the significance of this grouping do not seem to me persuasive ('Swift's *Mechanical Operation of the Spirit*', in *Pope and His Contemporaries: Essays Presented to George Sherburn* [Oxford 1949], pp. 135–46).

Jack's character in 'Section XI' of the *Tale*. But where the *Battle* dramatizes and enlarges a hint into a fresh, full, imaginative design, the *Mechanical Operation* takes a characterization which is heavy enough, and, without lightening its crudities, extends and labours its applications. Here is another case of Swift's obsessional violence drawing so much attention to itself that it distracts the reader from the author's satirical aim.

However, the parts compensate, to a degree, for the whole, since there are paragraphs in the *Mechanical Operation* as fine as any but the most brilliant passages of the companion works. One of these is the opening of 'Section I', based on the notable conceit of a reversed allegory. Swift pretends that he wishes to discuss the power attributed to an ass, by some authorities, of carrying its rider to heaven. He then says the problem is so tendentious that he will consider it 'by way of allegory', using Nonconformist preachers as a symbol of the ass and their congregations as a symbol of the rider. By this artifice he becomes free to speak as directly as he wishes about the Presbyterians, Independents, Baptists, and Quakers, and yet, within the frame of his irony, to claim that they are not his subject at all. Merely as exemplifying the skilful elaboration of a difficult rhetorical figure, the passage is of interest. As ridicule, however, it seems too broad for its purpose: the author sounds not as if he were disengaged but as if he were struggling to appear disengaged.

The best part of the essay is the long paragraph opening 'Section II'. Here Swift speaks with only the driest irony and with little disguise. Again, he makes the Puritans out to be but a special case of a general defect in humanity: our unwillingness to let 'right reason' work unimpeded, our itch to distort obvious moral judgments by the self-pleasing ratiocinations of 'discursive reason'. Comparing Europeans (and therefore Christians) with the wild Indians, he argues that at least the savages, however clumsy may be their conceptions of good and evil, never muddle the one with the other, 'nor ever suffering the liturgy of the *white* god, to cross or interfere with that of the *black*'.[1] The English, by contrast,

[1] *Tale*, p. 274.

have so troubled these boundaries that they cannot decide whether Nonconformity be the issue of divine or satanic powers. Swift characteristically suggests it is neither, though what he manifestly counts as absent is indeed the hand of God:

> Who, that sees a little paultry mortal, droning, and dreaming, and drivelling to a multitude, can think it agreeable to common good sense, that either Heaven or Hell should be put to the trouble of influence or inspection upon what he is about?[1]

What Swift means is that any body so contentious, stupid, and irrational as the 'modern saints' must be devoid of true piety or inspiration. In this proposition resides the dialectical premise of his argument. But it was to be a mark of his satirical style that Swift should, at some point in an essay, pretend to dismiss the positive teachings on which he based his attack. Therefore, just as, in the *Digression on Critics*, he had 'discarded' the two respectable meanings of *critic*, so also in 'Section I' of the *Mechanical Operation*, he had rejected the present proposition—actually the foundation of his rhetoric—as irrelevant:

> If [*spirit*] be understood for a supernatural assistance, approaching from without, the objectors have reason... But the *spirit* we treat of here, proceeding entirely from within, the argument of these adversaries is wholly eluded.[2]

By implication, he comes perilously near using Hobbes's tokens by which a true prophet is known: 'One is the doing of miracles; the other is the not teaching any other religion than that which is already established'.[3] Not only the discussion at the beginning of 'Section II' but the whole web of the *Mechanical Operation* seems involved with Hobbes's materialistic doctrines concerning 'Christian politics', spirit and inspiration, and prophets.[4] It is from the clash between the disillusioned psychology which these doctrines support, and the stern morality which the author in-

[1] *Tale*, p. 276. [2] *Ibid.*, p. 271.
[3] *Leviathan* III. xxxii (ed. A. R. Waller, p. 271).
[4] *Ibid.* III. xxxii, xxxiv, xxxvi.

vokes, that the energy of Swift's present discussion arises. As Professor French comments,

> [Swift] was a basically philanthropic man convinced against his will that Hobbes's *Leviathan* is truer to human nature than the Sermon on the Mount. As a result, he often intellectually accepted what he instinctively and emotionally disliked.[1]

iii

Except for these passages, however (and some fine aphorisms), Swift, in the *Mechanical Operation*, repeats, in a halting, crude form, what he had already and better expressed in *A Tale of a Tub*. The use of breaks and asides is neither witty nor meaningful. The puns, in the absence of comedy, seem more harsh than hilarious. The pervasive word-play smells stale because Swift discovered little of it. As Empson says, 'spiritual words are all derived from physical metaphors.'[2] The associations with the vocabulary of Hobbes further undermine the irony, since in that tradition Swift's words have already lost the figurative half of their meaning. The tone of the satire is obsessional; there is much heavy sarcasm, little comic irony, almost no humour.

One throws no lustre upon Swift by discovering, in the *Mechanical Operation* 'anticipations of Freudian theorems about anality, about sublimation, and about the universal neurosis of mankind'. Neither does it help to add that 'Swiftian psychoanalysis differs from the Freudian in that the vehicle for the exploration of the unconscious is not psychoanalysis but wit.'[3] Giving an important message to a work which as literature has been misconceived does not improve its literary design; a noble subject cannot make a poor speech into great oratory. This would be so even if Swift's adumbrations of Freud were deliberate. But they are not; they are unconscious. It would be more accurate to say Swift exemplified Freud's theorems than that he taught them,

[1] 'Swift and Hobbes—A Neglected Parallel', p. 243.
[2] William Empson, *Some Versions of Pastoral*, 1938, p. 60.
[3] Norman O. Brown, *Life against Death*, 1959, p. 186.

for what might appear to be demonstrations are in fact methods of ridicule: Swift employs 'anal' imagery as an aggressive, not a didactic, device. His meaning is not that anal preoccupations supply the energy for our loftiest principles but simply that the holder of lofty principles must not suppose they free him from the body.

The province of literary meaning belongs to the public domain. The unconscious, uncalculated aspects of literature are those which lump it together with the non-literary uses of language. Any angry man yelling chamberpot sarcasms at his enemy is anticipating and illustrating Freud.

Nevertheless, while Swift's violence distracts one from his meaning, it does not destroy that meaning; and a sympathetic critic will not misunderstand him. Swift never attacks the Nonconformists for having bodies, passions, faeces; he attacks them for confusing these with religion, for describing themselves as inspired when they are windy, or as charitable when they are lustful. On the other hand, he never argues that charity is a form of lust: when he says so ironically, he is employing a clumsy style of wit to ridicule false religion and false charity. To claim that what he says in irony is true in fact, neither makes Swift wise nor redeems his work.

However, this interpretation goes far to explain why men who can enjoy large doses of obscenity and blasphemy in other forms—certain commercial entertainments, party jokes, army humour—find works like the *Mechanical Operation* revolting. Swift's intensity and ingenuity bring readers so close to the Freudian truth that if they have already spent considerable energy dodging this truth in their own minds, the essay frightens them; and they find it not tedious or repetitious but noxious and unbearable.

Swift's originality in the *Mechanical Operation* lies where he sets it, in the treatment of Puritan zeal not as irresistible possession or as scheming hypocrisy, but as a deliberate method of obliterating one's perceptions and suspending one's intelligence so that one's fancy and passions may be free. With his natural guides removed, the practitioner of the exercises may confer upon himself such grace and spirituality that his body no longer appears to weigh him down. While in his outward acts he may then behave like a beast, his ecstasy persuades him that God is his inspirer.

To Swift, such zeal or enthusiasm seemed to blend a natural leaning with an artificial training, either of the two elements being the germ of the disorder. He recognized both those 'whose once conscious art in the creation of ecstatic states had now become a sincere and involuntary part of their nature' and those 'who were naturally enthusiastic but who employed artifice to arouse themselves and others':

> The idea that artifice became nature seems to have been original with Swift; in fact, his subtle distinction between types of enthusiasm is by far the most discerning of any of the seventeenth-century classifications.[1]

Although *The Mechanical Operation of the Spirit* is one of Swift's failures, it does suggest how much of his force as a writer originates in the fight between his reformer's temperament and his disillusioned, pessimistic philosophy of morals. While the 'fragment' is cast as a satire against the hypocrisy of the Dissenters, the Dissenters are treated in it as natural products of the English character; and the English are treated as no better than what one might expect of diseased humanity. Like the author of the *Digression on Madness*, this author must count himself among those possessed by corruption; and the last paradox, which nobody faced more directly than Swift, was how one of the damned themselves could retain sufficient integrity to recognize the general condition. Normally, Swift's resolution is ironical. By classifying himself among the accused, he forestalls the accusations of others; he also intimidates the reader into assuming the opposite; for one intuitively attributes virtue to the prophet who—even ironically—chastises himself.

[1] Clarence M. Webster, 'Swift and Some Earlier Satirists of Puritan Enthusiasm', *PMLA.*, XLVII (Dec. 1933), 1150.

Chapter Six

LAST YEARS AT MOOR PARK

i

To appreciate Swift's hopes while he was writing his first masterpieces we are helped by noting the situations of some contemporaries who were to share with him the vicissitudes of friendship and the honours of literature. Matthew Prior, three years older than Swift, belonged to a far humbler family; but he came of a generous father, had grown up near Whitehall, and had, from boyhood, drawn the interest of noble patrons. He could therefore go to the Westminster School and to St John's, Cambridge—fair parallels to Kilkenny and Trinity; and he took his B.A. degree the same year as Swift. The great Charles Montagu, later Earl of Halifax, went to school and university with Prior; and together they composed the burlesque of Dryden's *Hind and the Panther* which first gave Prior a reputation as a poet. After a few years in a college fellowship, Prior found himself chosen, through Montagu and other friends, as secretary to one of Temple's successors at The Hague: Lord Dursley, soon to become Earl of Berkeley. During the years when Swift sometimes saw William III at Moor Park, Prior was attending his majesty on official duties between Loo and Cleves. He played a small role in negotiating the Treaty of Ryswick, and it was he who carried that treaty from the Congress halls to London. By 1698 Prior not only was secretary of the English embassy in Paris, as well as secretary to the lords justices of Ireland (which he never visited); but he also was accustomed to the special protection, conversation, or correspondence of Montagu (now Chancellor of the Exchequer), the Earls of Dorset, Berkeley, Portland, and Jersey, and the Duke of Shrewsbury. He was well known to the king, to the main diplomatic corps of Europe, and to the officers of the English establishment. Yet he was only thirty-three years old.

Swift's school- and college-mate, Congreve, fled from Ireland about the same time as Swift, who was his senior by three years. Coming to London as a student of law, Congreve had still a father to support him, and close relatives—some, persons of rank and fashion—near at hand.[1] His charming manners and manifest genius carried him easily into the smartest set of Dryden's London. When his little novel *Incognita* appeared, he was just twenty-two. A year later, his brilliant first play received unusual applause. By 1698 he held a small sinecure from the government; seemed the climbing sun of comic and tragic drama; and had sufficient power to patronize newer-comers in the theatre. Jeremy Collier, in fixing him among the central objects attacked in *A Short View . . . of the English Stage* (1698), may have left Congreve's plays to suffer for decades under that censure[2]; but he also revealed the conspicuous height to which fame had so early lifted Swift's friend.

It was Congreve, according to Steele, who first brought Montagu and Addison together. With an ancestry as ecclesiastical as Swift's, Addison enjoyed the advantage of a scholarly, clergyman father, whose tastes outran his decent income. From Charterhouse, Addison had gone to distinguish himself at Magdalen College, Oxford; and he was still there, as tutor, and accomplished Latin poet, when he caught Dryden's notice with some flattering couplets. He soon appeared, like Congreve, in Tonson's series of miscellanies; and his contribution to the 1694 volume was a survey of English poets which included one panegyric of Congreve and another of Montagu. While Swift was serving his term in Kilroot, Addison produced a poem addressed to the king but dedicated, in verse, to Somers (then Lord Keeper). The great man saw it; and so, 'at the age of twenty-four, Ad-

[1] John C. Hodges, *William Congreve, the Man* (New York 1941), pp. 33–4.

[2] Emmett L. Avery, *Congreve's Plays on the Eighteenth-Century Stage* (New York 1951), p. 1.

dison had gained personal access to the two powerful political patrons who better than any others in that age could forward a young man's career'.[1] The most splendid literary event of 1697 was the publication of Dryden's Virgil; for this Addison supplied the preface to the *Georgics*; and in a postscript Dryden handsomely praised his talents as a translator. Upon the Treaty of Ryswick, the same year, Addison wrote a Latin poem celebrating *pax Guglielmi*, and dedicated it to Montagu. It seemed in the order of things, no doubt, that such a youth should succeed to a college fellowship. But he could thank his prudent prosody that the Treasury granted him two hundred pounds for travel, and that Montagu persuaded Magdalen to continue Addison's stipend while the young poet went on a grand tour of the Continent.

Meanwhile, Addison's friend Steele, five years younger than Swift, was still an officer in the Coldstream Guards. He had been born in the parish of St Bride's, Dublin, to which Swift's uncles Godwin, William, and Adam belonged: both Godwin and Adam were vestrymen at the church where Steele was baptized, and Steele's father was admitted an attorney at the King's Inns two years after Swift's. Not only must the families have been acquainted with one another, but Godwin may have helped the elder Richard Steele to obtain preferment from Ormonde[2]; however, since the great (first) duke's secretary was the elder Steele's brother-in-law, no further pressure may have been needed: certainly it was the duke himself who had young Richard (fatherless from the age of five) placed upon the foundation of the Charterhouse, where he first met Addison. From that school, Steele, with the aid of his influential uncle, went on to Christ Church, Oxford; but instead of staying long enough to collect a degree, he enlisted in the young (second) Duke of Ormonde's regiment of guards. Now he advanced his career by dedicating to Lord Cutts (Colonel of the Coldstream Guards) a poem on the death of Queen Mary; for Cutts soon made him an ensign in his own regiment and a member of his household. For a while Steele acted as

[1] Peter Smithers, *The Life of Joseph Addison* (Oxford 1954), p. 33.

[2] G. A. Aitken, *The Life of Sir Richard Steele* (1889), pp. 13–15.

his confidential secretary, performing services much like those which Swift, then in his last years at Moor Park, was performing for Temple.

If these men understood what elements had to be added to their natural endowment for them to gain the independence and recognition they desired, Swift was surely competent to draw the same inferences. He had something like their aims—a respectable income, an entrance into the great world, literary fame; he had a similar education, a similar power to charm those whom he wished to impress, and a superior genius. His 'backing' was equal to the average of theirs; his difficulties were no greater: Congreve and Steele came from Ireland; Prior's family and connections were notably meaner than Swift's; Addison was shy; Steele was an orphan. Unfortunately, Swift chose to work through the dying order of Temple's circle rather than through the instruments which belonged to the future. So in 1697—as we have seen—he approached the Earl of Sunderland, whose great gift was for surviving disgrace. In spite of his notorious treacheries and long retirement, Sunderland had been appointed Lord Chamberlain in April. But 'a House of Commons not distinguished for idealism, [or] even probity', displayed such mutinous distaste for his name that he resigned at the end of the year.[1] Swift commented, 'My lord Sunderland fell and I with him.'[2]

He immediately looked elsewhere, but we are not sure whom he approached. 'There have been other courses', he told Winder, 'which if they succeed, I shall be proud to own the methods, or if otherwise, very much ashamed.'[3] As Craik indicates, this is one of those hypocrite-in-reverse expressions by which Swift characteristically twists an interpretation of motives against himself: 'Its probable meaning', says Craik, 'is, that though he is sure of the honesty of his means, he will still be ashamed of having tried at all, if these means do not end successfully.'[4] We may guess from what happened a year later that Swift directed one application to Sunderland's handsome, middle-aged uncle, Henry Sidney, who, though now Earl of Romney, was still closer to Sir

[1] Ogg II. 441. [2] Ball I. 24. [3] *Ibid.* [4] Craik I. 76, n. 2.

William Temple than anybody else outside Moor Park; and we may further guess that Swift aspired to some well-endowed preferment in the church, such as the prebend of Westminster held by his own uncle Thomas's friend, Dr South. How his hopes were met, we shall see shortly.

ii

Although a career in England offered vistas which nothing in Ireland could match, the Established Church promised as little serenity in the one kingdom as in the other. On the contrary, the schisms now troubling the English clergy were soon to spread across the Irish Sea, so that wherever Swift settled he would be involved in them. Since these splits were both doctrinal and institutional, they opened the way for a heavy flow of polemical composition. In addition to the growing inroads of Nonconformity and the declining menace of Roman Catholicism, a new threat was looming: the congeries of rationalist attacks upon Anglican theology which are fuzzily associated with the rise of deism. In the adumbrative form of the Trinitarian controversy, this movement touched the institutional side of the church, since it supplied a weapon for the aggressive party in the quarrel over Convocation.

Between 1693 and 1695 the old system of licensing books before publication was allowed to die, and men could write boldly upon religious arguments that once would have exposed them to prosecutions. A government which necessarily distinguished its own policies from the intolerance of James II and Louis XIV found it difficult to set limits upon freedom of the press. Yet this was the time when Socinianism was spreading, Unitarianism was emerging, and orthodox churchmen were put to it to defend the Trinity without stumbling into Tritheism. Stephen Nye, a Hertfordshire parson, made propaganda for the 'Unitarians, called also Socinians'; William Sherlock, undertaking to vindicate the doctrine of the Trinity, found himself accused by Robert South of Tritheism; whereupon Nye charged South with Sabellianism.

The king intervened in 1695, and prohibited further speculations on the subject; but he only succeeded in shifting the focus of the incandescence to Arianism.[1]

In 1697, with the appearance of *A Letter to a Convocation Man*, the Trinitarian controversy joined streams with another. The war had deepened the usual breach between court followers and country landowners: while those in the king's employ could enrich themselves with places and perquisites, the agricultural gentry felt crushed by the land tax which was paying for the armies. Toward the middle of William's reign, furthermore, a natural reaction had turned the 'Country' and 'Church' parties against the principles which had inaugurated his reign. One Parliamentary group, with Robert Harley at its head, tried to limit the king both by reducing grants to the crown and army and by advocating the 'Place' and 'Triennial' bills, familiar Country programmes. Other opposition groups, led by the Earl of Rochester and the Earl of Nottingham, argued that the new order, through its tolerance, was undermining the Established Church. Since William, after the elections of 1695, relied increasingly upon 'Court Whigs' like Somers and Montagu, the forces of the opposition had good reason to draw together against him; and the counter-Revolutionary swing of the nation gave them support.[2] As part of their strategy, Harley, Nottingham, and Rochester encouraged sympathetic clergymen to write attacks upon the ecclesiastical policies of the government. 'From 1697 there is to be found the coming together of a recognizable set of divines, steadily encouraged by the anti-ministerial opposition and devoted to the task of bringing King, ministers, and their ecclesiastical appointees into popular disrepute.'[3]

When John Toland and Stephen Nye brought out some unusually provocative pamphlets teaching Socinian doctrines (1696, 1697), the clerical critics of the ministry used these among other excuses to demand a Convocation of the Canterbury Province of the Church of England. Although the machinery for

[1] Norman Sykes, *William Wake* (Cambridge 1957), II. 153–4.

[2] G. V. Bennett, *White Kennett* (1957), p. 26. [3] *Ibid.*, p. 29.

such a gathering existed, and although the York province met regularly (and quietly), no Convocation of Canterbury had assembled since 1664, apart from a brief and explosive sitting in 1689. Now Francis Atterbury, aided by associates,[1] produced a specious, ingenious alarum, *A Letter to a Convocation Man*. In Holland, he said, 'Socinians and other anti-Trinitarians' were claiming the English church for their camp; and in England there seemed to be 'an universal conspiracy' among Deists, Socinians, Latitudinarians, and other deniers of mysteries, 'to undermine and overthrow the Catholic Faith'. A secular Parliament was incompetent to strangle these monsters: the bishops (the upper house of Convocation) and other clergy (represented in the lower house) must meet to fight them.

That such a meeting would be turbulent, both sides knew. The court had regularly been giving bishoprics to co-operative men; and the nonjuror schism had widened the normal scope for such appointments. Among the old-fashioned lower clergy, however, distrust of the government had been growing, and they were baying for a heresy hunt. Obviously, whoever brought the two groups face to face would be inviting a mêlée.

Swift's exact sentiments are unknown; but it is safe to conjecture that while he would have supported the move to call a convocation, and would have welcomed any bridling of heretical or anti-clerical pamphleteers, he would have opposed a project to define the mysteries for dogmatic purposes, and would have discouraged an attempt to turn the clergy against the government. However, the issues were to travel much farther before he was compelled to face them directly. I notice them at this stage as important and provocative aspects of the environment in which he made his next decisions. If he persisted in seeking an ecclesiastical career, it would not be for thinking England an easy field for ghostly cultivation; and if he sought preferment without emulating Atterbury or Kennett (who answered Atterbury's book and was made Archdeacon of Huntingdon), it was not because their methods appeared foreign to their profession.

[1] Sykes, *William Wake* I. 81–2.

iii

Meanwhile, although Swift continued to exchange letters with Varina, he could still be reproached 'for the want of gallantry, and neglecting a close siege'; and he told Winder (April 1698) that some people in Ireland had written to him 'censuring [Swift's] truth in relation to a certain lady'.[1] Yet when Winder himself alluded to 'a dangerous rival for an absent lover', Swift responded as tranquilly as to a weather forecast: 'I must take my fortune. If the report proceeds, pray inform me.'[2]

He could afford such serenity because he owned other resources; a new and more steadfast star had risen for him:

> *—at sixteen*
> *The brightest virgin of the green.*[3]

This was the girl, nearly fourteen years his junior, whose moral code and literary taste he had modelled upon his own. She was, like Miss Waring, the eldest child of a widowed mother; and through the first years of Swift's friendship her health too was fragile. Not long before Esther Johnson's birth, Temple's only daughter—the 'child he was infinitely fond of'—had died of smallpox. Temple's sister says he enjoyed the company of children, whose 'imperfect language and natural and innocent way of talking' delighted him.[4] So he must have felt drawn to the little half-orphan of his late steward. In a document dated 1690, Temple acknowledged an indebtedness to Bridget Johnson of £140; and there are annual receipts, signed by her, for interest payments of six or seven pounds.[5] This may possibly have been his method of investing a nest-egg for mother and daughter and insuring it against his death.

On Swift's return in 1696 to Moor Park, he found Hetty Johnson to be 'beautiful, graceful, and agreeable'.[6] She had black,

[1] Ball I. 19, 22. [2] *Ibid.*, p. 30. [3] *Poems* II. 721.

[4] Temple, *Early Essays*, pp. 15, 21, 29.

[5] The documents are nos. 9 and 10 of the Temple family papers in the collection of Mr James Osborn. (In 1695 Mrs Johnson withdrew twenty pounds of her principal.)

[6] T. Scott XI. 128.

black hair and the enchanting gift of docility.[1] Almost twice her age, Swift could regard his own attitude as harmlessly tutorial. Even confined to the narrow dimensions of the same household, a priest in his fourth decade of life and a maid still in her teens might converse freely and frequently without inviting suspicion. When she had a mother, brother, and sister to live with, and he was studious, quippish, and chaste, what intrigue could follow? Swift's parental address to Esther, teasing when not didactic, must have misled him, her, and their friends. It was a quieter game than Héloïse and Abelard but not less tricky. With such pleasures in his reach (and rarely out of view), Swift was not languishing for Varina.

The closest friend Miss Johnson had besides Swift also belonged to the Temple circle. She was Rebecca Dingley, Sir William's spinster cousin. Although much older than Esther, Mrs Dingley had no adequate fortune, and probably relieved Lady Giffard of some housekeeping duties; she certainly was a companion and in emergencies waited on her ladyship. The status of 'Hetty' and 'Dingley' is sketched in Lady Giffard's masterly exposition of the servant problem; her ladyship has just dismissed a new maid for being too dainty to work properly:

> Papa [i.e., Temple] desires she may goe for fear he should be in love with her. she owns never to have wash'd a room in her life, & when she rose next morning asked if she must make her owne bed, complain'd yt she should not be able to wait & worke in a room with out a fire & you know I have no other, but ye cruel thing of all was dineing with the common servants, & yt she said she had never reckon'd upon & doubted she should not be able to bear. Indeed I beleeve nobody ever had a greater damp at heart yet when I spoke to her to day (how sorry I was to have put her upon what I doubted she yt had alwayes lived soe much better must thinke very hard, & she could not be more uneasy then I should be every time I did it, but twas such a servant I wanted), she said she had rather venter upon any service then live longer out & in yt I beleeve told ye true reason but she had lived I find in great places & bin an absolute gentle-

[1] We may doubt the report that when her remains were dug up in the nineteenth century her teeth were judged to be 'perhaps the most perfect ever witnessed in a skull' (*N. & Q.*, 12 Aug. 1871, p. 124).

woman & I dare say is one, by her name & her friends for I have had a great deal of talke with her her journey shall be pay'd for & Mrs Bradley yt came downe with her will goe up with her agin a Monday Nanny lagger who I had orderd to goe yt day says she is very happy to stay longer & soe I am going in search of my pussle again, 3 gentlewomen had bin a little too much state; for I make use of my cousin Dingley when ever I am in want, Hettys place being ye heigh[t] of her [i.e., Dingley's] ambition.[1]

Of course, friends and relatives were always visiting the family; and a grandson of Temple's brother later recalled to Swift how the young parson was sometimes drawn into those occasions:

When I was [a schoolboy], I remember I was committed to your care from Sheen to London. We took water at Mortlake, the commander of the little skiff was very drunk and insolent, put us ashore at Hammersmith, yet insisted, with very abusive language, on his fare, which you courageously refused; the mob gathered; I expected to see your gown stripped off, and for want of a blanket, to take a flight with you in it, but . . . by your powerful eloquence you saved your bacon and money, and we happily proceeded on our journey.[2]

Expeditions to London were not Swift's only errands for Temple. He kept the household accounts, acted as amanuensis, paid out moneys, and supported conversation. Of course, as Lady Giffard remarks, the great man was subject to periods of spleen and depression in his last years; and Swift felt their effect. 'Don't you remember', he wrote to Esther Johnson years later, 'how I used to be in pain when Sir William Temple would look cold and out of humour for three or four days, and I used to suspect a hundred reasons?'[3] But there was cosiness as well; and when Swift at forty-five, visiting the Lord Treasurer, was given a shilling to

[1] B.M. MS. Egerton 1705, ff. 17–18: letter of 30 Dec. [?1697], printed inaccurately in Longe, p. 215. A sign of Esther Johnson's status is that in the bills for mourning to be worn upon Temple's death she is entitled 'Mrs. Hetty'—suggesting a very young gentlewoman—whereas the ordinary servants' surnames, Christian names, or both, appear with no honorific. (See nos. 19 and 21 of the Temple family papers in Mr James Osborn's collection.)

[2] Ball IV. 66–7 (18 Mar. 1729). [3] *Journal* 4 Apr. 1711.

stake in a family game, he wrote, 'I was playing at one and thirty with him and his family tother night. he gave us all 12 pence apiece to begin with: it put me in mind of Sir W T.'[1]

Advancing years did not sharpen Temple's sense of responsibility to Swift, whose pursuit of knowledge and friendship left him as far as ever from a happy settlement. Glimpses of Moor Park during this time are given by Lady Giffard's letter to her niece:

> I have sent him [i.e., Swift] with another compliment from Papa [i.e., Temple] to the King, where I fancy he is not displeased with finding occasions of going. . . Thank God Papa is not very bad, I hear him just now going down stairs with a lame knee. . . Papa wishes you here too, at a piece of roast beef at dinner which he eat for the first time with a very good stomach and I must tell you he is now a great deal better, whatever comes after it. . . We are got hither [i.e., to Petworth] at last, and Papa I thank God very well, and insufferably pert with winning twelve guineas at crimp last night. The Duke of Somerset says he never remembers seeing him better.[2]

The Petworth visit, September 1698, was one of Temple's last holidays. Exhausted by what was called the gout, he had already begun his final struggle with illness. Swift, in a paper which he titled *Journal d'Estat de M^r^ T— devant sa Mort*, kept a register of his dying friend's fluctuations, from 1 July until 27 January following, when a closing note recorded his immediate reaction to Temple's end: 'He dyed at one o'clock in the morning and with him all that was great and good among men.'[3] When he had time for a fuller appreciation, Swift's language was even more extravagant:

> He was a person of the greatest wisdom, justice, liberality, politeness, eloquence, of his age and nation; the truest lover of his country, and one that deserved more from it by his eminent public services, than any man before or since: besides his great deserving of the commonwealth of learning; having been universally esteemed the most accomplished writer of his time.[4]

[1] *Journal* 9 Oct. 1712. [2] Longe, pp. 216, 198, 202, 227.
[3] Lyon, preliminaries, f. 6v. [4] W. Scott I. 43.

Besides such formal though honest tributes, Swift expressed less gracious sentiments upon his master's death. These appear on an odd leaf headed, 'When I come to be old 1699—'. Although Swift does not in fact indicate their occasion, the resolutions sound like the suppressed conclusions of a young man's close, prolonged observation of one or perhaps several old men. Most of the animadversions could reflect upon Temple; others may allude to visitors like Romney.

Not to marry a young Woman.
Not to keep young Company unless they realy desire it.
Not to be peevish or morose, or suspicious
Not to scorn present Ways, or Wits, or Fashions, or Men, or [?War], &c—
Not to be fond of Children, ⌈or let them come near me hardly⌉
Not to tell the same Story over & over to the same People
Not to be covetous
Not to neglect decency, or cleanlyness, for fear of falling into Nastyness
Not to be over severe with young People, but give Allowances for their youthfull follyes, and Weaknesses
Not to be influenced by, or give ear to knavish tatling Servants, or others.
Not to be too free of advise nor trouble any but those that desire it.
To ⌈?Compel⌉ \desire/ some good Friends to inform me wch of these Resolutions I break, or neglect, & wherein; and reform accordingly.
Not to talk much, nor of my self.
Not to boast of my former beauty, or Strength, or favor with Ladyes, &c
Not to hearken to Flatteryes, nor conceive I can be beloved by a young woman. et eos qui herdeditatem [*sic*] captant ⌈?omnes ?de⌉ odisse ac vitare
Not to be positive or opiniatre
Not to sett up for observing all these Rules, for fear I should observe none.[1]

[1] The MS. (often printed) is in the Forster Collection of the Victoria and Albert Museum. I have queried doubtful readings and put them between square brackets, used half-brackets around cancelled words, and used half strokes around inserted words.

Obligatory attendance upon Sir William would provoke the resolutions against seeking the company of young people, against peevishness, against scorning modern manners, against repeating stories, against too much talking and boasting. We know how vain Temple was and how much he enjoyed his own anecdotes; we have seen that he was notably old-fashioned, sometimes morose, and extremely fond of children. Temple's pride in his gallantries may account for the January–May theme, or it may be due to the conversation of rakish guests. Other motifs are probably casual thoughts on old age, called up by the common associations of the subject. Some cautions smell of literary sources: the Latin warning about legacy-hunters, the desire for friends' admonitions.[1] Finally, the attitude towards servants suggests that Swift, having to deal directly with the humbler members of the establishment, came to the traditional view of life below stairs.

More significant than the particular opinions expounded is the act of writing them down. Only to certain minds would such a compilation appear a wise method of regulating one's conduct. Swift's taste for this sort of list is characteristic of him. Not only manners but morality, he thought, could be codified in sets of instructions. Although the habit belongs to an epoch, and we find Descartes, Locke, and Franklin among the manufacturers of such programmes, we expect a great moralist to have reserves of insight that would line Swift's dicta with irony. Here again is evidence that his nobility was intuitive, that his soaring moral indignation starts from another spring than his explicit, didactic propositions. So I think the reverently admiring tone of the eulogies of Temple reveal more of Swift's essential nature than the naïveté of his resolutions.

In Temple's rosary of virtues, however, Swift could not count a zeal to further the interests of a dependent. Instead of providing his secretary with an income or a start in public life, Temple left him a modest acquaintance with court circles, the disposition of several unprinted works, and a legacy of a hundred pounds. Of

[1] Cf. *Gil Blas* VII. iii–iv.

these advantages, the only one mentioned by Temple in his will is the money, 'to Mr. Jonathan Swift, now dwelling with me'. Bridget Johnson, who continued to work for Lady Giffard, received twenty pounds and half a year's wages; young Esther, identified as 'servant to my sister', received the valuable lease of certain lands in Ireland. Except for Swift, all the legatees were servants or relatives; nothing went to Thomas Swift, although he witnessed the main part of the will.[1]

Swift stayed on briefly at Moor Park, settling Temple's affairs and paying off legacies. A batch of receipts is preserved, endorsed by him, for such disbursements as a journey by himself to London, and a waistcoat and breeches for himself; books bought by Temple; funeral clothes for Rebecca Dingley, Mrs Johnson, Swift, and others; a quarter-year's land tax; and the interment fee for Temple's burial in Westminster Abbey.[2]

Next, he had to look after his own fortune; and on this step we have no guide but Swift's words. He still hoped the king might present him to a prebend. Romney seemed a proper person to put William in mind of Mr Swift's merit. But the noble lord either failed or never tried to do the business. After months of profitless waiting, Swift took an unattractive post as private chaplain to a new lord justice of Ireland. (This at the very time when Matthew Prior, though still in Paris, held the place of first secretary to the lords justices of Ireland.) Swift's account has the ring of bias:

> Upon this event [i.e., Temple's death] Mr Swift removed to London, and applyed by petition to King William, upon the claym of a promise his majesty had mad[e] to Sir W[illiam] T[emple] that he would give Mr Swift a prebend of Canterbury or Westminster. The Earl of Rumney who professed much friendship for him, promised

[1] Because of the many deaths in his family, Temple drew up several wills, of which this was the last. Dated 8 Mar. 1694/5, it in turn had to be emended when one of his brothers died; so he added a codicil dated 2 Feb. 1697/8. Thomas Swift witnessed only the original version of 1695; Jonathan Swift's legacy is defined in the codicil (Courtenay II. 484–6).

[2] Documents in the collection of Mr James Osborn. Since the books may have been read by Swift while he was writing the *Battle of the Books*, I have listed them in Appendix G.

> to second his petition, but, as he was an old vitious illiterate rake without any sense of truth or honor, said not a word to the King: And Mr Swift after long attendance in vain; thought it better to comply with an invitation given him by the E[arl] of Berkeley to attend him to Ireland as his chaplain and private secretary; his lordship having been appointed one of the Lords Justices of that Kingdom.[1]

No prebend of either cathedral had in fact fallen vacant during the time of suspense. Of course the king could have promoted one of the prebendaries to free a stall for a petitioner. But Swift had no right to consider himself a correct object for such distinguished care. Furthermore, it is just possible that Romney introduced him to Berkeley. Temple and his sister were indeed familiar with the earl; but that they were on visiting terms, or friendly enough for a recommendation from either to succeed with him, is not certain. Romney, however, had been a lord deputy of Ireland (though a blundering one) 1692–3; and he might have directed Swift to the modest opportunity when it arose. Berkeley was fifty years old at the time. Short, fat, and gouty, he had waded through a mediocre *cursus honorum* of lord lieutenancies, commissions, and envoyships, but never held a post of ministerial rank. In a record of minor diplomatic missions, his greatest state had been as Envoy Extraordinary at The Hague, 1689–94, where his secretary for most of the time had been Prior. With Berkeley, Swift left for Dublin, sailing from Bristol in August 1699.

iv

Why did Swift not push his chance more shrewdly? He published nothing dedicated to men in real power; he performed no service that might be rewarded by the ministry; he attached himself to no one besides Temple; he won no college fellowship; he took no parochial living. Perhaps his ineptness reflects a half-conscious wish to prolong the *sollicitae iucunda oblivia vitae* of Moor Park—

[1] *Autob.*, f. 9^{v}.

'which no time', he said eight years afterward, 'will make me forget and love less'.[1] To the excitement of Hetty's presence and the amenities of Temple's household, he might add the pleasant landscape, the nearness to London, the advantage of meeting distinguished company. When he was an old man, his memory could still dwell upon the grounds fronting the mansion: 'The tree on which I carved those words, *factura nepotibus umbram*, is one of those elms that stand in the hollow ground just before the house.'[2] However, there are so many signs of his longing, at thirty, for advancement, that a contrary wish should not be stressed.

Perhaps Temple advised him foolishly. No doubt. But why did he take the advice? Retired courtiers, like exiles, always underestimate the decline of men whom they knew in place and the rise of those they did not. For Swift to have laid his money on such sway-backed jades as Sunderland and Romney, when all the world could see that Montagu, Somers, Wharton, and Portland were rising, bespeaks either the most cloistered innocence or darkening counsel.

We must ask how Swift might have preferred this guidance to the judgment born of his own observation. He had seen Atterbury, long before the Phalaris controversy, gain a pulpit in London and a royal chaplaincy for defending their church against Roman Catholic polemics[3]; he knew the details of Congreve's success; he heard of others'. Obviously, to find glory or preferment, one should first have identified oneself with the leader of an active party in literature, the church, or the government, and should then have studied to make oneself appear indispensable. If one neither contributed to controversy, nor brought lustre to a patron's name, nor did draught-horse work for a party project, nor caught the affection of a great, great personage, the road up was an impasse. Swift could have written on the Convocation affair; he could have defended the Trinity; he could have glori-

[1] Ball I. 57. [2] *Ibid.* v. 417.

[3] I assume that Atterbury's lectureship at St Bride's (1691) was largely a reward for his Anglican apologetics of 1687.

fied the Peace of Ryswick; he could have dedicated to somebody other than the king. But he chose not to.

From Swift's actions and remarks in the decade which followed, we may believe that he had ample intuition of all this. He should also have had enough experience of Temple to distrust the baronet's precepts—supposing they were in fact what Swift relied upon. I think he left too much to Temple; or, in a practical—not moral—sense, expected too much from him. Ignoring ten years of evidence, Swift was pretending to believe that Sir William would act as the father Swift would like to have had. In the disappointment which followed, he poured over Romney's character the acid which ought to have fallen on Temple's. This transfer of blame may suggest that Swift realized, underneath, that his own miscalculation, and not Temple's inertia, was the effective source of his disappointment. A quarter-century later, in a spasm of anger, he adjusted the implicit balance between Romney and Romney's old friend:

> I own myself indebted to Sir William Temple, for recommending me to the late King, although without success. . . [But] I was at his death as far to seek as ever, and perhaps you will allow that I was of some use to him. This I will venture to say, that in the time when I had some little credit I did fifty times more for fifty people, from whom I never received the least service or assistance.[1]

In view of this outburst, I think it fair to suspect that Swift had originally sacrificed his small faith in Romney to save his deep admiration for Temple. It was an excellent bargain.

On one account, however, Swift possessed little freedom to choose a path; for he had already done what few of his contemporaries dared to try before their careers were established: he had risked the effects of independence. Prior clung, without swerving, to Montagu; Congreve never broke with Dryden or the court; Addison and Somers kept up, to the end, a cordial, if sometimes thin, friendship; even the quixotic Richard Steele only left Lord Cutts after a dedication to Lady Albemarle won him a captaincy.

[1] Ball III. 301.

But Swift had not only followed the evening rather than the morning star: he had abandoned Temple's shelter without the resource of another patron. In his own native city, however, he had needed Temple's good word to admit him even into a course which Temple himself had discouraged. At Kilroot the desolation of Swift's life had refurbished the appeals of Moor Park. When the offer of renewed 'acquaintance with greatness' arrived, Swift seized it. By returning to his master, however, he gave up the power to act without Temple's approval. He locked himself within a circle which the old man's death would have to break.

Ultimately, moreover, the questioner is flung back upon an interpretation of Swift's own character. Whether or not he took advice from Temple, Swift certainly committed faults of strategy which were corrected in succeeding years. I think that he was fundamentally so unsure of himself, though aware of his gifts, at this era, that he held passively to the appearance of calm and strength. 'Little disguises', he wished to believe, 'were infinitely beneath persons of [my] pride . . . paltry maxims that they are, calculated for the rabble of humanity.'[1] Without appeasing the usual gods, he was offering up the usual prayers. He looked for the blessings of prudence but hugged the words of his Muse:

Stoop not to int'rest, flattery, or deceit;
Nor with hir'd thoughts be thy devotion paid.[2]

Unfortunately, if 'dirty paths where vulgar feet have trod'[3] are not the way to Parnassus, they are, for a man in Swift's case, the way to a thousand pounds a year. Yet he could hardly disdain others for taking it unless he refused it himself. It was to be his lesson for the next ten years that genius, charm, and integrity, all together, could not exempt him from the common doom.

[1] Ball I. 20. [2] *Poems* I. 55. [3] *Ibid.*, p. 49.

Appendices

APPENDIX A

The Family of Swift's Father

These are the children of Thomas Swift, vicar of Goodrich, Herefordshire, as their baptisms are recorded in the MS. parish register. The original entries are in Latin. Where the English form of the name is not perfectly certain, I give the Latin as well. It is possible but unlikely that other children of Thomas Swift were baptized elsewhere. The Abraham Swift (died in Dublin 1686) listed by Ball (VI. 215) among the sons of Thomas Swift of Goodrich does not seem to belong to this family. He is not among the children baptized at Goodrich; he is not named in Thomas Swift's will; and he is not mentioned in Jonathan Swift's autobiographical essay, or in his correspondence or works.

Mary ('Maria'): 12 July 1626
Godwin: 23 January 1627/8
Dryden: 15 November 1629
Emily ('Aemilia'): 9 July 1631
Elizabeth: 4 November 1632
Thomas: 8 December 1633
Sarah: 7 February 1635/6
William: 13 August 1637
Katherine ('Katherina'): 24 March 1638/9
Jonathan: 24 May 1640
Adam: 21 March 1641/2

The following events, relating to Thomas Swift's family, are also recorded in the Goodrich register:

4 May 1658: Thomas Swift buried.
5 May 1662: Thomas Vaughan and Elizabeth Swift married.
28 December 1664: Jonathan, son of Thomas Vaughan and Elizabeth his wife, baptized.
26 December 1666: Godwyn, son of Thomas Vaughan and Elizabeth his wife, baptized.
25 September 1670: James, son of Thomas Vaughan and Elizabeth his wife, baptized.

APPENDIX B

The Will of Thomas Swift of Goodrich[1]

Thomas Swift cler[icus]

In the name of God amen. I Thomas Swift of Goodridge in the county of Hereford beinge sick in bodie but of sound and good memorie (blessed be the allmighty God for it) doe make and ordaine this my last will and testament in manner followinge: ffirst I giue and bequeath my soule to allmighty God trustinge to be saued by the merritts of my redeemer Jesus Christ And my body to be buried at the will and discrecōn of my welbeloued wife and my executor herein afternamed And as for that smale personall estate wherewith god hath blessed mee I giue and devise the same in manner following Vizt) I giue and devise all my corne now groweinge vpon all or anie of my landes togeather with all my householdstuffe as plate, brasse, pewter, linnen, of all sorts bedds and beddinge woodden vessells, tables chaires stooles and other the necessaries of the house and all provisions of all sorts as bacon, beefe, butter, cheese, wheate, rye, barley, mault, and beere of all sorts to my deare and welbeloued wife Item I giue and devise vnto my foure sonnes Thomas William Jonathan and Adam, and to my foure daughters their seuerall porcōns beinge already paid or secured to them) the summe of fiue shillings a peece Lastly I giue and devise that my eldest sonne Godwin shall pay all my debtes of what kinde soever and to enable him herevnto I giue vnto my said sonne Godwin all the rest of my personall estate as horses, oxen, sheepe, lambes, swine hopps in the house ready sacked woods cutt and corded on my lands, waines, carts ploughes, plough timber and other implements and necessaries of husbandry and other my personall estate not herein before bequeathed and I doe alsoe make and appointe my said sonne Godwin executor of this my last will and testament In witnes whereof I haue herevnto sett my hand and seale the foure and twentieth day of Aprill one thousand six hundred ffiftie eight: Thom: Swift: Sealed and published. In the

[1] Principal Probate Registry, Somerset House, 1658, f. 697, Wootton.

presence of Elizabeth Swift the marke of Edward Lambert the marke of Jane Howells the marke of Mary Williams Katherine Swift.

This will was proved at London the sixth day of the moneth of December in the yeare of our lord God one thousand sixe hundred ffiftie and eight: before the judges for probate of wills and grantinge administrations lawfully authorized by the oath of Godwin Swift the naturall and lawfull sonne of the said deceased and sole executor named in the said will: to whome was committed administration of all and singular the goodes chattles and debtes of the said deceased: hee the said Godwin Swift beinge first sworne in due forme of lawe by vertue of a commission well and truly to administer the same.

APPENDIX C

Swift's Maternal Grandfather

The identity of Swift's mother's father has been an object of investigation at least since John Nichols took up the search while working upon his *History of Leicestershire*. Until recently, however, little progress was made beyond what Nichols himself suggested. Though his statements are not all consistent with one another, the drift of the argument is that Abigail Erick was sister to Thomas Errick, vicar (1664–81) of Frisby-on-the-Wreake, Leicestershire, and that her niece, Thomas Errick's daughter, married John Kendall, vicar (1684–1717) of Thornton, Leicestershire.[1] If we can substantiate these conclusions, we can identify Abigail Erick's father, since it is now known that Thomas Errick was the son of James Ericke, vicar (1627–34) of Thornton, Leicestershire.[2] By showing her to be James Ericke's daughter, we can account for two further puzzles which have plagued Swift's biographers: first, why no record of Abigail Erick's baptism has been found in Leicestershire; secondly, how a woman from that county happened to marry, in Dublin, a recent immigrant from Herefordshire. For it will appear that James Ericke emigrated to Ireland toward the end of 1634. Although Swift described his mother as 'M[rs] Abigail Erick of Leicester-shire',[3] her wedding licence describes her as 'of the city of Dublin spinster'.[4] According to the record of her burial, she was seventy years old at her death in 1710, and therefore born in 1640.[5] If her father moved to Ireland in 1634, and she was born there in 1640, no record of her baptism would of course be found in Leicestershire; and Swift's father would have met her after he arrived in Ireland, and not before. Since, however, she moved to her ancestral county when Swift was still a child, and he re-

[1] Nichols, *Leicestershire* II. ii. 620–1 and n. 3. But cf. III. i. 261, n. 10; IV. ii. 982, n. 7, and 985.

[2] Venn. [3] *Autob.*, f. 6[v]. [4] Ball IV. 475.

[5] Parish register of St Martin's, Leicester, 27 Apr. 1710.

peatedly visited her in Leicester, he naturally thought of her as native to Leicestershire.

James Ericke certainly married Elizabeth Imins, daughter of William Imins of Ibstock, Leicestershire, in the church of Thornton 16 October 1627.[1] His sister Anne married Nicholas Berkett in St Martin's, Leicester, 16 January 1626/7.[2] James and Elizabeth Ericke witnessed the will of William Imyn of Ibstock on 21 October 1629.[3]

We have thus established a connection of three families. The name of each appears unfortunately in many variant spellings: Erick, Eyricke, Herrick, etc.; Birkhead, Berket, Burkett, etc.; Imminges, Imin, Imaine, etc. These names corroborate the tie between James Ericke and Thomas Errick; for when the administration of Thomas Errick's estate was granted to Jane, his widow (October 1681), the sureties named were William Immyn and Josiah Birkhead.[4]

Nichols's statement that Abigail Erick's niece—Thomas Errick's daughter—married John Kendall is corroborated, though not proved, by a few facts. The marriage is so described in W. G. D. Fletcher's *Pedigrees of Leicestershire*.[5] Although Fletcher was probably following Nichols's *Leicestershire*, he was a wide searcher; and it is significant that he found no evidence to contradict Nichols. Kendall's wife certainly bore the Christian name of her putative mother, Jane.[6] Furthermore, a book has been noticed which was signed 'Jane Ericke, her book, 1677' on the flyleaf, with 'John Kendall, his book' written below.[7] It also seems significant that Swift's sister was named Jane: for though Swift had many female relatives in his father's family, none was so called; but if Nichols is right, this sister was the namesake of both an aunt (Thomas Errick's wife) and a cousin (John Kendall's wife) in Swift's mother's family. To clinch this argument, Swift, in a letter to John Kendall, addresses him as 'cousin', and directs the letter to be left 'at Mr. Birkhead's'.[8] Finally, and corroboratively, when

[1] Thornton parish register. In the marriage bond, 1 Oct. 1627, she is described as 'Elizabeth Imins of Tilton' (Leicester City Museum, Archives 1 D 41/38/III/81).

[2] St Martin's parish register.

[3] Leicester City Museum, Archives 14 D 57/112/9, p. 36.

[4] Leicester County Record Office.

[5] Leicester, 1886, p. 160, 'Kendall of Twycross'.

[6] She is so named in the records of his children's baptisms in the Thornton parish register, and she is so named in his will, 27 June 1717 (Leicester County Record Office).

[7] *Transactions of the Leicestershire Archaeological Society*, VI, pt. 1 (1884), 10–11.

[8] Ball I. 6.

Elizabeth Jones, whom Swift described as his mother's cousin, was married at Thurcaston, the surety was Josiah Birkhead.[1]

James Ericke was made vicar of Thornton in 1627.[2] The following baptisms of the children of 'James Ericke minist^r^' are recorded in the parish register:

25 July 1628	Thomas
30 March 1630	James
28 December 1631	William[3]

Although no further record of his family appears here, and there is a gap in the original register after 1634, the bishop's transcripts give further baptisms:

8 October 1633	Grace
18 September 1634	Mary[4]

Mary is described as the daughter not of the minister but of 'Mr James Ericke', and the bishop's transcript for 1634/5 is signed not by Ericke, as in earlier years, but by 'John Sommerfeild Vicar', his successor. There are bishop's transcripts annually until March 1641/2, still preserved, but no mention, in them, of Ericke or his family.

In the induction mandate for his successor at Thornton, the benefice is said to be vacant 'per cessionem derelictionem sive depriuationem Jacobi Ericke'.[5] What had happened is made clear elsewhere. In January 1633/4 Ericke was accused of having held an unlawful conventicle, and he confessed that 'in the house of Nicholas Birkhead who married his sister . . . in the presence of some of his neire kinsfolk he did then and there repeat the sermon which he had that morninge preached at St Maries in Leicester and that they did singe a psalme before and one after the said repetition'[6]. He was prosecuted in the Court of High Commission, and one of the decisions is recorded under the date 8 May 1634:

> This day after severall motions made by the Counsell of both sydes the Court at last resolued to referre the finall hearing and ending of this cause

[1] Ball IV. 55–6.

[2] Induction mandate dated 22 July 1627 (Leicester City Museum, 1 D 41/28/373).

[3] Possibly the alleged uncle of Swift identified as William Herrick of Stamford, Lincolnshire (*N. & Q.*, 4 Apr. 1885, pp. 264–5; 30 May 1885, p. 435).

[4] Leicester City Museum.

[5] Leicester City Museum, Archives 1 D 41/28/442.

[6] Helen Stocks and W. H. Stevenson, edd., *Records of the Borough of Leicester 1603–1688* (Cambridge 1923), pp. 271–2. In this text 'Richard' Birkhead is an error for 'Nicholas', occasioned by a misreading of the contraction 'Nich'.

to Sr John Lambe Knight Comissary of Leicester yet wth this Reservation that the Articles shall still remaine in Court and the Cause not as yet to be finally dismissed in reguard the Court resolued to make tryall of him for a tyme to see how and in what manner he did demeane and Carry him selfe in the execution of his ministry and so for the present he was lycensed to depart paying first the costs of the suite.[1]

In the autumn, during a visitation by Archbishop Laud, reports were made on the three parishes of which Ericke's benefice was constituted: Stanton, Bagworth, and Thornton. At Stanton, 15 September 1634, the chancel of the church was found to be 'out of repaire' and 'Mr. Jacobus Herricke Rector' was ordered to repair it.[2] At Thornton, three successive notes were made: the presentment of the church-wardens (in English); the sentence of the court, added later and dated; and a final note of four words in a slightly different hand:

Mr. James Errycke vicar there presented for not readinge prayers on Wedensdaies and Frydayes and Sonday Eves.
15. September 1634: contra Mr. Eyricke quem dominus monet ad perlegendum preces publicas diebus predictis etc et ad certificandum etc in proxima omnium sanctorum

vertit solum in Hiberniam[3]

The final four words ('He has emigrated to Ireland') are paralleled in the report on Bagworth, 22 November 1634: according to this, not only is the church 'uncovered and out of repaire', but also 'The Minister is absent and gone into Ireland and they have noe prayers there nor divine service.'[4] It would thus appear that Ericke remained in Thornton until after his daughter Mary was born, September 1634, but left for Ireland before the date of the Bagworth entry, 22 November.

If my account is reliable, later events may be inferred from the wills of some relatives of Elizabeth Ericke. To see the pertinence of the material, we must recognize a connection among the Tarlton, Hooker, and Immings families. This is established by a will dated 21 January 1687, in which Samuel Tarlton of London names as

[1] P.R.O. SP 16/261, f. 26^{v}. I have preserved the spelling, etc., of the MS.

[2] A. Percival Moore, 'The Metropolitical Visitation of Archdeacon [*sic*] Laud', *Associated Architectural Societies' Reports*, XXIX, pt. II (1908), 493. I have expanded contractions, and spelled the name as in the MS. (Leicester City Museum, Archives 1 D 41/13/61, f. 32^{v}).

[3] Leicester City Museum, Archives 1 D 41/13/61, f. 33^{v} (contractions expanded).

[4] A. P. Moore, p. 492, corrected from MS., as above (f. 28).

cousins—i.e., relatives of some sort—William Immyn of Maresfield, Leics., and John Hooker of [?Massworth],[1] Leics.

These hints are repeated and enlarged by a will dated 1 January 1654/5, in which John Hooker of Maresfield, Leics., names as cousins William Immings and also Samuel Hooker, student in New England; he names as well other members of the Hooker and Immings families; and he describes Frances Tarlton of the City of London as his sister. His executor is William Immings of Maresfield; the will was proved 26 November 1655.[2] For us, the most important remarks in this will are two bequests: a hundred pounds to 'Cosin Elizabeth Errick' and five pounds to 'her daur. Abigail'. From the concatenation of names, places, and dates, it seems that this Elizabeth Errick was James Ericke's wife, and that Abigail was Swift's mother.

Furthermore, in a will dated 16 March 1652/3, John Tarlton of the parish of St Olave, Southwark, Surrey, and citizen and brewer of London, names Frances Tarlton as his wife; he is therefore probably the brother-in-law of the John Hooker whose will we have just looked at. He also names his sons, among them Samuel, who is probably testator of the will of 1687 seen above. One of John Tarlton's bequests is three pounds to 'Cozen Elizabeth Erricke widow of Leicester'. Since this will was proved 23 February 1653/4,[3] we may assume that James Ericke died before 1654.

Finally, an 'Elizabeth Errick' was buried 4 September 1663 in St John's church, Dublin[4]; this was probably James Ericke's widow, and Swift's grandmother. Her death would presumably have hastened the marriage of her daughter, Abigail, the following year; and it may be significant that her son, Thomas, took his final orders as a priest in December 1663, three months after her death, although his Cambridge B.A. degree is dated 1648 (and his deacon's orders, 7 August 1662).[5]

[1] Probably a misreading of 'Maresfield'.

[2] Somerset House, Registry of Wills, P.C.C., Aylett, 403. [3] *Ibid.*, 246.

[4] W. H. Welply, in *TLS.*, 17 Jul. 1959. The late Mr Welply, with great generosity, gave me abstracts of the Tarlton and Hooker wills, the discovery of which was due to his patient and exact research.

[5] Venn.

APPENDIX D

[St George Ashe's Speech to Lord Clarendon 25 January 1685/6[1]]

While the whole nation aemulosly crowds to kis your excellencyes hands, and the most differing parties agree in joynt congratulations, loud expressions of joy for your wished for arrivall, and the happiness they all promise themselves under your auspicious government; shall philosophy alone (how stoicall soever) remain insensible? and the [poets] and muses continue silent? who are proud to call you theire own, and glory in hauing form'd your mind to that rare pitch of wisdome and knowledge which is admired by all men. And from whome indeed, but persons of your excellencyes illustrius character and inquisitiue genius can philosophy expect its advance and propagation? whose larger souls and more refin'd parts are most fitt to comprehend and cultivate the vastest truthes, whose more liberall education, innate grandeur of mind, and exalted station in ye world, gives 'em a more extended prospect, a farther veiw [*sic*] over the whole intelligible world; To such therefore it belongs (whose plenty secures from the sordid considerations of gain and profit, and whose usuall generosity makes them disdain to bound their thoughts wholly by others precepts) to reason and philosophize above the common rate of man-kind, at least to protect those that do so, by their authority and example. 'Tis true, knowledge was of old for the most part only the study of the sullen and the poor, who thought it the gravest peice of science to contemn the use of man-kind, and to differ in habit and manners from all others; It was heretofore condemn'd to melancholy retirements, kept as a minor under the tuition of ambitious and arrogant guardians, buried in cloysters, or the more dark obscurity of affected jargon and unintelligable cant; Antiquity too was ador'd with such superstitious reverence, as if the beauty of truth, like that of a picture cou'd not be known or perceived but at a distance, as if

[1] T.C.D. MS. Molyneux I. 4. 17, no. 2. The date is given in the minutes of the D.P.S.

theire eyes, like ye praepostrus animalls, were behind them, and their intellectuall motions retrograde; No wonder then that knowledge did not outgrow the dwarfishness of its pristine stature, and that the intellectuall world did continue such a microcosm: for while they were slaves to the dictiates [*sic*] of their forefathers, their discoveries, like water, cou'd never rise higher then the fountains, from whence they were derived.

But when by the generous care and noble designe of his late majty and our present soveraign, and the never to be forgotten zeall of your illustrius father, in instituting the Royall Society; Captive truth was rescued from its former bondage, & clouded knowledge began to shine more bright; when instead of words and empty speculations were introduc'd things and experiments, and the beautifull bosome of nature was exposed to veiw, where we might enter into its guarden, tast of its fruits, satisfy our selves with its plenty, instead of idle talking and wandering under its fruitless shadows; Then philosophy was admitted into our palaces and our courts, began to keep the best company, to refine its fashion and appearance, and to become the employment of the rich and of the great.

Now, my lord, if your noble fathers patronage was so successfull in our neighbouring iland, how happy an omen would it be to us, cou'd we obtaine your excellencies tuition for our young orphan society? how powerfull an influence wou'd so great an example have upon all the nobility and gentry of our nation? what a royatt of philosophers might we justly expect from such encouragement? And this we presume not only to beg, but even challenge, since in it is concluded the publick interest and good of ye kingdome, which (we are sure) 'twill be your excellencyes care allways to promote and advance, for tho fabulous tradition will have this to have been ye iland as well of learned men as saints, and the western Athens; Yet so few tracks and foot steps thereof remain'd, that 'tis not long since a mathematicion and a conjurer were aequivalent terms, and a telescope and quadrant were things as unknown as a frog or a toad. So that considering whence we began, our progress for so short a time has not been wholly inconsiderable, and some not unsuccessfull essays have been made in many usefull parts of knowledge; Yet we have nothing truly to boast of, but the extreme honour that is done us by this noble lord's vouchsafing to be our president, concerning whom his presents and modesty forbids me to add more, then that if every member of our company did contribute half the zeall and abilities for the promoting naturall and mathematicall knowledge, wch our worthy president does, we then assure our selves, that we shou'd throughly meritt your excellencyes protection. Thus, my lord, tho our designe seems very fair and usefull, at least to give offence to no one, yet even in our cradle, like Hercules, we have suffer'd persecution, and been fircely oppos'd by a loud and numerous; tho (God be thanked) an impudent sort of adversaries, ye railleurs and the witts; But to gain their good will and do them honour, I must inform 'em, that the railleurs and philosophers are derived from the same originall, the confessed author as well of irony as philosophy being Socrates; Methinks therefore they should be tender, where the honour of their comon parent is concern'd, and value their own friends and relations, at least above their jest; we are told by them that our time is spent in vulgar experiments, in empty useless speculations, which (suppose true) is it not necessary that many loads of unprofitable earth shou'd be thrown by, before we come at a vain of gold, yet certainly the contemplation even of flies and shells and the most trifling works of nature (which they so much redicule) is more manly then downright idleness and ignorance, and the extreams of raillery are more offensive then those of stupidity; They should reflect that all things are capable of abuse from the same topicks by which they may be comended, that (besides the ill manners in discountenancing such studies as our great master has declared himself the founder of and promoter) burlasque and [laughter] is ye easiest and the slenderest fruit of witt, that it proceeds from ye observation of the deformity of things, whereas there is a nobler and more masculin pleasure wch is rais'd from beholding their orders and beauty; Then they wou'd perceive how great a difference is between them and true philosophers, for while nature has only form'd them to be pleas'd with its irregularities and monsters, it has given the other the delight of knowing and studying its most beautifull works. All usefull enterprizes among ingenious good natur'd people should find assistance wn they are begun, applaus [when] they succeed and even pitty and prais when they fail; true railery shoud only intend the derision of extravagant, and the disgrace of vile and dishonourable things; and this kind of witt ought to have the nature of salt, to which tis usually compared, wch preserves and keeps sweet the good and sound parts of our bodies, and only fretts and dries up, and destroys those humours which putrify and corrupt.

My Lord, you'l pardon this digression, to which we have had sufficient provocation, but we shall have no longer reason to [dread] these pleasant gentlemen, if your excellencye will be our patron, wch high honour I am [com̄anded] here most humbly to implore; All our inventions and discoveries shall be consecrated to your fame, and 'twas by such arts that the [antient] heroes and demy-[gods] gain'd their temples and their alters; and all studies and endeavours shall tend to render (if possible) the great names of *Hyde* and *Clarendon* more illustrious and renown'd.

APPENDIX E

Roll of Students' Marks on the Terminal Examinations at Trinity College, Dublin, Easter, 1685[1]

(Abbreviations: *D*=dominus [i.e., graduate], *G*=Greek, *L*=Latin, *Log*=logic, *med*=mediocriter, *neglig*=negligenter, *Ph*=physics, *Phil*=philosophie, *Th*=thema.)

Wilson	Ph: male GL male Th: med
Wade	Ph: med G:L bene Th: negligenter
Lambert	
Meridith	
Drysdall	Ph: med: GL med Th: vix med:
Richardson	Ph: male GL med Th: med
Banks	Ph: med G:L med Th: neglig
Blany	Ph: med G:L bene Th: neglig
Jones	[Ph: male Th: bene[2]]
Chandler	Ph: med GL: med Th: Med
Stratford	Ph: vix med: GL vix med. Th Med
Swift [i.e., Thomas]	Ph: Med: GL: Med. Th: Med
Swift [i.e., Jonathan]	Ph: male G:L bene Th: Neglig:
Lange	Ph: Med: GL Med Th: vix med
Ward	
Norman	
Hassett	Ph: bene G:L Med Th: med
Ruffin	Ph: med: G:L med Th: vix med
Fitsimmons	Ph: med: GL vix med
Winn	Ph: med GL: med Th: vix med
Jones	Ph: male. GL. med. Th: Med
[St]amp	
Brown	Ph: med: G:L Med The: med
Dixy	
Baly	Ph: med. GL med. Th: Negligent[er]

[1] MS. in the library of Trinity College. [2] Line scratched through.

Kirton	Ph: med. GL vix med Th: med
Wilson	Ph: med: GL Med: Th: male neglig
Vandelure	Ph: male GL Med: Th: mal: neglig
Townly	
Brereton	
Conolly	Ph: med: G:L Med Th: vix med
Browne	Ph: male. G:L. Med Th male
Hamilton	Ph: Med GL: bene Th: bene vix
Hamilton	Ph: med: GL med. Th: vix med
Hamilton	Ph: med. GL med Th: vix med
Cox	Ph: med GL med Th: vix med
Wittingham	Ph: bene. GL. Med: Th: Med
Moore	
[?Uiseant[1]]	Ph: pessime
D: Marsh	Med: Ph:
D. Richesy	Ph: Male
D: Hassett	
D: Savage	Ph: male
Cardiffe	Ph: pessime
Tenisson	Ph: Med
Sheridon	Ph: pessime
Muchall	Ph: Med
Slingsby	Ph: Med
Ottoway	Ph: Med
Ker[in][1]	Ph: bene
Berry	Log bene: G:L Med Th: Med
Law	
Brereton	
Berckly	
Merriman	
ffulton	
Walk[ara][1]	Log: mal: Phy: mal: GL med Th: med
Travers	
Charlton	
Bishope	
Yarner	
Mussendine	Log: mal. Phy: mal GL Med Th: Med
Bradshaw	

[1] Doubtful reading.

Price	
Thomas	Log Med Ph: med G:L: Med Th: Med
Tovey	Log & Phil: med Gr: L bene Th: bene
Ayton	L: & Phil: Med Gr:L: Med Th: Med
Ward:	Phil: Med: GL: [?et][1] Med Th bene
Leeds	Log: Med [Phys][1]: med: GL: med Th: Med
Hamilton	Log & Phy: Med: GL vix med: Th: Med
Brady	Log: & Phys: vix med: G:L: Med: Th Med
Parker	
Dixon	
Brady	Log: & Phys: vix med: G:L: Med Ph Med
Parker	
Dixon	
Maxwell	Log: Med Phy: med: G:L: Med Th: Med
Bates	Log: vix med: Phy: med GL: Med Th: Med
Hassett	Log & Phy: Med G:L Med: Th: Med
Conner	Phys: med G:L: [obliterated] Th: Med
Mossum	
Wacham	Log mal: Phy: mal: G:L: med Th: med
D: Harrison	
D: Brewster	Log: Med: Th: Med
D: Ram	Log: Med: Th: Med
D: Warren	
Perse	Log: Med: Th: Med
Mallery	Log: Med: Th: bene
Bates	Ph: vix med: Th: bene
Shaddow	Ph: vix med: Th: Med
Squire	
R[ichar]dson	Ph: med: Th: Med
R[ichar]dson	Ph: Med: Th: Med
Bolton	
Parkes	
Grattan	
Tarlton	Ph: Med: Th: Med
Maxwell	Ph: vix med: Th: bene
Maxwell	Ph: bene: Th: Med
Bates	Ph: med: Th: Med
Crump	Ph: Med: Th: Med

[1] Doubtful reading.

Procter	
Sutton	Ph: mal (Mr. Patrickson contradicts this censure) medioc GL & Theme
Lea[thes][1]	Ph: Med: L: med. G bene Th: bene
Bland	
Mathews	L: bene G: Med: Th: Med
Galbreth	Ph: G:L: Med: Th: bene
Jones	
Maddin	
Ashe	
Mongumry	Ph: Med: L: bene. G: Med: Th: Med
Travers	Ph: Med: L: Med: G: bene: Th: Med
Dean	
Phipps	Ph: Med: L: bene. G: Med: Th: Med
Drury	Mediocriter in omnibus
Mullins	Mediocriter in omnibus
Southel	Ph: Med: L: Med: G. bene Th: bene
Mullan	Ph: Med: L: Med: G: bene Th: Med
King	Ph: Med G:L med: Th: male
Morris	mediocriter in omnibus
Revett	mediocriter in omnibus
Webb	
Goodlett	Log: Med: L:G: bene. Th: Med
fflemmin	mediocriter in omnibus
R[ichar]dson	Med: in omnib[us]
Bredy	Med: in omnib[us]
Ayton	Med: in omnib[us]
Moor	Med in omnib[us]
Beecher	Log: med: L:G: bene. Th: Med
Touse	Log. bene L:G: bene. Th: med
Prin	Log. Med: L:G: bene. Th: med
Warring	Med: in omnib[us]
Browning	Log. optime: L:G: bene. Th: Med
Vaughen	Log: Med: L:G: Med. Th: bene
Luther	Log. bene. L:G. bene. Th: Med
Ormsby	
Quin	Ph: Med. G:L. bene Th: bene
Garner	Log: Med: G:L: bene Th: Med
Williams	log: Med: GL: bene. Th: Med

[1] Doubtful reading.

Norris	
Law.	
D: Ware	Med in omnibus
D: Ray	
Creamer	Ph: bene. Th: Med
Donavan	Ph: bene G L bene: Th: Med
Johnson	
Ince	Med: in omnibus
Shaw	
Alcock	Ph: bene GL bene Th: Med
Warrall	
Thewles	bene in omnibus
Brian	Ph: bene GL: bene: Th: Med
Edgworth	
Kerny	vix med: in omnibus
Weale	
Perry	Log: bene GL Med Th: med
Ambrose	vix med: in omnibus
Edrington	Mediocriter
Smith	
Jones	Mediocriter
Pratt	
Pratt	
Pratt	
Aikins	
Gray	
Hartis	Log: med: GL: Med: Th: Med
Purifoy	
Johnson	Log: med GL med: Th: med
Hill	log: med GL med: Th: med
Downing	log: med: GL. bene Th: med
Wilson	
Gibbins	Log: Med. GL Med Th: Med
Bishope	G:L Med Th: med
Co[wron][1]	Log. med GL Med Th: Med
Ash	
Banks	Log. med GL med Th: Med
Stewart	
ffrench	Log: med GL med: Th: med

[1] Doubtful reading.

APPENDIX F

Disciplinary Fines of Swift and Other Students at Trinity College: Further Examples

I do not repeat here those figures which have been used above, in Part I, Chapter Seven. The records are taken from the MSS. *Junior Buttery Book* (14 Nov. 1685 to 14 Oct. 1687) and *Senior Buttery Books* (14 Nov. 1685 to 18 Sept. 1691) of the College[1]; Swift is entered only in the former. Generally, the date of a week's accounts appears on each recto; but it is not clear whether each verso is the same date as the preceding or the following recto; I have assumed the latter, because terms seem to begin and to end together on facing pages. There are regrettably few periods when circumstances seem sufficiently parallel, between Swift and the other students, for him to be significantly matched against them. (Non-disciplinary fees or expenses are not counted here.)

Two weeks, 3–16 July 1686: Swift fined 1s. 1d.; Thomas Swift, 1s.; Congreve, 1s. 3d.; Thomas Wilson, 5d. (not counting 5s. cancelled, for missing roll-call).

Five weeks, 17 July to 20 August 1686: Swift fined 4s. 4d.; Congreve, 1s. 7d.

Three weeks, 10 September to 1 October 1686: Swift fined 3s. 4d.; Stratford, 4s. (not counting 5s. cancelled, for missing roll-call).

Three weeks, 27 November to 17 December 1686: Swift fined 2s. 7d. (not counting 4s. 11d. cancelled, for missing ordinary chapel and services requiring a surplice); Thomas Swift, 5s. 8d. (not counting 3s. 9d. cancelled, for missing declamations and chapel); Stratford, 1s. (not counting 9s. 8d. cancelled, for missing ordinary chapel, services requiring a surplice, and roll-call).

[1] I am deeply indebted to the officers of Trinity College for permitting me to use these MSS. and the *General Registry*.

Three weeks, 19 February to 11 March 1687: Swift fined 2s. 4d. (not counting 7s. 2d. cancelled, for missing roll-call, chapel, and services requiring a surplice); Stratford, 10d. (not counting 13s. 2d., cancelled).

APPENDIX G

Books Bought by Sir William Temple from Ralph Sympson in 1698

[I have copied the items on Sympson's bill, which is no. 78 in Mr James Osborn's collection of Temple family papers. The dates are apparently of delivery. After each of Sympson's entries I have given, in square brackets, enough information to identify the book and, where possible, the number in Donald Wing's *Short-Title Catalogue*. For Brice I have used the catalogue of the Bibliothèque Nationale; the note on this book is in Swift's hand and is probably addressed to Lady Giffard. The significance of the list is of course the possible use of these books by Swift, who certainly read some of them (not necessarily, to be sure, in these copies) while he was writing the *Battle of the Books*. Cf. the list in the *Tale*, pp. liii–liv.]

Jul. 21, 1698 1 Answer to Mullineaux book 0: 2: 0
[William Atwood, *An Answer to Mr. Molyneux His Case*. 1698. Wing A 4167.]

1 Essay Concerning Critical Learning 0: 1: 0
[Thomas Rymer, *An Essay, concerning Critical and Curious Learning*. 1698. Wing R 2425.]

1 Answer to it 0: 0: 4
[*An Answer to a Late Pamphlet, Called An Essay Concerning Critical . . . Learning*. 1698. Wing A 3306.]

Aug. 23, 1698 1 Embassy from Moscow to China 0: 2: 0
[Adam Brand, *Journal of the Embassy from Muscovy . . . into China*. 1698. Wing B 4246.]

1 Hist: of Muscovy in 2 Vol[s] 0: 6: 0
[Jodocus Crull, *The Antient and Present State of Muscovy*. 2 vols. 1698. Wing C 7424.]

	I Boyles Answer to Bentley 3[d] Edit:	0: 4: 0

[Charles Boyle, Earl of Orrery, *Dr. Bentley's Dissertations*, 3rd ed. 1699. Wing O 471.]

	I Wafers Discription of y[e] Isthmus	0: 3: 6

[Lionel Wafer, *A New Voyage and Description of the Isthmus of America*. 1699. Wing W 193.]

	I Vindication of an Essay	0: 0: 6

[Thomas Rymer, *A Vindication of an Essay concerning Critical . . . Learning*. 1698. Wing R 2434.]

	I Account of Pennsilvania	0: I: 0

[Gabriel Thomas, *An Historical and Geographical Account of . . . Pensilvania*. 1698. Wing T 964.]

	I Life of Milton	0: 2: 0

[John Toland, *The Life of John Milton*. 1699. Wing T 1766.]

	I History of Standing Armies	0: 0: 6

[John Trenchard and W. Moyle, *A Short History of Standing Armies*. 1698. Wing T 2115.]

	for Binding Divine Plate Cal: pl[n]:	0: 3: 0
	I Æsop at Tunbridge	0: I: 0

[*Æsop at Tunbridge*. 1698. Wing A 739 or 739A.]

	I View of ye Dissertations on phalris	0: I: 0

[John Milner, *A View of the Dissertation upon the Epistles of Phalaris*. 1698. Wing M 2082.]

×For y[r] Ladyship	I ×Discription of Paris	0: 2: 6

[*Germain Brice, Description nouvelle de la ville de Paris*. 2 vols. Paris 1698. Bibl. Nat. cat., vol. XIX, p. 603.]

	I Character of a Trimer	0: 0: I
		I: II: I

[George Savile, Marquess of Halifax, *The Character of a Trimmer*, '3rd' ed. 1697. Wing H 300.]

APPENDIX H

Abbreviated References and a Note on the Quotations

In quotations I have followed the spelling and punctuation of the originals, using ellipses to indicate any deletions made within the passage quoted. But I have not preserved the old usage in capitals, italics, superior letters, or the long *s*; I have not indicated omissions at the opening or the close of a quotation; and I have generally spelled out ampersands, 'ym', and a few other contractions. In some passages from unpublished manuscripts I have followed the originals more closely; but several quotations, in which the substance alone was important, I have condensed rather freely, calling attention to such treatment in my notes.

In the following list of abbreviated references, the place of publication is London if no place is named.

Autob.
Jonathan Swift's unfinished autobiographical essay, headed by him, 'Family of Swift'. MS. in the library of Trinity College, Dublin.

B.M.
The British Museum.

Bagwell
Richard Bagwell, *Ireland under the Stuarts*. 3 vols. 1909–16.

Ball
The Correspondence of Jonathan Swift, ed. F. Elrington Ball. 6 vols. 1910–14.

Barrett
John Barrett, *An Essay on the Earlier Part of the Life of Swift*. 1808.

Black Book
The Black Book. MS. in the library of the King's Inns, Dublin.

Bodl.
The Bodleian Library, Oxford.

Bolton
Robert Bolton, *A Translation of the Charter and Statutes of Trinity-College*. Dublin 1749.

Boyle's *Examination*
Dr. Bentley's Dissertations on the Epistles of Phalaris, and the Fables of Æsop, Examin'd by the Honourable Charles Boyle, Esq;, 2nd ed. 1698.

Burnet
Gilbert Burnet, *Bishop Burnet's History of His Own Time*, ed. M. J. Routh. 6 vols. Oxford 1824.

Burtschaell
George Dames Burtschaell and T.U. Sadleir, comps., *Alumni Dublinenses*, new ed. Dublin 1935.

Carte
Thomas Carte, *The Life of James, Duke of Ormond*, new ed. 6 vols. Oxford 1851.

Clark
G. N. Clark, *The Later Stuarts 1660–1714*. Oxford 1934.

Colie
Rosalie L. Colie, *Light and Enlightenment*. Cambridge 1957.

Connell
Kenneth Hugh Connell, *The Population of Ireland 1750–1845*. Oxford 1950.

Cotton
Henry Cotton, *Fasti Ecclesiæ Hibernicæ*. 5 vols. Dublin 1847–60.

Courtenay
Thomas Peregrine Courtenay, *Memoirs of the Life, Works, and Correspondence of Sir William Temple*. 2 vols. 1836.

Craik
Henry Craik, *The Life of Jonathan Swift*, 2nd ed. 2 vols. 1894.

D.U.M.
The Dublin University Magazine, vol. XVIII, 1841.

Davis
The Prose Works of Jonathan Swift, ed. Herbert Davis. Oxford 1939– .

Davis, *Drapier*

Jonathan Swift, *The Drapier's Letters*, ed. Herbert Davis. Oxford 1935.

Dunlop

Robert Dunlop, *Ireland from the Earliest Times to the Present Day*. Oxford 1923.

Fletcher, *Gray's Inn*

Reginald James Fletcher, ed., *The Pension Book of Gray's Inn*. 2 vols. 1901–10.

Ford

The Letters of Jonathan Swift to Charles Ford, ed. D. Nichol Smith. Oxford 1935.

Forster

John Forster, *The Life of Jonathan Swift*, Volume I [no more published]. 1875.

Foster

Alumni Oxonienses, ed. Joseph Foster. 8 vols. 1887–92.

Froude

James Anthony Froude, *The English in Ireland in the Eighteenth Century*. 3 vols. 1872–4.

Gilbert

John Thomas Gilbert, *A History of the City of Dublin*. 3 vols. Dublin 1854–9.

HMC.

Historical Manuscripts Commission, Reports.

Hodges

John C. Hodges, *William Congreve the Man*. New York 1941.

JEGP.

The Journal of English and Germanic Philology.

J.H.C.

The Journals of the House of Commons.

J.H.I.

Journal of the History of Ideas.

J.H.L.

The Journals of the House of Lords.

Journal

Jonathan Swift, *Journal to Stella*, ed. Sir Harold Williams. 2 vols. Oxford 1948.

Jouvin

Albert Jouvin, 'M. Jouvin de Rocheford's Description', in C. Litton Falkiner, ed., *Illustrations of Irish History and Topography*. 1904.

Kearney

Hugh F. Kearney, *Strafford in Ireland*. Manchester 1959.

Keble

John Keble, *The Life of Thomas Wilson*. 2 vols. 1863.

Landa

Louis A. Landa, *Swift and the Church of Ireland*. Oxford 1954.

Locke, *Works*

The Works of John Locke, 5th ed. 3 vols. 1751.

Longe

Julia S. Longe, *Martha, Lady Giffard, Her Life and Correspondence*, 1911.

Luce

A. A. Luce, *The Life of George Berkeley*. 1949.

Luttrell

Narcissus Luttrell, *A Brief Historical Relation of State Affairs*. 6 vols. Oxford 1857.

Lyon

John Lyon, MS. notes in a copy of J. Hawkesworth, *The Life of the Revd. Jonathan Swift*, 1755, in the Victoria and Albert Museum, Forster Collection, no. 579 [48. D. 39].

MLN.

Modern Language Notes.

Mason

William Monck Mason, *The History and Antiquities of the Collegiate and Cathedral Church of St. Patrick*. Dublin 1820.

Maxwell

Constantia E. Maxwell, *A History of Trinity College, Dublin*. Dublin 1946.

McSkimin

Samuel McSkimin, *The History and Antiquities of . . . Carrickfergus*, 3rd ed. Belfast 1829.

N. & Q.

Notes and Queries.

Nichols
The Works of the Rev. Jonathan Swift, ed. John Nichols. 19 vols. 1808.

Ogg I
David Ogg, *England in the Reign of Charles II*, 2nd ed. 2 vols. Oxford 1955–6.

Ogg II
David Ogg, *England in the Reigns of James II and William III*. Oxford 1955.

P.C.C.
Prerogative Court of Canterbury.

PMLA.
Publications of the Modern Language Association.

P.R.O.
Public Record Office.

Petty
Sir William Petty, *Economic Writings*, ed. C. H. Hull. 2 vols. Cambridge 1899.

Phillips
Walter Alison Phillips, ed., *A History of the Church of Ireland*. 3 vols. 1933–4.

Pilkington
Memoirs of Mrs Laetitia Pilkington, ed. Iris Barry. 1928.

Poems
The Poems of Jonathan Swift, ed. Sir Harold Williams, 2nd ed. 3 vols. Oxford 1958.

Pons
Emile Pons, *Swift, Les Années de jeunesse et le "Conte du tonneau"*. Strasbourg 1925.

SPD.
Calendar of State Papers, Domestic.

SPI.
Calendar of State Papers, Ireland.

T. Scott
The Prose Works of Jonathan Swift, ed. Temple Scott [i.e., J. H. Isaacs]. 12 vols. 1897–1908.

W. Scott

The Works of Jonathan Swift, ed. Sir Walter Scott. 19 vols. Edinburgh 1814.

Sherburn

The Correspondence of Alexander Pope, ed. George Sherburn. 5 vols. Oxford 1956.

Simms

John Gerald Simms, *The Williamite Confiscation in Ireland*. 1956.

Spingarn

Critical Essays of the Seventeenth Century, ed. J. E. Spingarn. 3 vols. Oxford 1908.

Starkman

Miriam K. Starkman, *Swift's Satire on Learning in A Tale of a Tub*. Princeton 1950.

Stubbs

John William Stubbs, *The History of the University of Dublin*. Dublin 1889.

D. Swift

Deane Swift, *An Essay upon the Life, Writings, and Character, of Dr. Jonathan Swift*. 1755.

Sykes, *William Wake*

Norman Sykes, *William Wake*. 2 vols. Cambridge 1957.

T.C.D.

Trinity College, Dublin.

Tale

Jonathan Swift, *A Tale of a Tub*, ed. A. C. Guthkelch and D. Nichol Smith, 2nd ed. Oxford 1958.

Temple, *Early Essays*

The Early Essays and Romances of Sir William Temple, ed. G. C. Moore Smith. Oxford 1930.

——, *Introduction to the History of England*.

An Introduction to the History of England. 1695.

——, *Letters* I–II

Letters Written by Sir W. Temple, ed. Jonathan Swift. 2 vols. 1700.

——, *Letters* III

Letters to the King . . . by Sir W. Temple, ed. Jonathan Swift. 1703.

Temple, *Memoirs* II

Memoirs of What Past in Christendom. 1692.

——, *Memoirs* III

Memoirs. Part III . . . by Sir William Temple, ed. Jonathan Swift. 1709.

——, *Miscellanea* I

Miscellanea. 1680.

——, *Miscellanea* II

Miscellanea. The Second Part. 2nd ed. 1690.

——, *Miscellanea* III

Miscellanea. The Third Part . . . by the Late Sir William Temple, ed. Jonathan Swift. 1701.

——, *Observations upon the U.P.*

Observations upon the United Provinces of the Netherlands, 6th ed. 1693.

——, *Of Poetry*

Essay IV. Of Poetry, in *Miscellanea* II. 279–341.

——, *Select Letters*

Select Letters to the Prince of Orange. . . . To Which Is Added An Essay upon . . . Ireland. 1701.

Venn

John Venn and John Archibald Venn, comps., *Alumni Cantabrigienses.* 10 vols. Cambridge 1922–54.

Ware

The Whole Works of Sir James Ware, ed. Walter Harris. 3 vols. Dublin 1739–46.

K. Williams

Kathleen Williams, *Jonathan Swift and the Age of Compromise.* 1958.

Woodbridge

Homer Edwards Woodbridge, *Sir William Temple.* New York 1940.

Wotton, *Reflections*

William Wotton, *Reflections upon Ancient and Modern Learning*, 2nd ed. 1697.